Hiking Trails of Ottawa, the National Capital Region, and Beyond
2nd Edition

Hiking
Trails
of Ottawa,
the National Capital Region,
and Beyond 2nd EDITION

MICHAEL HAYNES

Edited by Charles Stuart.
Cover and page design by Julie Scriver.
Cover photograph by Ross Dunn, *Autumn in Gatineau Park overlooking the Ottawa Valley*, CC BY-SA 2.0, Flickr.com.
Interior photographs by Michael Haynes unless otherwise noted.
Maps by Todd Graphic, toddgraphic.ns.ca.
Printed in China by MCRL Overseas Group.
10 9 8 7 6 5 4 3 2 1

Goose Lane Editions
500 Beaverbrook Court, Suite 330
Fredericton, New Brunswick
CANADA E3B 5X4
gooselane.com

Library and Archives Canada Cataloguing in Publication

Title: Hiking trails of Ottawa, the National Capital Region and beyond / Michael Haynes.
Names: Haynes, Michael, 1955- author.
Description: 2nd edition.
Identifiers: Canadiana 20200308114 | ISBN 9781773101842 (softcover)
Subjects: LCSH: Trails—Ottawa River Valley (Québec and Ont.)—Guidebooks. | LCSH: Trails—National Capital Region (Ont. and Québec)—Guidebooks. | LCSH: Hiking—Ottawa River Valley (Québec and Ont.)—Guidebooks. | LCSH: Hiking—National Capital Region (Ont. and Québec)—Guidebooks. | LCSH: Ottawa River Valley (Québec and Ont.)—Guidebooks. | LCSH: National Capital Region (Ont. and Québec)—Guidebooks. | LCGFT: Guidebooks.
Classification: LCC GV199.44.C22 O88 2021 | DDC 796.5109713/8—dc23

Goose Lane Editions is located on the traditional unceded territory of the Wəlastəkwiyik whose ancestors along with the Mi'kmaq and Peskotomuhkati Nations signed Peace and Friendship Treaties with the British Crown in the 1700s.

Goose Lane Editions acknowledges the generous financial support of the Government of Canada, the Canada Council for the Arts, and the Province of New Brunswick.

Contents

Michael Haynes

Preface

Since the publication of the first edition of *Hiking Trails of Ottawa* in 2010, much has changed in outdoors activity. Hiking has been growing steadily in popularity, especially winter snowshoeing, and many of the most popular trails are almost as busy as Highway 417 during rush hour. Practically everyone now owns a smartphone, so being out of communication is increasingly rare – and yet progressively more uncomfortable. Fitness tracking devices have meant that relatively accurate information on distance and elevation change in addition to other hike data is available instantly on your wrist. Improved online mapping data and websites have almost entirely replaced paper maps.

New trails are constantly being developed, and existing trails upgraded; fourteen of the routes in the second edition did not exist when the first edition was written, while many other trails have experienced significant changes. In total forty-three out of the fifty routes in this book are partially or significantly different from what they were in the first edition. The Great Trail (formerly Trans Canada Trail), as of 2017, has mapped a route connecting the Atlantic, Pacific, and Arctic Oceans that is more than 25,000 km in length, and every year more and more people traverse long portions of it.

Near the cities of Ottawa and Gatineau, the Gatineau Hills are foremost in people's affection, particularly the park with its magnificent networks of summer and winter trails. Its high escarpment dominating Ottawa's northwestern skyline, Gatineau Park's 361 km² natural spaces, extending into the urban core of Gatineau, is the forest playground of choice for tens of thousands of outdoors enthusiasts. And, with its rugged hills, lakes, and winding river valleys, many other options for outdoor activity are available throughout this section of Western Quebec.

Perhaps even more central to the region's identity are its rivers. The Ottawa, Rideau, and Gatineau Rivers were once major routes for industry and trade, and now their banks are home to numerous parks and conservation areas, and many of the most popular trails. Smaller tributaries such as the Mississippi, Petite Nation, Madawaska, Lièvre, and South Nation Rivers helped define the pattern of settlement and are themselves major recreational corridors for canoeists and kayakers.

Circling Ottawa to the west, the Opeongo Hills and the Frontenac Arch are extreme southern extensions of the Canadian Shield. Once as high as the Himalayas, the eroded remains of the Shield are made up of some of the most ancient rock on earth, nearly four billion years old. The granite and gneiss-type rocks of this area produce thin, acidic soils, which have prevented much agricultural development or dense settlement. However, its hills and lakes have attracted hikers and other recreationists for decades.

In sharp contrast to much of the region, the sedimentary lowlands extending south and east of Ottawa are some of Ontario's flattest land. Largely the result of glacial deposition when the entire area was submerged during the last ice age, this steppe-like area supports extensive agricultural activity and its trails present extended view planes reminiscent of the Prairie provinces.

In short, Ottawa offers a considerable variety of natural landscapes and experiences, and its residents respond by hiking, biking, canoeing, cross-country skiing, and participating in every form of outdoor recreation available. The city is home to one of the largest hiking clubs in Canada, the Rideau Trail Association, as well as the Ottawa Outdoor Club, Ottawa Rambling Club, and Oxygène Club de Randonnée – just to name a few. Nakkertok Nordic Cross Country Ski Club may be the largest skiing club in the country, with more than one thousand members. Many more informal group hikes are available online through Meetup. Online resources, by contrast, although steadily improving, are not always easy to use, especially by those wishing to get started, and too often don't differentiate between public and private.

Yet, despite all this organized outdoors activity, and the online resources published by parks, tourist associations, independents, and the National Capital Commission, many still often find it difficult to know how and where to start to enjoy the outdoors. This may be particularly true for new Canadians who previously lived in a large urban environment. But for too many Canadians, no matter their origins, stories about bears and bobcats, coyotes and cougars, can make the outdoors appear primeval and even dangerous, a place to be avoided rather than explored. Happily, the National Capital Region's network of managed footpaths is one of the easiest and safest ways to introduce oneself to "Outdoor" Canada. Almost all the paths profiled in this book are maintained by either professional staff or volunteers and are well signed and easy to follow. Many of them are rated at an easy or moderate level of difficulty suitable for all first-time hikers.

The winter of 2020 introduced a major element of disruption: COVID-19. From periods of trail closures to constantly changing regulations about whether facilities such as outhouses, picnic grounds, or nearby restaurants and grocery stores would be open, hikers and cyclists had their ability to access the outdoors severely restricted. The closing of the Ontario/Quebec border, and Gatineau Park, was unprecedented. At the time of my writing this in May 2020, many of these restrictions are gradually being lifted, but the possibility of their being reimposed, weeks, months, or even years later remains until an effective vaccine for COVID-19 is developed and in widespread use. "Social distancing" (or "physical distancing"), a term that suggests maintaining a 2 m distance from non-family members at all times – even on the trail – to reduce the chances of spreading this highly infectious virus, is likely to remain as a legacy of this public health crisis. Even as parks reopen, some trails may be designated as one-way only and services like restaurants and washrooms may not be available at all times. As always, check the current state of play before heading out.

The purpose of this book is to make starting to hike easier by providing a resource compiled and evaluated by a single knowledgeable and experienced trail developer and profiling them in a consistent manner. Over my thirty years of work in trails, I have been a trail user, a volunteer, executive director of a provincial trail organization, trail director of a national not-for-profit, a consultant, a conference presenter in eight different countries, a broadcaster responsible for more than three hundred radio segments about trails, and author of twelve published trail guides and numerous magazine articles. I have hiked and/or biked every route profiled in this book, and many others that were not. So, like the curator of an art gallery, I have selected a collection – a sample – of the region's trails, in order to provide a wide range of experience to potential users.

Eastern Ontario and Western Quebec are blessed with thousands of kilometres of managed trails. *Hiking Trails of Ottawa* does not attempt to list them all. Instead, it provides a detailed profile of fifty representative routes, distributed throughout a circle radiating from downtown Ottawa. I have divided this circle into five districts:

- Ottawa - Greenbelt and City
- Gatineau Park
- Quebec - Outside Gatineau Park
- Ontario - North of Highway 7
- Ontario - South of Highway 7

I chose to balance the number of selections in each of the five districts, and to ensure that each region contained variety by selecting ten hiking trails: a few easy, some moderately challenging, and at least one or two more demanding. This occasionally meant that I left out many very good routes – in Gatineau Park, for example – but was able to profile a wider geographic area than I might if I had attempted to mention every trail found inside the National Capital Region.

The selection of the routes in *Hiking Trails of Ottawa* is mine alone. If I left out your favourite trail, please let me know.

I hope that you all enjoy your outdoors experiences and find in them as much beauty, tranquility, and admiration for the natural world as I have.

WAYPOINT
POINT DE REPÈRE

44
B

N 45.35056   W 75.58643

↑ 44
C

P
18   2.4 km
     2,4 km

← CH. Hawthorne RD.

For your safety
[text illegible]

Be aware of your
environmental impact
[text illegible]

Pour votre sécurité
[text illegible]

Ayez conscience de votre
impact sur l'environnement
[text illegible]

6. Pine Grove Forestry Trail

Introduction

There have been significant changes in this work from the first edition, published in 2010. The majority of the routes are either different or have been changed somewhat from how they were presented then. That doesn't mean that the trails in the first edition can no longer be used, simply that I made different selections for this edition.

The following list outlines all these changes. Where I indicate that these routes are essentially similar to how they were in 2010, owners of the first edition can continue to use the trail descriptions in that volume to hike them.

OTTAWA – Greenbelt and City

Mer Bleue (Mer Bleue – Trail 51 in current edition): Eliminated the section east of Anderson Road. Traffic is much heavier than in 2010, and I found crossing it stressful and dangerous. The first edition version can still be used.

Old Quarry Trail: Significantly shortened. The first edition version can still be used; I simply decided to profile a shorter, less navigationally confusing option.

Ottawa River – Britannia Park: Dropped, but essentially unchanged. A more current route description can be found in *The Best of The Great Trail, Volume 1.*

Ottawa River – Green Creek (Ottawa River – Green's Creek in current edition): Slightly shortened. First edition version can still be used.

Rideau River: Significantly changed, with a different start/finish, though using some of the same route as the first edition.

Rideau Trail – Lime Kiln Loop (Lime Kiln Loop in current edition): Shortened, and with a different start/finish. The first edition version can still be used.

Shirleys Bay – Trail 10: Dropped because it has been affected by the flooding in recent years. It was actually closed for repairs when I did the research for the second edition.

WESTERN QUEBEC – Gatineau Park (Gatineau Park in current ediiton)

Herridge Shelter: Essentially the same, except that I now end this route at the nearby Healey Shelter.

King Mountain (Mont King in current ediiton): Significantly shortened. The first edition version can still be used.

Pink Lake: Dropped. The first edition version can still be used.

Lauriault Trail: Dropped. The first edition version can still be used.

Luskville Falls (Chute de Luskville in current edition): Lengthened by adding the section from the fire tower to McKinstry Shelter.

Trail 62 (Sentier des Loups/Wolf Trail): Dropped. The first edition version can still be used.

Skyline: Dropped. The first edition version can still be used.

Trail 56: Replaced by Lac Taylor (Taylor Lake). Chemin Eardley-Masham was damaged by flooding and closed for more than a year, preventing access to the Trail 56 start.

Western Shelter: Dropped. The first edition version can still be used.

WESTERN QUEBEC – Beyond Gatineau Park (Outside Gatineau Park in current edition)

Cycloparc PPJ: This has been replaced by the new route, from Shawville to Campbell's Bay. However, the first edition route can still be used.

Lac Leamy to Museum of Civilization: The Gatineau River and Voyageur Pathways have been dropped. The first edition version can still be used.

Parc du Lac Beauchamp: Dropped. The first edition version can probably still be used, although there have been some changes.

Parc national de Plaisance – Sentier des Outaouais: Dropped. The first edition version can still be used.

Parc linéaire de la Vallée-de-la-Gatineau: Renamed as the Véloroute des Draveurs.

Sentier des Montagnes Noires: Most trails have been renumbered, and new ones built. The route profiled is significantly different from the first edition.

Sentiers L'Escapade: Dropped. A more current version can be found in my *Hiking Trails of Montréal*.

Wakefield to Lac Brown: Dropped. A more current version of the section through Wakefield can be found in *The Best of The Great Trail, Volume 1*.

EASTERN ONTARIO – Beyond Greenbelt (North of Highway 7 in current edition)

Glengarry Trails – Alexandria: Dropped. There have been significant changes to this route.

K&P Trail – Calabogie: Dropped, but the first edition version can still be used.

Manitou Mountain: Modified. Because of residential development, the trailhead used in the first edition has changed. I have also lengthened the route somewhat.

Marlborough Forest: Dropped. The first edition version can still be used, but there have been some changes. Follow the Rideau Trail signage.

New York Central Fitness Trail: Essentially unchanged, but now accounting for the road changes and building development near Embrun.

Ottawa-Carleton Trailway: Dropped. The first edition version can still be used.

Prescott-Russell Recreational Trail: Hammond to Bourget: Replaced by the Vankleek Hill route. However, the description in the first edition can still be used.

47. Rideau Trail – Westport

St. Lawrence Recreational Path: Modified at the Upper Canada Village end.

Stonebridge Trail: Changed to account for park development in recent years.

EASTERN ONTARIO – Frontenac Arch (South of Highway 7 in current edition)

Cataraqui Trail – Chaffeys Locks: Dropped. A more current and extended version can be found in *The Best of The Great Trail, Volume 1.*

Charleston Lake Provincial Park – Tallow Rock Bay Trail (Charleston Lake Provincial Park in current edition): Extended to Bach's Lookout. However, the first edition version can still be used.

Frontenac Provincial Park – Doe Lake and Arab Gorge: Dropped. The first edition version can still be used.

Frontenac Provincial Park – Slide Lake Loop: Dropped. The first edition version can still be used.

Mac Johnson Wildlife Area – Brockville: Dropped. The first edition version can still be used, although there are minor changes to the trails.

Marble Rock: Dropped. The first edition version can still be used.

Murphys Point Provincial Park: The new route description has been changed from the first edition. Do not use the previous route description.

Rideau Trail – Tay Towpath: Dropped. This trail here has significantly changed, and the description in the first edition is no longer usable.

Rideau Trail – Westport: Lengthened in the current edition.

Rock Dunder: Dropped. The first edition version can still be used.

How to Use This Book

Begin your exploration with the Trails at a Glance section (p. 31). This provides summary information on each of the fifty routes found in *Hiking Trails of Ottawa*. In table format, it displays each section's length; indicates the uses permitted when there is snow and when there is not; whether dogs are permitted off leash, on leash, or are prohibited altogether; and if there are fees required to use the trail. Finally, it lists the page in the book where the full route description is found.

The Trails at a Glance section uses a number of abbreviations and notations with which you should be familiar.

Uses:

These are the uses either formally permitted, or likely possible, anywhere on the route being profiled during those times of the year when the trail is not covered by snow. Typically, that means most of the spring, all of the summer, and the majority of the fall.

Any item marked with an asterisk means that it is permitted, and might be encountered, along some sections of the profiled route, but not throughout the entire distance.

- **W** = walking/hiking
- **B** = bicycling, either touring or mountain biking
- **I** = inline skating, skateboarding
- **H** = equestrian/horseback use
- **A** = ATV and other off-highway vehicles

Uses [in snow]:

These are the uses either formally permitted, or likely possible, anywhere on the route being profiled during those times of the year when the trail is covered by snow. Typically, that means the late fall, winter, and early spring. Many trails have official opening and closing dates for summer and winter uses; check each trail's website for details.

I have not attempted to include which routes permit fat-tire bicycling, a relatively new and rapidly evolving winter trail activity. Again, check with the trail manager for confirmation.

- **S** = snowshoeing
- **X** = cross-country/Nordic skiing
- **Sm** = snowmobiles and other motorized winter vehicles

Dogs: The majority of trails profiled have strict rules about dog use, particularly trails within national and provincial park properties and in urban areas. Please respect non-dog owners and observe these regulations – and always "poop & scoop"! Whenever the rules vary for different sections of a route, I will highlight the most restrictive rules and mark with an asterisk.

- **N** = no dogs permitted
- **L** = dogs permitted on leash
- **L/N** = dogs permitted on leash when no snow/not permitted with snow uses
- **0** = dogs permitted off leash

Fees: Several of the pathways are either entirely located within or pass through portions of provincial and national parks. These charge a daily visitor fee. Others, such as the Sentier des Montagnes Noires are not park trails but a fee is required to use them. In some trails in Gatineau Park, there is a fee associated only with winter uses or for the parking area at the trailhead.

Fees vary from park to park and year to year, so I have chosen to indicate where fees will be required by using a "$". Where they apply to only a portion of the route, or only for some uses, I use "$*".

Carbide Wilson Ruins	1	3.5	1+	W, B* [X]	L/N	$*

In the example above, the section of the Carbide Wilson Ruins route is profiled (p. 86):

- It is rated a Level 1, a relatively easy path suitable for beginners and most casual walkers.
- It is 3.5 km in length.
- It requires at least one hour to complete.
- It permits walking throughout its entire length and biking on some sections, during non-snow months.
- In winter, it is open only to cross-country skiing.
- Dogs are permitted when on leash, except in winter when they are not permitted at all.
- A fee is required for winter use, but the parking area charges a fee as well during the summer months.

Individual Route Listings

Once you have selected a route from the Trails at a Glance, turn to the page indicated. Here, at the start of each path profile, is a capsule synopsis. Every route description follows the same basic format:

- **Name of Trail:** Where possible, I use the official name of the pathway(s) or park on which all or most of the profiled route is found. For the other routes, I use other prominent features, such as the names of the communities where it starts and finishes (e.g., Wilno-Barry's Bay), the destination (e.g., Keogan Shelter), or a geographic reference (e.g., Rideau River).

- **Distance:** The return trip distance is given in kilometres. To convert to miles, multiply by 0.62.
- **Type:** This is a description of whether the trail is linear or a loop.
- **Difficulty:** Trails are rated by the relative level of the degree of difficulty represented by the profiled route. Level 1 is considered open to most people without physical or mobility challenges, followed by relatively increasing levels of difficulty, with level 5 suitable only for those who are quite fit or are experienced hikers. Routes ranked levels 4 and 5 are followed by a short descriptor of why they were given that rating, such as "distance," "rugged terrain," or "navigation."
- **Ascent/descent:** This figure provides the total ascent and descent, measured in metres of the profiled route. It is always based on a return trip; reduce figures by half if you are going only one way on a linear route.
- **Hiking Time:** This is the likely minimum time required to walk the profiled route, based on an average pace of 4 km per hour. This does not include time for rests, snacks, or calls of nature. The reason I add the plus sign is because this is the minimum time required for "average" people to complete this. If they dawdle, decide to snack, or do anything other than march along briskly, it will require additional time. So I added the plus sign to reflect that fact, as I did with all the routes.
- **Trail conditions:** This indicates all the types of treadway – trail surface – that will be encountered along the route profiled. Many pathways incorporate more than one surface type, although some of them often do so only for short distances, such as a paved section when it passes through a community. The possibilities include asphalt (paved roadway, concrete sidewalk), crushed stone (gravel or limestone crusher fines), compacted earth (dirt road, former forest roadway), and natural surface (woodland footpath, rock, sand).
- **Cellphone coverage:** This provides a brief overview of the cell reception when I traversed this route in 2019. Please note that the coverage varies considerably depending upon the service provider. I used Bell Canada, but be sure to consult your own provider's coverage map if you use a different service.
- **Uses:** This indicates what uses are permitted on all, or portions, of the profiled route.
- **Facilities:** All the amenities, such as picnic tables or interpretive panels, found either at the trailhead or along the route are listed here.

- **Hazards:** This offers information on possible hazards that might be encountered along the route. Some, such as road crossings, are certain to be met. Others, such as ticks and poison ivy, are known to occur along the route but can be avoided with caution. A fuller list of potential hazards and an explanation of each may be found on page 19.

Following this capsule synopsis is the detailed description of the route being profiled. This detailed trail outline is divided into the following sections:
- **Finding the trailhead:** This item offers directions on how to drive to the trail's starting point from a convenient landmark:
  - › directions for trails in Gatineau Park and Quebec begin from the mid-point of the Macdonald-Cartier Bridge;
  - › directions for trails west of Ottawa begin at the junction, known locally as the "split" of Highway 417 and Highway 416;
  - › directions for trails east of Ottawa begin at the split of Highway 417 and Highway 174; and
  - › directions for trails within or close to the city of Ottawa begin at the closest exit of Highway 417.
- **Trailhead:** Here you find the GPS coordinates for the start of each profiled route. In a few cases of longer linear routes, the GPS of the finish will be provided as well.
- **Introduction:** This features some background about the trail, possibly including historical, natural, or geographical information, as well as some additional detail on its regulations or restrictions.
- **Trail Description:** This offers a walk-through of the route, relating what I found when I travelled it in 2019. In every case I describe junctions and landmarks from the perspective of someone following the trail in the direction I have indicated. If you are travelling in the opposite direction, remember to reverse my bearings.

Sidebar Notes: Scattered throughout the book are brief capsule descriptions of some of the plants, animals, geological features, and human history that you might encounter on the various trails. These are intended to be brief samples to whet your curiosity about the terrain through which you are hiking/biking, and to encourage you to learn more.

In addition, each route features a short capsule story about one of its salient features, or a short story associated with that particular trail.

Safety and Other Considerations

Accompanying each route description is a list of hazards, provided in brief descriptions. Though some might include mosquitoes and blackflies in this list, I consider them simply part of the Canadian landscape, unavoidable and inescapable. Expect to encounter them in all but the most urban routes; late spring and early summer are usually when they are at their worst.

Hazards:

- **Cliffs:** When I list "cliffs" as a hazard, it is because that particular trail features a section with at least one high, vertical drop with no guardrails – and where you are usually a long way from help.
- **High Usage:** On a few of the routes, particularly those in Ottawa's urban area, the sheer number of people using the pathways is a significant hazard. Particular care must be taken by cyclists in these locations. Where so many people share the trail, reduced speed is the only correct response.
- **Hunting:** In some cases trails pass through areas where hunting deer and/or moose is permitted, usually during October and early November. For safety, don an orange vest/jacket, stay on posted, public trails, and avoid hiking/biking at dawn/dusk.
- **Motorized Uses:** Many trails are shared use, which means that more than just hikers might be encountered when using them. And while there are conflicts between hikers and bicyclists, some people make a clear distinction between those uses and motorized recreation, such as ATVs. Where ATVs might be using a portion of a route, I mention it so that extra caution may be taken on those sections.
- **Poison Ivy:** These toxic plants (see p. 21) are increasingly found along the edges of many trails and fields. Managed trails will usually post warning signs, but as both poison ivy and other noxious plants, such as giant hogweed, are spreading and extending their range, poison ivy could be growing anywhere alongside the pathway. The best way to avoid poison ivy is to stay on the path.
- **Road Crossings:** Most long trails, particularly those that have been created on former railways, require multiple road crossings. Quite often these will be over highways where the speed limits are 80 or 90 kph,

and in many cases road and trail cross each other at a diagonal, making visibility difficult for either the trail user or approaching automobile traffic. Of all the hazards trail users face, this is actually the most commonly encountered and truly dangerous.

- **Rugged Terrain:** Some of the paths profiled in this book are wide, level, and surfaced in crushed stone. Others, however, wander over the landscape regardless of hills, rocks, rivers, or any other obstacle. When I think that the terrain is of a greater than average challenge, I mention it.

- **Ticks:** These tiny spider-like insects climb onto grass and scrub and latch onto animals and people when they rub against the plants. Although a tick bite is usually painless, ticks can transfer several diseases, including the serious Lyme disease, while they feed.

In the Ottawa area, tests of ticks in 2019 revealed that roughly one in three carried Lyme disease. Should a tick become embedded, remove it as soon as possible and save it. See a doctor immediately and bring the tick with you.

For more information about Lyme disease, visit www.phac-aspc.gc.ca/id-mi/tickinfo-eng.php. Black-legged ticks are extending their range through much of southern Canada; consult a provincial website for the most up-to-date information.

- **Wildlife:** Wildlife encounters tend to be what most people fear when hiking or biking on trails. Stories of bear attacks, though extremely rare, are usually gruesome and always captivating to hear about. But in addition to bears, the wrong interaction with any wild animal can result in injury or death. For example, in 2013, in Belarus, a man died after an attack by a beaver! Nor are wild animals found only in the wilderness. Even in urban areas in Canada, non-domestic animals such as coyotes, raccoons, and skunks can be routinely found. Caution is always advisable around wild animals. However, for the purposes of this book, I have only listed "wildlife" as a hazard where larger, more aggressive species such as bear, bobcat, and/or wolf are known to commonly roam.

Poison Ivy

This nasty little plant is found throughout the National Capital Region, and if you brush into it you might end up in the emergency room. Despite its typical three-leafed appearance, poison ivy can be difficult to recognize, as it can creep along the ground, grow as a bush, or even climb like a vine. Usually found near the edges of fields and forests, if you come into contact with it, you have less than thirty minutes to thoroughly wash the affected skin with cold water to avoid symptoms.

Trail Etiquette

Many of the routes in *Hiking Trails of Ottawa* are shared-use pathways, which require all users to be aware of and follow basic rules of courtesy that will enhance the safety of themselves and everyone else. Detailed codes of conduct are usually posted at trailheads, and many excellent ones can be found online with a simple search.

Generally, follow the rule that "wheels yield to heels." Cyclists should slow when passing oncoming walkers, and slow while ringing a bell when overtaking from behind. Both walkers and cyclists should yield to horseback riders, and should defer to the rider's judgement, as horse behaviour can be unpredictable. (Once, while cycling, I had to stop, dismount, and remove my helmet before a horse would sidle past me.)

On some routes ATVs are permitted. Although these should defer to walkers and cyclists, I found it easier as a walker just to stop, stand aside, and let them pass.

In addition, some trails are just a thin ribbon of public right-of-way bordered by private land. The easiest way to respect landowners is to stay on the trail, and only leave it at designated access points.

Outdoor Tips

Backpack: You need something to carry your water, first aid kit, garbage bag, etc. A light day pack with adjustable shoulder straps, a hip belt, back pad, a large inner pouch, and roomy outer pockets should do. After footwear, a pack is probably the most important piece of equipment you require. Get help to select the right pack for you.

Bandana: Bandanas are useful and versatile items that make great headbands or neck protectors. A bandana can even substitute for a hat to provide shade from the sun. During hot weather, soaking your bandana and wetting your hair and face can be pleasingly invigorating.

Bear Encounter: A bear encounter is every new hiker's nightmare, but such encounters are surprisingly uncommon, and even then are usually rather uneventful. In forty years of hiking I have encountered bears many times, but have never had a problem. For advice on what to do, visit www.ontario.ca/page/prevent-bear-encounters-bear-wise.

39. Shaw Woods

Johnny's Lookout Trail 1.4 km. ←

S.R. Portage .270 km. →

Johnny's Lookout Trail 1.4 km. →

ALL DOGS MUST BE KEPT ON A LEASH

Shaw Woods

BE AWARE OF WEATHER RELATED HAZARDS

USE TRAILS AT YOUR OWN RISK

Shaw Woods

Monarchs and Milkweed

Probably the most well-known North American butterfly, the monarch is also the continent's insect undertaking the longest migration. Starting from northern Mexico and the southern United States in the spring, these fragile butterflies travel thousands of kilometres to Canada, where several generations reproduce in the summer and early fall.

The health of this beautiful butterfly's population depends on the availability of milkweed plants. The monarch caterpillar will only eat milkweed because it produces a toxin that defends them from predators, and adult monarchs lay their eggs on the underside of milkweed leaves.

Blisters: Even the most careful hiker will get blisters occasionally. Left untreated, they can turn the shortest walk into a painful nightmare. Treat them like an open wound: clean with soap and water and dress with Second Skin. If your feet are dirty or sweaty, clean with an alcohol swipe to help adhesive tape adhere.

Blue Jeans: These pants are great at home, but less so in the outdoors. Blue jeans are usually constricting compared to hiking pants, and should they get wet they can triple in weight – and take forever to dry. Choose something else for your walks.

Call of Nature: No, not a loon's call. Sometimes you just must…"s**t in the woods." If this happens, move well off the path, stay 25 m away from water, and if you can, dig a scat hole. When finished, cover it up. Sanitary napkins, tampons, disposable diapers, and toilet paper should be packed out. (Remember that garbage bag?)

First Aid Kit: When you are out in the woods, even minor wounds can be debilitating. A small first aid kit with bandages, gauze, tape, moleskin, etc., can permit you to deal with any blisters or scrapes that might require immediate attention.

Food: I always carry something, even for short hikes. If, like me, you prefer to nibble, carry nuts, dried fruit, and heavy breads. And while anything is better than nothing, try to stay away from chips, chocolate bars, and similar fare, which don't always pair well with a person's metabolism during physical activity.

Footwear: Proper footwear can enhance your comfort and safety. Even the best-maintained trail might have rocks and roots, and the chance to twist your ankle. The options are endless, so care is essential in making your selection. But I can give one bit of advice: do not rely on footwear you use on roads and sidewalks.

Garbage Bag: Always, always pack out your trash. And unless you want to make a mess of your pack, you will probably need a waterproof bag to do so. As a responsible member of the outdoor community, you might even pick up other garbage you find along the trail, make hiking a better experience for everyone.

GPS/Compass: Few things have revolutionized outdoor travel as much as Global Positioning System satellite navigation. With GPS, either on your smartphone or a separate device, you can travel directly to any location for which you have the coordinates. I use one, especially when researching for my books, but also carry a compass as a backup.

Hunting Season: In the fall, hikers often share the woods with hunters. If this worries you, restrict your excursions to Gatineau Park, most provincial parks, and other similarly restricted areas. For safety, don an orange vest/jacket; stay on posted, public trails; and avoid hiking/biking at dawn/dusk.

Hypothermia: Teeth chattering? Shivering uncontrollably? Hands numb? You may be entering Stage 1 hypothermia. Hypothermia is a condition in which the body's temperature drops below that required for normal metabolism and bodily functions, and it can happen in spring and fall as well as winter – even in summer, too, if the water is cold and the exposure long enough. If you experience these symptoms, end your hike immediately. If you are far away from help, a mildly hypothermic person can be effectively rewarmed through close body contact and by drinking warm, sweet liquids.

Layering: Instead of having a separate outfit for each weather condition, put together a variety of clothes for different purposes: base (underwear), insulation, and outer shell. Mix and match according to conditions, adding, removing, or changing items as you warm up or cool down and if weather conditions change. Synthetic clothes for layering tend to be lighter and more durable, and provide greater flexibility.

Map: Hiking without a map is like walking with one eye closed. What is the name of that lake? How high is that hill? How much further to walk? In most cases, online maps on your smartphone work well, but it is wise to carry a hard-copy backup for places with no reception or in case of accident. A physical map remains a valuable safety tool.

Old Shoelaces: It sounds silly, but they take up very little room and when needed can be very useful. (If you think none of your equipment will ever break, good luck!) For example, if you carry a small tarp, you can quickly erect a shelter by tying it between trees using the old laces.

Rain Gear: Choose fabrics that are highly breathable. Completely waterproof clothing traps perspiration, resulting in it becoming wet from the inside out. If possible, have two sets of gear, one for summer and something heavier for spring/fall.

Smartphone: Most of the region is well covered by the major service providers. However, there are still a few areas without coverage and dead zones even on some of the most popular trails. Carry your phone, of course, but always tell someone where you are hiking, and when you are expecting to return. (And please turn off receiving calls/texts, etc. You are walking to enjoy nature.)

Spare Socks: After walking for a couple of hours, changing into a fresh pair of socks is almost as refreshing as bathing your feet, and you will find a new spring in your step. I carry two extra pairs so I also have a pair to change into at the end of the hike.

Sunscreen: Sadly, skin cancer as a consequence of unprotected sun exposure is all too common and the rate of cases continues to rise. Use SPF 15 or higher sunscreen frequently and reapply liberally every two hours as long as you stay in the outdoors, even on overcast days, and especially at peak times: 11:00 a.m. to 3:00 p.m.

Vaseline: Prone to blisters? My grandfather taught me to thickly smear my feet with Vaseline, especially between my toes. He told me that if I did so, I would never get a blister, no matter how far I walked: I never have, whenever I followed his advice, even when I ran marathons.

Water: Summers in Ottawa can be very hot and dehydration can occur quickly. It is essential when hiking to have enough water on hand. Safe refill sources are rarely available on the trail, so I like to carry two litres in two bottles as well as purification tablets so that I may refill one bottle from natural water sources and sanitize it while consuming the second.

Water Purification: Finding safe drinking water while you are hiking is unlikely, and on hot, summer days you can rarely carry enough. Portable water filtration units, or purification tablets, are compact, easy to use, and should ensure that you are able to stay hydrated without running the risk of beaver fever – or worse!

Whistle: Lost? Injured? Cellphone battery dead? Carry a whistle. It is much louder and carries further than your voice, and it is less tiring to blow on the whistle than to yell. I carry mine clipped to the strap of my pack, within easy reach.

Batteries and Freezing Temperatures: Lithium-ion batteries, the usual recharge-ables in smartphones, hate cold weather. If exposed to freezing winds, a fully charged phone can stop working in minutes – not hours. It will work fine once thawed, but until then is unlikely to function. When winter hiking, having a backup – a map and compass – is very important. Don't rely on your phone as the only navigation source.

Everything Is More Difficult: Snowshoeing is more difficult, and slower, than walking, especially if the snow is deep and soft. Do not plan to complete a winter hike as quickly as you would the same hike when there is no snow – and expect to be more fatigued than usual for a similar distance.

The Days Are Short: In Ottawa, there is almost a seven-hour daylight difference between the longest day in June and the shortest day in December. And with the sun so low in the sky, it can become dark in east- and north-facing ravines much sooner. Start early and always plan to finish well before sunset. I always carry my headlamp, just in case; it doesn't require much space.

19. Snowshoe Trail 73

Turn Back: The mountaineer Ed Viesturs once said: "Getting to the top is optional. Getting down is mandatory." Sometimes conditions are different than you expected: the snow is deeper or the trail is icier, someone in the group is struggling, or – worst of all – the weather changes suddenly for the worse. Be prepared to turn back. The trail will still be there tomorrow.

Winter Hydration: Keeping hydrated is just as important in winter as in summer, but water can freeze quite quickly. Carry your bottle in the middle of your pack or inside your coat close to your body. Also, since water freezes from the top down, carry it upside down, so that when you want a drink there is no layer of ice on top.

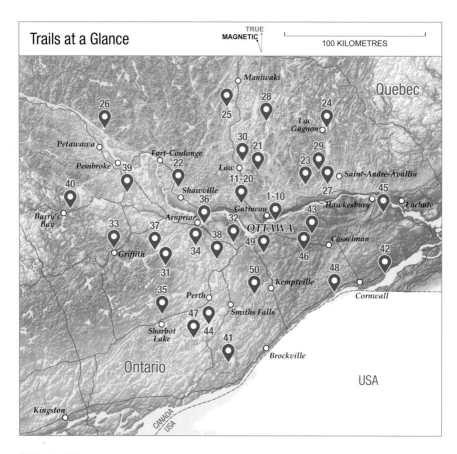

Trails at a Glance

TRUE
MAGNETIC

100 KILOMETRES

Trail amenities:

⋈	Bridge	?	Information	S	Services (gas, $, etc.)
🏠	Camping	🚽	Outhouse	🚇	Tunnel
🚰	Drinking water	P	Parking	🚻	Washroom
F	Ford	🏠	Rustic cabin		

Trails at a Glance

All trails in this guide are rated by the relative level of the degree of difficulty represented by the profiled route. **Level 1** is considered open to most people without physical or mobility challenges, followed by relatively increasing levels of difficulty, with **level 5** suitable only for those who are quite fit or are experienced hikers. Routes ranked levels 4 and 5 are followed by a short descriptor of why they were given that rating, such as "distance," "rugged terrain," or "navigation."

| Trail Name | Level 1-5 | Features | | | | | |
		Length km	Time to Complete (hours)	Uses [in snow]	Dog Use	Fees $	Page

Uses: W = Walk, **B** = Bike, **A** = ATV, **H** = Horseback Riding, **I** = Inline Skating
Uses [in snow]: **S** = Snowshoe/Walk, **X** = Cross-Country Ski, **Sm** = Snowmobile
* = Permitted on some sections of the route, but not all
N = no dogs permitted
L = dogs permitted on leash
L/N = dogs permitted on leash when no snow/not permitted with snow uses
O = dogs permitted off leash
N/A = not applicable

OTTAWA – GREENBELT AND CITY

Trail Name	Level 1-5	Length km	Time to Complete (hours)	Uses [in snow]	Dog Use	Fees $	Page
1. Lime Kiln Loop	2	8.9	2+	W [S, X]	L/N	N/A	38
2. Mer Bleue – Trail 51	2	7.1	2+	W [S, X]	L/N	N/A	42
3. Old Quarry Trail	1	5.5	1+	W, B* [S, X]	N	N/A	48
4. Ottawa River – Aviation Museum	2	7.8	2+	W, B, I* [S, X]	L	N/A	52
5. Ottawa River – Green's Creek	2	6.2	1.5+	W, B, I* [S, X]	L	N/A	58
6. Pine Grove Forestry Trail	1	5.5	1.5+	W, B* [S, X]	L/N	N/A	62
7. Prescott-Russell Pathway Link	5	25.4	7+	W, B, H [S, X, Sm*]	L	N/A	66
8. Rideau Canal	2	8	2+	W, B*, I* [S, X]	L	N/A	70

Trail Name	Level 1-5	Features					
		Length km	Time to complete (hours)	Permitted Uses [in snow]	Dog use	Fees	Page
9. Rideau River	2	10.5	2.5+	W, B*, I* [S, X]	L	N/A	74
10. Rideau River Nature Trail	1	5.8	1.5+	W, B* [S, X]	L	N/A	78
GATINEAU PARK							
11. Carbide Wilson Ruins	1	3.5	1+	W, B* [X]	L/N	$*	86
12. Caverne Lusk (Lusk Cave)	4	12.7	3+	W, B* [S*, X*]	L/N	$*	90
13. Chute de Luskville (Luskville Falls)	4	9.8	3+	W, B* [X*]	L/N	N/A	96
14. Healey Shelter	2	9.2	2.5+	W, B [X]	L/N	N/A	100
15. Keogan Shelter	3	8.4	2.5+	W, B [X]	L/N	N/A	104
16. Lac Brown (Brown Lake)	2	6	1.5+	W, B* [X]	L/N	N/A	108
17. Lac Taylor (Taylor Lake)	5	16	4+	W, B* [X]	L/N	$*	112
18. Mont King (King Mountain)	1	1.8	1+	W [N/A]	N	N/A	118
19. Snowshoe Trail 73	4	13.5	4+	N/A [S]	N	$	122
20. Tawadina Lookout	3	12.8	3+	W, B* [S*, X*]	L/N	N/A	128
QUEBEC – OUTSIDE GATINEAU PARK							
21. Chutes-de-Denholm	2	4.6	1.5+	W, A* [S]	N	N/A	134
22. Cycloparc PPJ	5	36.8	10+	W, B [Sm]	O	N/A	138
23. Forêt-la-Blanche	2	8	2+	W [S, X]	N	$	144
24. La Route des Zingues	5	26.5	7+	W [S]	N	N/A	148
25. Mont Morissette	2	6.4	2+	W [S]	L	N/A	154
26. Parcours Louis-Joseph-Papineau	5	21.8	6+	W, B [S, X]	L*	N/A	158
27. Poisson Blanc	4	9.4	3+	W [S]	L	N/A	162
28. Rocher à l'Oiseau	3	10.8	3+	W, H [S, X]	O	$	168
29. Sentier des Montagnes Noires	3	9.4	2.5+	W, B* [S, X]	L	$	172
30. Véloroute des Draveurs	4	20.4	5+	W, B [Sm]	L	N/A	176

ONTARIO – NORTH OF HIGHWAY 7

31. Blueberry Mountain	1	4.4	1+	W, B [S, X]	L*	N/A	182
32. Crazy Horse Trail	2	6.8	2+	W [S, X]	L	N/A	186
33. Griffith Uplands Trail	3	8.3	2.5+	W, A* [S, Sm*]	O	N/A	190
34. High Lonesome Nature Preserve	1	4.8	1.5+	W [S, X]	L	N/A	194
35. K&P Trail – Sharbot Lake	5	28.4	8+	W, B, H, A [S, X, Sm]	O	N/A	198
36. Macnamara Nature Trail	1	4.1	1+	W [S]	N	N/A	204
37. Manitou Mountain	4	13.9	4+	W [S]	O	N/A	208
38. Ottawa Valley Recreational Trail	5	22.5	6+	W, B, H, A [S, X, Sm]	L*	N/A	212
39. Shaw Woods	2	7.1	2+	W [S]	L	N/A	216
40. Wilno – Barry's Bay	4	19.4	5+	W, B, H, A [S, X, Sm]	O	N/A	222

ONTARIO – SOUTH OF HIGHWAY 7

41. Charleston Lake Provincial Park	4	12.2	3+	W [S]	L	$	228
42. Cooper Marsh	1	4.6	1+	W [S]	L	N/A	234
43. Forêt Larose	2	9.2	2+	W, B [S, X]	L	N/A	238
44. Murphys Point Provincial Park	2	10.1	2+	W, B* [S, X]	L	$	244
45. New York Central Fitness Trail	2	12	3+	W, B, I [S, X]	L	N/A	248
46. Prescott-Russell Recreational Trail: Vankleek Hill	5	30.4	8+	W, B [S, Sm]	L*	N/A	252
47. Rideau Trail – Westport	3	11.8	3+	W [S, X*]	L	N/A	256
48. St. Lawrence Recreational Path	4	21.6	6+	W, B [S, X]	L	N/A	262
49. Stonebridge Trail	2	8.8	2+	W, B [S, X]	L*	N/A	266
50. Tip to Tip Trail	1	4.8	1+	W [S, X]	L	N/A	270

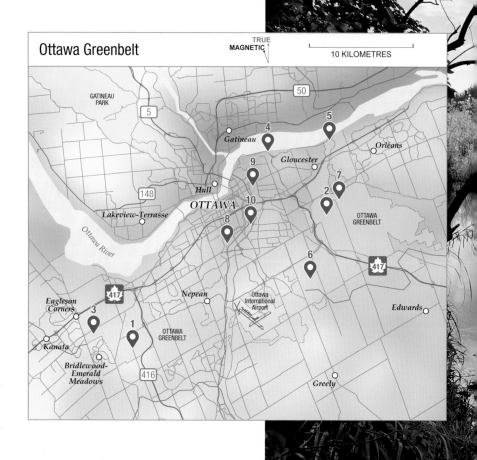

Ottawa Greenbelt

TRUE
MAGNETIC

10 KILOMETRES

GATINEAU PARK

5

50

5

Gatineau

4

Orléans

9

Gloucester

7

Hull

148

2

OTTAWA
GREENBELT

OTTAWA

10

8

Lakeview-Terrasse

Ottawa River

6

417

Eagleson
Corners

3

417

Nepean

Ottawa
International
Airport

Edwards

Kanata

1

OTTAWA
GREENBELT

Bridlewood-
Emerald
Meadows

416

Greely

**6. Pine Grove
Forestry Trail**

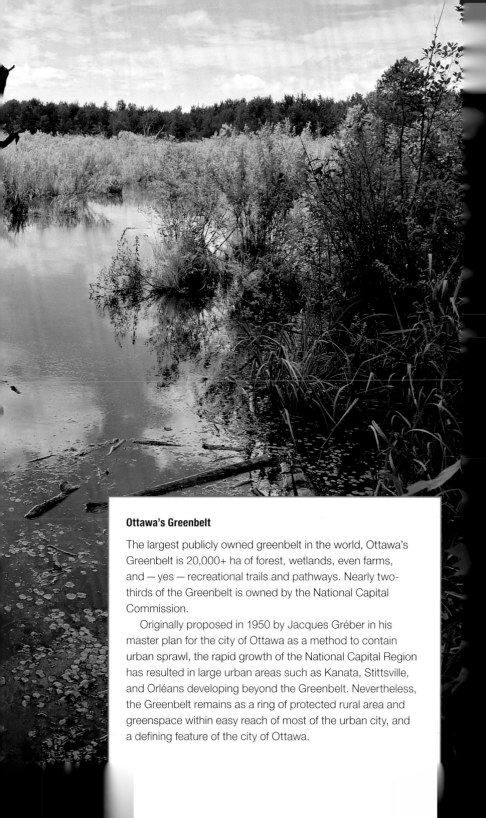

Ottawa's Greenbelt

The largest publicly owned greenbelt in the world, Ottawa's Greenbelt is 20,000+ ha of forest, wetlands, even farms, and — yes — recreational trails and pathways. Nearly two-thirds of the Greenbelt is owned by the National Capital Commission.

Originally proposed in 1950 by Jacques Gréber in his master plan for the city of Ottawa as a method to contain urban sprawl, the rapid growth of the National Capital Region has resulted in large urban areas such as Kanata, Stittsville, and Orléans developing beyond the Greenbelt. Nevertheless, the Greenbelt remains as a ring of protected rural area and greenspace within easy reach of most of the urban city, and a defining feature of the city of Ottawa.

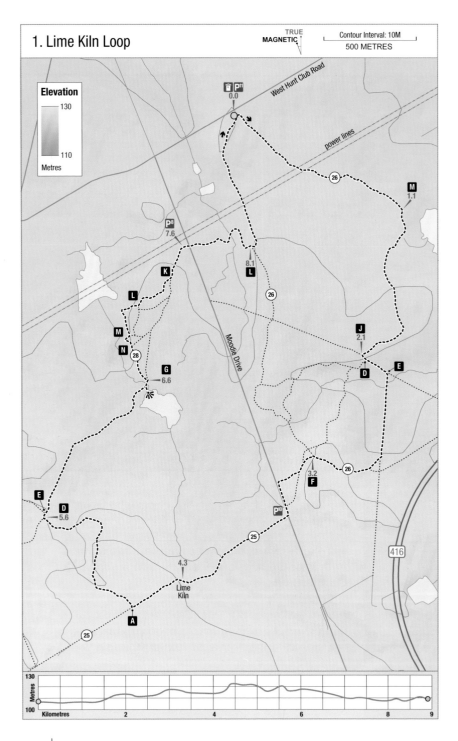

1. Lime Kiln Loop

TRUE
MAGNETIC

Contour Interval: 10M
500 METRES

West Hunt Club Road

power lines

Elevation
130
110
Metres

Moodie Drive

Lime
Kiln

416

130
Metres
100 | Kilometres | 2 | 4 | 6 | 8 | 9

1. Lime Kiln Loop

Distance: 8.9 km
Type: loop
Difficulty: 2
Ascent/descent: 21 m
Hiking time: 2+ hrs
Trail conditions: compacted earth, crushed stone, natural surface
Cellphone coverage: excellent

Uses: walking, snowshoeing, cross-country skiing
Facilities: benches, garbage cans, interpretive panels, outhouses, picnic tables
Hazards: poison ivy, road crossing, ticks

Finding the trailhead: From the Highway 416/417 split, follow Highway 416 for 3.5 km to exit 72. Turn right onto West Hunt Club Road and follow it for 1.2 km. Turn left into parking area P11.

Trailhead: 45°18'23.1" N, 75°49'01.4" W

Introduction: Experienced hikers know that the Rideau Trail connects the cities of Kingston and Ottawa with a hiking path more than 300 km long. However, it is less commonly known that, in addition to the main route, there are a number of signed side trails. One of these is the Lime Kiln Loop, which uses several of the National Capital Commission's Greenbelt trails. This is an excellent route for nature watching, especially for viewing waterfowl. It also passes its namesake lime kiln, a historical site featuring several interpretive display panels.

The Lime Kiln Loop is a good choice for those wishing to hike for a couple of hours and who want something easier than rugged Gatineau Park, but do not wish to drive too far. This can be good for families with children capable of two to three hours of walking.

Dogs are permitted on leash during non-snow months but prohibited during snow season (December 1–April 14).

Route description: From P11, where there are garbage cans, an outhouse, and a trailhead kiosk – including a map – take the leftmost of the two available paths, both Trail 26. The treadway is extremely clear, a well-worn track through the thick vegetation. You should notice blue triangles affixed to some trees; these are the markers of the Rideau Trail Association, which signs their main route with orange triangles, and uses blue ones for side trails. Views are few until at 450 m, where the trail crosses the cleared space beneath two power lines.

On the opposite side the path enters a dense stand of cedar, evoking unbidden images of haunted forests, especially when the sun hides behind clouds.

From time to time, the remains of stone fences can be glimpsed among the trees. The path is moving closer to busy Highway 416, so the drone of automobiles will probably be strong for the first few kilometres.

After a pleasant meander through the trees, at 1.1 km I encountered junction post M. These posts are excellent, compact yet providing a map of the nearby trail system. But this one is noteworthy because it isn't at a trail junction, and it mistakenly stated that it was 500 m from P11. Hopefully this has been corrected.

About 150 m further, the trail turns distinctly right and crosses a wet area on a boardwalk, and at 2.1 km it arrives at junction J. Turn left, now on a very wide track, toward junction D, which is only 200 m further. Continue straight, toward junction E. Very quickly the trail narrows, then crosses a series of short boardwalks/drainage culverts. Turn right at junction E. To the right lies a large marsh, and for the next 400 m the path is quite straight as it uses an impoundment embankment for its route. Just beyond this marsh, where some informal paths branch left, Trail 26 then curves right into a lovely stand of young hardwoods.

📍**3.2 km** Junction F is critical, because this is the final decision point between a shorter hike along the remainder of Trail 26 or the full Lime Kiln Loop. For the latter, turn left; in 200 m the path ends at Moodie Drive. This is a busy road that must be crossed, but first turn left and remain on the same side for 200 m. Once opposite the Lime Kiln parking area (P10), cross there carefully.

Continue through the parking area, where there are garbage cans and a trailhead kiosk with map. (Notice that these trails are for cross-country skiing in winter.) The pathway, Trail 25, is wide at first with wetlands on both sides.

An interpretive panel, at a bench, explains the purpose of a lime kiln. After 400 m, the trail narrows then crosses some boardwalks, becoming simply a well-defined footpath until it reaches the Lime Kiln ruins at 4.3 km. There are several additional interpretive panels here.

Beyond the ruins, the trail enters an area ravaged by a 2012 forest fire, where the reconstructed pathway becomes a wide crushed-stone path. About 300 m further, it arrives at junction A. This sits in a large open area created by the fire, and three interpretive panels describe how much the fire has altered the area.

Turn right, and head toward junction D. Because of the fire, the route on the ground doesn't match what is shown on the map. However, the wide track, on natural surface, meanders through this extensively fire-damaged area and should be easy to follow: watch for the blue triangles. This route is interesting enough, though not particularly scenic.

5.6 km Arrive at junction D, which is the connection to the main route of the Rideau Trail. Keep straight/right, heading toward junction E, which is so close that you might miss it. From here, head toward junction G. This pleasant section, though often wide, shows no evidence of fire damage, and so looks delightful by comparison. An easy walk continues until, just after reaching a boardwalk, at 6.6 km, Trail 25 arrives at junction G and Trail 28.

What follows is a small area with an extensive network of paths, the Chipmunk Trail and the Beaver Trail. To keep it simple, turn left at junction G, and again at junctions N, M, L, and K, all of which will be reached in the following 700 m. (This is a busy place.) Along the way are some lovely hardwood ridges, a viewing platform overlooking a wetland, and the former home of the Wild Bird Care Centre.

7.6 km After junction K, where once again you keep left, the path soon emerges into the Beaver Trail parking area (P8), where there are outhouses, then Moodie Drive. Trail 28 ends at this parking lot, but the blue route of the Rideau Trail continues across the road and enters the forest on its far side.

The next section is trail built and maintained by Rideau Trail volunteers, so is at a slightly different standard than those of the National Capital Commission. The treadway is narrow: well defined but rougher, with more roots and rocks intruding. After about 200 m, the footpath reaches the John Bennett Boardwalk, named for a long-time volunteer, then passes through an interesting cedar stand before reconnecting, at 8.1 km, with Trail 26 at junction L.

Turn left, and an easy 800 m stroll remains to your starting point at P11.

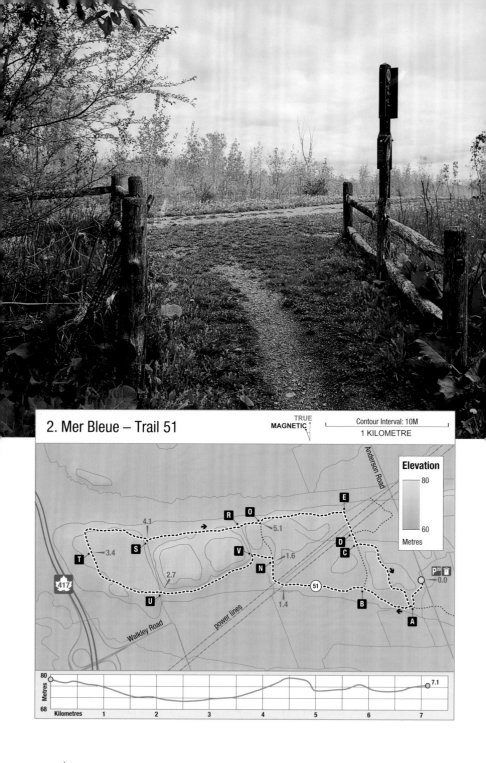

2. Mer Bleue – Trail 51

TRUE
MAGNETIC

Contour Interval: 10M
1 KILOMETRE

Elevation

80

60

Metres

2. Mer Bleue – Trail 51

Distance: 7.1 km
Type: loop
Difficulty: 2
Ascent/descent: 41 m
Hiking time: 2+ hrs
Trail conditions: compacted earth, crushed stone, natural surface

Cellphone coverage: excellent
Uses: walking, snowshoeing, cross-country skiing
Facilities: benches, garbage cans, picnic tables, outhouse
Hazards: poison ivy, ticks

Finding the trailhead: From the Highway 417/174 split, head east on Highway 417 for 1.7 km to exit 112 Innes Road. Turn left onto Innes Road and follow it for 2.3 km to Anderson Road. Turn right onto Anderson Road, and follow it for 1.6 km to a roundabout, keeping right on Anderson Road for an additional 1.8 km to parking area P20, on the right.

Trailhead: 45°24'15.4" N, 75°33'31.5" W

Introduction: There are a number of walking trails in the Mer Bleue area, not all connected. They are situated on a series of low, sandy ridges that are separated by extensive wetlands. I have selected Trail 51, which is organized into four connected trails that are also known as "stacked loops." This permits users to select the distance appropriate for them. I have profiled the outer perimeter, providing the longest hike possible without repeating any sections.

One of my favourite features of Trail 51 is its many bird feeders, which have been put up by local residents. Scattered throughout the route, these attract dozens of chickadees, nuthatches, and other species, especially in the winter. Spread a few sunflower seeds in your palm, hold very still, and within a minute you will have a procession of these featherlight diners perching delicately on your fingertips. Dogs are permitted on leash during non-snow months but prohibited during snow season (December 1-April 14).

Route description: In P20, a wood rail fence separates the path from the parking lot. At its opening is an array of regulatory signs, and a kiosk where a trail map is posted. A bear-proof garbage can and an outhouse are there, and beneath the pines to the right there are several picnic tables positioned near bird feeders.

The wide, compacted earth pathway wends through hardwoods for 200 m to the first junction, which is signed as "A" and features another map. Continue straight toward junction B. This easy path works along near the edge of the ridge, with the wetlands of Mer Bleue to your left and below. Very quickly you will encounter the first, for want of a better description, bird feeder tree. This is an old, tall cedar decorated with perhaps two dozen bird feeders, many of them brightly coloured. As you might expect, bird – and squirrel – activity in this area is usually quite high. In May, look for purple trilliums blossoming on the right side of the path in this area.

At 700 m, in a small clearing fringed by birch, with more bird boxes, sits junction B. Continue straight, toward junction M. Through this next section you pass several stands of red pine, their ordered ranks filing off to your right. Occasional yellow circles affixed to trees sign the cross-country ski route. At 1.4 km, the trail curves right and passes through the open area beneath two high electrical towers. Junction M, directly ahead, is the site of a junction with a future trail. Continue straight toward junction N.

1.6 km After stepping carefully through an area that can be soggy after a rainfall, the trail arrives at junction N. For a shorter walk and to remain on (mostly) dry trail, continue straight. The profiled route turns left, toward junction V. This next 200 m, crossing a swampy area, has some wet spots, even though a long boardwalk traverses most of it.

But then, as you climb up a low slope to junction V, the trail becomes a wide, crushed-stone track. Turn left again, heading toward junction U. Trail 51 works around the south side of a low hill, thick vegetation to the left and semi-open slope to your right, for a gentle, easy stroll

2.7 km The wide pathway ends at junction U. To your left, about 300 m away, is an access point on Walkley Road, the only available exit option. Continue straight, toward post T. The experience changes significantly, as the trail narrows to a natural-surface footpath shaded by enfolding hardwoods. Even though it remains wide enough for two, it feels much more inviting.

Trail 51 continues in a more or less straight line, though gradually curving right. Despite the thickly forested surroundings, the traffic noise from nearby Highway 417 grows regrettably louder. At 3.4 km, and not at a junction, sits post T. Perhaps it is here because this is about the furthest point from P20. After another 200 m, the path turns distinctly right. You should notice that the route has returned to a ridge crest, with cultivated fields left and below. The next 500 m are among my most favourite, with the path making small turns and passing over low undulations, tiny mounds that have not been levelled. Unfortunately, there is a short area that is often poorly drained. Expect wet feet, particularly in the spring or after a rainfall.

At 4.1 km, the path emerges from the trees to return to open ground at junction S. Continue straight (left), toward junction R, on the wide crushed-stone track with the open hillside to the right. The nearby apartment towers of Blackburn Hamlet look incongruous sprouting above the distant trees. For 800 m the route remains in the open, until it reaches junction R.

Keep straight, toward junction O, where the path re-enters the forest, and another stretch of wet ground. There is a boardwalk, but when I was there in late May there was considerably more water than board. By junction O, at 5.1 km, the route returns to drier ground and a wide compacted earth tread-way. Continue straight, following the ridgeline as before, as the trees on the slope change to include more cedar and some stands of hemlock. This is a particularly magnificent section to walk in the fall, when the leaves are so vividly colourful.

After 600 m, at junction E, turn right toward junction D. The trail again crosses beneath the power lines 100 m later, then reaches junction D about 50 m beyond that. Continue straight, crossing a small bridge – and popular feeding location for squirrels and birds; expect to be "mugged." On the far end is junction C, where you turn left.

I particularly enjoyed the next 800 m, with its many boardwalks and attractive woodlands. The ground through which the trail passes is often low and wet – mosquitoes can be plentiful here – but the route weaves through this soggy area, skirting the wettest spots.

At 6.9 km, the path returns to junction A, and the broad, dry pathway. Turn left and retrace the route back to P20.

Chickadees

Tiny, energetic birds flitting among the pines and hardwoods, emitting their easily recognizable call of "chik-a-dee-dee," are a common hiking companion. Black-capped chickadees are quite curious and very comfortable around people. Stand motionless and make a low, steady "pish-pish-pish" sound; this should soon result in several of the little birds alighting on nearby trees to get a closer look. Place sunflower seeds in your palm and remain motionless, and they may land momentarily to feed.

Eastern White Cedar

One of the most valuable trees for wildlife habitat in Ontario, eastern white cedar, sometimes called the "tree of life," grows in abundance in the Ottawa Valley. With its thick evergreen foliage, white cedar provides shelter and food to deer, small mammals, and many species of birds. It can grow to 15 m high and live up to four hundred years in swamps.

White cedar grows best in moist, well-drained soil over limestone bedrock, and often develops in pure stands in old fields and pastures. It thrives in areas of thin soil. As a result, much of Ottawa's Greenbelt, in particular Stoney Swamp, features extensive and dense stands of white cedar.

3. Old Quarry Trail

TRUE
MAGNETIC

Contour Interval: 10M
500 METRES

Elevation

130

100

Metres

Robertson Road

Eaglesons Corners

Eagleson Road

E

G — 3.2

D   1.9

C

A

1.5

4.9

B

23

24

H — 2.5

TRAIL

0.0   0.15

117

Metres

102

Kilometres   1   2   3   4   5   6

5.5

3. Old Quarry Trail

Distance: 5.5 km
Type: loop
Difficulty: 1
Ascent/descent: 14 m
Hiking time: 1+ hrs
Trail conditions: compacted earth, crushed stone, natural surface

Cellphone coverage: excellent
Uses: walking, biking*, snowshoeing, cross-country skiing
Facilities: benches, garbage cans, interpretive panels, picnic tables, outhouse
Hazards: poison ivy, ticks

Finding the trailhead: From the Highway 417/416 split, follow Highway 417 west for 6.5 km to exit 138. Turn left onto Eagleson Road, and follow it for 2.5 km. Turn left into parking area P5.

OC Transpo route 88, and several others, stops 250 m from P5, at the Eagleson/Hazeldean Mall stop.

Trailhead: 45°18'06.2" N, 75°52'27.1" W

Introduction: The Old Quarry Trail is located in the Stoney Swamp area, where the most extensive network of the Greenbelt's walking routes can be found. In the first edition of *Hiking Trails of Ottawa*, I included extensive portions of Trails 23, 24, and 25, as well as segments of the Rideau Trail and the Ottawa-Carleton Trailway. However, I found that route somewhat difficult to follow, especially for newer walkers, so I chose instead to profile only the two loops of Trail 23.

Walking the Old Quarry Trail is ideal for a pleasant family outing or an excellent introductory hike for those just starting their outdoor explorations. The route can be considerably shortened, if desired, by turning left at either junction 23B or 23C and completing only one loop, rather than turning right for the second, as I recommend.

Dogs are not permitted on Trail 23, even on leash.

Route description: The trailhead area has been significantly improved since 2010, particularly with regard to signage, although I saw no map. A pleasant picnic area and an outhouse are also there. Begin your Trail 23 walk on what appears to be the middle of three possible tracks. This is partially surfaced with a narrow strip of crushed stone.

The path quickly enters the forest, and in 150 m reaches a short side path, to the left, that leads to an interpretive panel. As this describes the topography of the area, definitely read it. From here, the trail crosses a former field, at the end of which an informal footpath – the first of many – branches to the right.

Remain on the crushed stone, which briefly curves left, reaches another interpretive panel, then turns right nearly 180°.

Now in a little grove of cedar, Trail 23 runs behind a low stony ridge (explained by the first interpretive panel), with a wetland visible to the left. At 700 m, Trail 23 curves left, an informal path – connecting to a nearby neighbourhood – branching right. Almost immediately, Trail 23 crosses a wetland on a fairly long boardwalk. Once across, there is a short stretch of rock and natural-surface trail – at least, there was in 2019 – but the crushed stone soon resumes. Lower ground and a swamp are to the left, but the terrain on the right is only marginally higher, so there was some evidence that this part of the trail gets submerged occasionally. As the path skirts the edge of this large wetland, there is at least one more interpretive panel, which explains why the swamp is here.

1.5 km The trail reaches junction B, which has a signpost that includes a map. (All the junction signposts feature a map – an excellent improvement.) To add the second loop, turn right here, and right again at junction C, which is only 300 m distant. From here, the path reduces to a narrow track through the grass. Junction D is barely 100 m further, where you turn right once again.

Forest soon encloses the footpath, often providing overhead shade. Stands of cedar, groves of pine, and dense thickets of young hardwoods alternate as the natural-surfaced track meanders through the woods. No distant views are available, imparting this section with a more remote quality.

At 2.5 km, junction H is reached. Directly ahead, it connects to The Great Trail (Trans Canada) connector between Ottawa and Carleton Place. Trail 23 turns left, and for the next 700 m runs roughly parallel to – and sometimes in sight of – this broad crushed-stone-surfaced former railway line. This is a more open section, a wider trail which passes through several small grass-covered open areas.

3.2 km Junction G provides another connection to The Great Trail, and other Greenbelt trails beyond that, but turn left toward junction E. The wide, straight path appears to be a former road, and the traffic on busy Robertson Road can be seen in the distance. However, the bordering trees are tall and provide shade, and junction E is reached in only 250 m, where you turn left and head back toward junction D.

Once again on a crushed-stone surface, this section passes through some stands of lovely pine, with their fallen needles often covering the pathway. It is an uncomplicated and pleasing stroll back to junction D, at 4.4 km, and the completion of this loop.

Keep straight (right) at junction D, and retrace the 150 m to junction C, the only section you will repeat. From there continue straight/right, through more stands of cedar and small rocky outcroppings. The route nearly touches Robertson Road, crossing a very small bridge, before curving left and away to climb over a low ridge.

At 4.9 km, the trail reaches junction A: to the right only a flat 600 m remains before Trail 23 ends at P5.

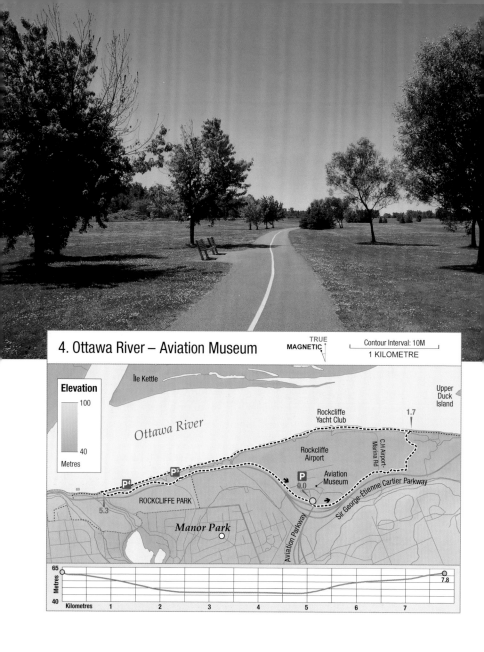

4. Ottawa River – Aviation Museum

TRUE
MAGNETIC

Contour Interval: 10M
1 KILOMETRE

Île Kettle

Ottawa River

Elevation
100
40
Metres

Upper
Duck
Island

Rockcliffe
Yacht Club

1.7

Rockcliffe
Airport

C.H Airport-
Marina Rd.

Aviation
Museum

P
0.0

P⁴

P⁵

ROCKCLIFFE PARK

5.3

Aviation Parkway

Sir George-Étienne Cartier Parkway

Manor Park

65
Metres
40

Kilometres   1   2   3   4   5   6   7

7.8

4. Ottawa River – Aviation Museum

Distance: 7.8 km
Type: loop
Difficulty: 2
Ascent/descent: 18 m
Hiking time: 2+ hrs
Trail conditions: asphalt, crushed stone

Cellphone coverage: excellent
Uses: walking, biking, inline skating*, snowshoeing, cross-country skiing
Facilities: benches, garbage cans, picnic tables
Hazards: high usage, poison ivy, road crossing, ticks

Finding the trailhead: The Aviation Museum is at the north end of the Aviation Parkway, 4.9 km from the Highway 417/174 split. However, the only direction from which Aviation Parkway can be accessed is from exit 112/Innes Road on Highway 417. There is no access from Highway 417 from the west, nor from Highway 174 to the east. Park in the south end of the pay parking lot; the trail starts in the southwest corner.

Trailhead: 45°27'24.5" N, 75°38'41.6" W

Introduction: Few hikes offer the possibility of combining your walk with a visit to a nationally famous museum. By itself the loop, which includes 3.5 km of the most exquisite scenery along the banks of the Ottawa River, is one of the better options available within the Greenbelt. Add to that the possibility of spending a few additional hours exploring the Aviation Museum, and I think you have a most enjoyable way to spend a day.

This is a very good walk for families, but those with small children should be aware that the asphalt sections are heavily used by cyclists, particularly on the weekends. Limiting your travel to the crushed-stone track along the river will probably result in a more relaxing experience. To do that, start from an alternative parking area, 1.6 km along the Aviation Parkway to the left of the museum.

Route description: Next to the Aviation Museum parking lot is a map pavilion, which often contains free brochures outlining the National Capital Region's bike paths, and a few other regulatory and informational signs. Turn left and follow the paved Aviation Pathway – keeping to the right of the yellow centre line, of course – as it crosses Aviation Parkway and heads through a very large grassy field. To your right is the Sir George-Étienne Cartier Parkway (formerly Rockcliffe Parkway), which your route will parallel; to the left are the huge hangers of the Aviation Museum and behind that, Rockcliffe Airport.

For the next 900 m you march across the wide-open grassland. A few ornamental trees have been planted, and two benches at 500 m permit you

to watch the continual procession of small aircraft taking off and landing. At the far end of the open ground you cross Polaris Avenue, finally obtaining a little forest cover, although mostly young trees. The paved pathway also begins to curve somewhat, but still follows alongside Sir George-Étienne Cartier Parkway for another 300 m before turning sharply left, away from the road and toward the Ottawa River. The trail coils pleasantly through the young hardwoods, crossing a small railed bridge at 1.6 km.

1.7 km Immediately afterwards, it curves right and then descends a short slope to connect with the Ottawa River Pathway. The asphalt surface ends here, and a wide crushed-stone pathway stretches off in both directions. Directly across the broad river is the province of Quebec; to your right are Upper and Lower Duck Islands and the Ottawa River stretching toward Montréal.

A directional sign says that Parliament is to our left, 9 km away. We will not be going that far, but that is the direction of our hike. You may wish to shut your conscious mind off for the next little while. The crushed-stone-surfaced Ottawa River Pathway traces the banks of the river closely, tree-covered hill-side on your left, water less than 5 m to your right. The broad, smooth pathway is level and without tree roots or rocks to trip you, so you have little to divert your attention from the lovely view.

One of the most striking characteristics of this route is how little evidence you can see of human habitation. You are in the middle of one of the largest metropolitan regions in Canada, yet visible are only a few houses at river level on the Quebec side, possibly one or two office towers far ahead, and the steam from the pulp and paper mills pushing above the trees of Île Kettle.

After 900 m, the trail passes through the Rockcliffe Yacht Club, crossing its launch ramp. (Those wishing a shorter walk can turn left here and walk along Polaris Avenue back to the Aviation Pathway.) On the far side of the RYC is the first of many benches, so you may wish to sit and enjoy the view. But there is also a sobering sign warning of the presence of poison ivy.

For the next 2.6 km there is little additional to relate. Numerous benches, always on your left, facing the water, provide the possibility to relax and contemplate the scenery. There are several possible exits, well signed and announcing a steadily decreasing distance to Parliament. Take any of these up the hillside to shorten your trip. But I consider the river view so pleasing that I recommend that you continue until you are almost within hailing distance of a large white building, once home to the Ottawa New Edinburgh Club.

Just 200 m beyond the Hillside Road exit, which states that Parliament is only 5.7 km further, an unmarked, but paved, route heads left up the slope: climb.

5.3 km At the top of the short hill, you rejoin the paved Aviation Pathway. Turn left and follow this as it parallels Sir George-Étienne Cartier Parkway back to the Aviation Museum. Your route now remains on the embankment above the river and mostly on open ground. Occasional benches look toward the water whenever any view presents itself, and you will pass parking areas P4 and P5, crossing their entranceways, which are often very busy. The only services at each are garbage cans, picnic tables, and trail maps.

There are three other connecting paths back to the river track, should you wish to return alongside the water, with the final one at 6.6 km. On your right, across Sir George-Étienne Cartier Parkway, you can see the fields and structures of the Canadian Police College and the Home of the RCMP Musical Ride Stables. Directly ahead, the massive buildings of the Aviation Museum dominate.

In its final 800 m, the asphalt pathway curves away from the river, veering right to avoid the end of Rockcliffe Airport's runway. Small aircraft regularly fly directly overhead, and a few benches provide ideal viewing. The path continues across the open fields, close to the Aviation Parkway, before returning to the museum's parking lot.

Canada Goose

Ottawa sits on one of North America's main migratory flyways, and every spring and fall the region's watercourses and farmers' fields are dimpled with tens of thousands of these raucous visitors.

Canada geese are easy to identify as large, plump birds with black heads and necks and contrasting white throats. They are noisy, constantly making low honking sounds that rise in volume considerably when they become airborne. Their long V-formations, often heard before they are seen, easily evoke a sense of awe and wonder.

On trails near water, geese are frequently a hazard, either because of their violent territorial defence when approached — they show little fear of humans — or their extravagant and lush droppings (bikers especially beware!).

Trillium

The white trillium, the provincial flower of Ontario, carpets the hardwood forest floor of Gatineau Park and much of the region for a few weeks each spring from late April through early May. Usually blossoming before leaves have opened on hardwood trees, these distinctive, three-leafed trilliums glow brightly in the spring sunlight, in clusters of hundreds or thousands.

The less common purple trillium, shyly hiding its flower, may also often be found mixed among its more visible relative, and the painted trillium — far rarer still — is usually found in the shade of acid-loving trees.

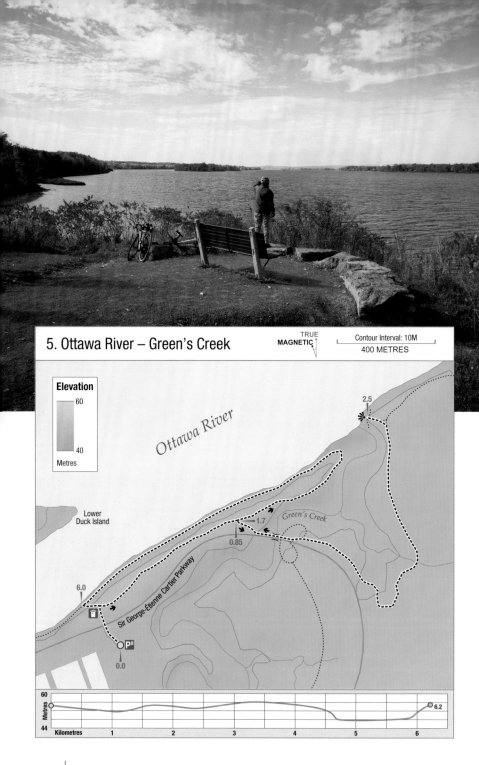

5. Ottawa River – Green's Creek

TRUE
MAGNETIC

Contour Interval: 10M
400 METRES

Elevation
60
40
Metres

Ottawa River

Lower
Duck Island

Green's Creek

2.5

1.7

0.85

6.0

Sir George-Étienne Cartier Parkway

0.0

60
Metres
44
Kilometres   1   2   3   4   5   6

6.2

5. Ottawa River – Green's Creek

Distance: 6.2 km
Type: loop
Difficulty: 2
Ascent/descent: 10 m
Hiking time: 1.5+ hrs
Trail conditions: asphalt, compacted earth

Cellphone coverage: excellent
Uses: walking, biking, inline skating*, snowshoeing, cross-country skiing
Facilities: benches, garbage cans, outhouse
Hazards: poison ivy, road crossing, ticks

Finding the trailhead: From the Highway 417/174 split, follow Highway 174 for 4.5 km to the Montreal Road exit. Turn right onto Montreal Road, and in 1 km turn left onto Sir George-Étienne Cartier Parkway (formerly Rockcliffe Parkway). Follow Sir George-Étienne Parkway for 3.2 km; turn left into parking area P8. The trail starts on the east side of the lot.

Trailhead: 45°28'00.3" N, 75°34'53.7" W

Introduction: One of the most striking characteristics of the city of Ottawa is how much of its shoreline along the Ottawa River is preserved as public space. In the east, from Rockcliffe Park to Petrie Island, a distance of nearly 18 km, the shoreline is public land, and trails run almost the entire distance.

In my opinion, these are among the most scenic pathways in the city, and all are worth visiting any time of the year. I have profiled a section that leads from the parking lot at Green's Creek toward Orléans, which includes the best view of the river. This route is best hiked late in the day, when the sun is setting behind the Gatineau Hills and the river is a ribbon of gold stretching from your feet toward the horizon.

Route description: From P8, cross Sir George-Étienne Cartier Parkway and head onto the paved pathway in the direction of the river. At 150 m, you reach a junction, with an outhouse and a trail map, and the Ottawa River can be seen to the left and below. Turn right instead, and head into the forest, in the direction indicated by the sign saying Orléans is 3 km. Do not worry! You will see the river on the return walk.

These woods are very attractive, especially in the late afternoon, even though they do thin out after another 150 m. The paved trail meanders nicely, never settling into an extended straightaway for long, and with vegetation growing lushly to the edge of the asphalt.

By the way, pay attention to the yellow line in the middle and stay to the right. This is a busy bicycle route, and sharing the trail means staying in the proper lane. Bikes are required by law to have bells, so if you suddenly hear

jingling, freeze — or at least continue in a straight line and let the cyclists pass safely.

Regrettably, this path parallels Sir George-Etienne Cartier Parkway, traffic on which can sometimes be busy, and within 20 m. However, when there are leaves on the hardwoods, it is usually well buffered. After 850 m, you reach a junction with a crushed-stone-covered path. Keep right, and follow the asphalt pathway as it emerges from the forest and crosses Green's Creek on the sidewalk of the road bridge.

On the opposite side, another gravel path branches left, and you might notice another trail on the far side of the road, but there is another map sign here if you are unsure of your route. There is also a sign warning about poison ivy; take that very seriously. (I know from personal experience!)

Continue on the paved pathway, which crosses a field while edging further from the parkway. Within a few hundred metres it enters an area beneath towering hemlock and other softwoods. On summer days it is always much cooler here, under their shade. The trail skirts around the edge of several ravines while also curving wildly around several large trees: if you are riding a bicycle, be attentive.

Though pretty, it is an all too brief 250 m before you emerge from the forest, already into a long sweeping curve that arcs through 180° and crosses a tiny brook. Cultivated fields stretch from the far-off Highway 174 almost onto the path's edge. The trail describes two more curves and crosses another tiny brook before settling into a long straightaway, 1.9 km from P8. For the next 600 m the path passes through open grassland, farmland to the right, trees left.

2.5 km You reach a junction. On your left, it is a short 80 m side trail to a lookout situated above Green's Creek where it enters the Ottawa River. The view from this knoll, facing toward the Gatineau Hills but with sight lines north and east as well, is grand. Quite possibly it is the finest view along the entire river, particularly at sunset. Unofficial but distinct footpaths enable you to drop down to river level. The benches here are almost always occupied by someone enjoying the scenic vista.

The paved pathway continues all the way to Petrie Islands, another 8.2 km. If you are feeling energetic, go for it! Otherwise, retrace your route back, across Green's Creek, until the intersection with the crushed-stone path, about 1.7 km from the lookout. A directional sign, next to a garbage can, says that this is an alternate route to Parliament, 14.7 km away. Turn right; you will only be walking 2 km of this trail.

This track is a little narrower than the main route, with vegetation crowding closer to its edge. It starts on the top of a small ridge above Green's Creek, which is soon visible to the right, but within 500 m drops down to pass closer to the narrow, slow-moving stream. Within another 100 m, the trail swings 180° in a tight curve, to fetch up against the bank of the broad Ottawa River, at this point more than 1 km wide. Only a few houses are visible in Gatineau, on the far bank, and there are often numerous recreational boaters. Ahead, in the middle of the river, lie the low bulks of Upper and Lower Duck Islands.

For the next 1.2 km, the wide crushed-stone pathway traces the bank of the river, your view unobstructed. Several benches invite one to sit and spend a few extra tranquil moments.

♀ **6 km** Too quickly, the trail reaches an intersection with a paved trail descending the hill on the left: the return route. Of course, the Ottawa River Pathway continues ahead, stretching all the way, almost, to the urban core, and all along the water: tempting! But that's for another day. Turn left and head the 200 m back to P8.

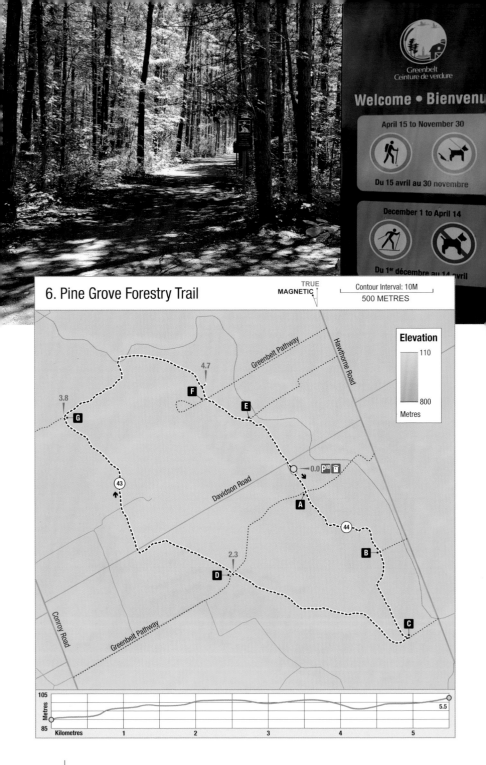

6. Pine Grove Forestry Trail

TRUE
MAGNETIC

Contour Interval: 10M
500 METRES

Elevation
110
800
Metres

Greenbelt Pathway

Hawthorne Road

4.7

F

E

3.8

G

43

Davidson Road

0.0

A

44

B

2.3

D

C

Conroy Road

Greenbelt Pathway

105
Metres
85
Kilometres   1   2   3   4   5
5.5

Greenbelt
Ceinture de verdure

Welcome • Bienvenu

April 15 to November 30

Du 15 avril au 30 novembre

December 1 to April 14

Du 1er décembre au 14 avril

6. Pine Grove Forestry Trail

Distance: 5.5 km
Type: loop
Difficulty: 1
Ascent/descent: 3 m
Hiking time: 1.5+ hrs
Trail conditions: compacted earth, crushed stone, natural surface
Cellphone coverage: excellent

Uses: walking, biking*, snowshoeing, cross-country skiing
Facilities: benches, garbage cans, interpretive panels, outhouse, picnic tables
Hazards: poison ivy, road crossings, ticks

Finding the trailhead: From the Highway 417/174 split, follow Highway 417 east 5.3 km to the Hunt Club Road exit. Turn right onto Hunt Club Road for 1.4 km, then turn left onto Hawthorne Road. Follow Hawthorne for an additional 2.1 km, then turn right onto Davidson Road. P18, well signed, is on the left in 500 m.

Trailhead: 45°21'15.3" N, 75°35'31.6" W

Introduction: The majority of trails in the Greenbelt use former forestry or farming roads as their foundation. This means that they are often wide and level, comfortable for sharing with a companion. And enough time has passed that in most cases the vegetation has grown onto and around them, making them seem rather naturalized. The Pine Grove Forestry Trail is ideal for an evening's amble in sylvan surroundings, for those who walk more slowly or not so far, or for those who simply wish a gentle, relaxing stroll. An additional feature, for those wishing to combine some education with their exercise, is a number of interpretive panels that identify the trees and explain various forest management techniques.

Portions of both Trails 43 and 44 are part of the Greenbelt Eastern Pathway, an initiative to create an off-road recreational pathway that will circle the city of Ottawa. Cycling is permitted on these sections.

Dogs are permitted on leash during hiking season, officially posted as being from April 15 to November 30, but not at all from December 1 to April 14.

Route description: From the parking area, where there are garbage cans, picnic tables, an outhouse, and a trailhead kiosk with a map, begin your walk down the wide, crushed-stone pathway on the other side of a metal gate. However, barely 100 m later, at junction A – where there is another map – the Greenbelt Pathway turns right. Trail 44 continues straight, and the crushed-stone surface ends.

This is still quite easy walking, through an attractive forest that provides considerable overhead shade, although by 300 m an increasing number of tree roots peek up through the treadway and the path has narrowed somewhat. Soon it narrows even more, as it crosses the first of several boardwalks. To the right, a large wetland is clearly visible.

At 700 m, the trail reaches junction B. To the left, and in sight, is Hawthorne Road. Continue straight toward junction C; the sign also states that it is 2.4 km back to P18. The footpath, grass covered or natural surface, continues through the thick vegetation, providing occasional glimpses of the wetland as it crosses more boardwalks.

Upon reaching junction C, 500 m further, turn right again, onto a wide track. This soon curves right, and soon there is wet ground on both sides. Thick alders often line the path, particularly on the right. But by about 1.7 km, the trail moves onto drier ground, and into attractive stands of tall pine. This enables viewing into the forest for a considerable distance. The path also becomes very wide.

2.3 km Trail 44 arrives at junction D, where there is a bench, and it also intersects the Greenbelt Pathway. Those wishing a short loop should turn right here; it is about 750 m back to P18. Otherwise, continue straight, toward junction 43G, which will be across Davidson Road.

The wide pathway soon becomes grass-surfaced, though with a centre strip of bare earth: dry and flat. In 400 m, it reaches Davidson Road, where there is a wooden gate. Just before reaching the pavement, an arrow directs walkers to the left, and a slender footpath – with a few soggy spots – cuts through the trees parallel to the highway. In less than 200 m, this exits onto the road opposite another wooden gate: cross here.

Once across, Trail 43 resumes as a wide, compacted earth pathway, on quite sandy soil, lined by tall hardwoods that shade the route. There is minimal signage, and several informal paths branching from it, but Trail 43 remains on the very wide track.

3.8 km Junction 43G is in a small open, grassy area, at a T-junction with another wide track. Conroy Road is to the left; Trail 43 heads right. The easy stroll through the attractive forest continues. About 400 m from junction 43 G, the trail turns left to avoid a small wetland, but it soon curves right around it until it finally settles into its return route toward P18.

At 4.7 km, you will encounter the first interpretive panels, which are in a short side track on the left. Just 200 m further, at junction F, the Greenbelt Pathway connects from the left, and shares Trail 43 back to P18. On the right is the short Arboretum Loop, with another collection of interpretive panels.

During the remaining 600 m to Davidson Road, interpretive panels alongside the path are frequent; at the highway a large pavilion on your left profiles a history of the region. It also contains a map outlining the tree populations found along the route. Much of the information was provided by the Eastern Ontario Model Forest, which administers the silvacultural maintenance of this property. Text may be found on all sides of the pavilion; do not overlook the part turned away from the trail.

Cross Davidson Road one final time, and finish your hike at P18 directly ahead.

White-tailed Deer

Sighting one of these graceful delicate-looking animals can be the highlight of anyone's hike, despite its being the most numerous of all large mammals. Reddish brown on its back and sides during the summer, darker grey brown in the winter, most recognize its long, brilliantly white tail raised in alarm as it flees from people. If you encounter a spotted-coat young deer unattended, do not touch! Does frequently leave fawns alone for hours and will return to feed them, but might abandon them if they smell human scent on their coat.

The Greenbelt surrounding Ottawa is home to one of the densest populations of white-tailed deer in North America.

7. Prescott – Russell Pathway Link

TRUE
MAGNETIC

Contour Interval: 10M

4 KILOMETRES

Blackburn Hamlet

Renaud Road

Blackburn Hamlet Bypass

power line

10th Line Road

Navan

Elevation
100
600
Metres

P 0.0

1.6 2.0

4.7

6.4

8.1

10.0

12.7

Anderson Road

Mer Bleue Trail

2

417

Milton Road

Frank Kenny Road

90
Metres
65

Kilometres   2   4   6   8   10   12

12.7

7. Prescott-Russell Pathway Link

Distance: 25.4 km return
Type: linear
Difficulty: 5 (distance)
Ascent/descent: 56 m
Hiking time: 7+ hrs
Trail conditions: crushed stone
Cellphone coverage: excellent

Uses: walking, biking, horseback riding, snowshoeing, cross-country skiing, snowmobiling*
Facilities: bench, garbage cans, interpretive panels
Hazards: poison ivy, road crossings, ticks, wildlife

Finding the trailhead: From the Highway 417/174 split, head east on Highway 417 for 1.7 km to exit 112/Innes Road. Turn left onto Innes Road and follow it for 2.3 km to Anderson Road. Turn right onto Anderson Road and follow it for 1.6 km to a roundabout, keeping right on Anderson Road for an additional 300 m. The parking area is on the left.

Trailhead: 45°25'01.9" N, 75°33'54.5" W

Introduction: Over the past decade, the city of Ottawa developed and now maintains a number of abandoned railway lines as recreation pathways. The Prescott-Russell Pathway Link, utilizing a right-of-way still owned by VIA Rail, runs 22.4 km from Anderson Road to connect with the 72 km Prescott-Russell Recreational Path, creating one of the longest hiking and bicycling corridors in Eastern Ontario. Future plans include the possibility of extending into Rigaud, Quebec, and accessing that province's extensive cycling network, and of connecting with the National Capital Commission's Greenbelt Pathway, which will eventually circle the city of Ottawa.

This path is broad, surfaced entirely in crushed stone, almost level, and very easy walking. Ideal for cyclists, it is also popular with trail runners. The first several kilometres, and the section between Renaud Road and the former landfill, are excellent for families with small children.

Route description: From the parking area, follow the broad, crushed-stone pathway away from Anderson Road. The straight, level track heads immediately into a thickly wooded area, although there is no overhead shade, with low wet ground on either side. A few houses can be seen through the trees on the left at about 600 m, and the trail opens considerably when it passes beneath two power lines at 1.6 km, but otherwise it is uneventful until it reaches Renaud Road at 2 km.

This increasingly busy highway must be crossed twice in the next 300 m, and caution should be exercised, particularly at the second crossing, which is diagonal, rather than perpendicular, to traffic.

Once safely across, views open up in both directions as the trail passes through a farmed portion of the Greenbelt. New housing developments sprawl to the left, crowding right to the edge of the protected space. The first bridge, over a small stream, is crossed 250 m further.

The pathway begins a very slight curve to the right as it approaches the houses. Few trees line the trail through here, but there is a series of artificial ponds, seemingly quite popular with geese and ducks, between it and the homes. To the right, the ground is low and swampy. Side trails connect residential areas to the pathway at 3.8 km and 500 m further. New housing is still being built, so there might be additional linkages in the future.

📍**4.7 km** When the trail reaches the low hill on the left, the former landfill, it is time to consider whether to continue. Beyond this point it becomes increasingly rural. The former landfill continues for a considerable distance, and regrettably, nearly every time I passed it – more than a dozen times – there were at least a couple hundred metres of noxious odours. Cyclists enjoy a definite advantage in their ability to speed through this section!

By 5.8 km, the landfill has been passed, and soon afterwards a small golf course is visible on the left. At 6.4 km, a side path, which is actually an extension of Mer Bleue Road, connects – also on the left. After this is a somewhat larger pond, complete with wood duck boxes and a beaver lodge.

The trail reaches Tenth Line Road at 8.1 km. By this point, the Greenbelt has been left and both cultivated land and farm buildings are visible to the right. Also on the left, a low ridge parallels the route, and houses can often be seen atop it. Frequent paths connect adjacent horse paddocks to the pathway, and it is in this section that the most horseback riders – and their mounts' droppings – will probably be encountered. At 9.7 km, Milton Road must be crossed.

📍**10 km** At the Km 10 marker, just across Smith Road, is the Navan Parking Lot, the first formal trailhead since Anderson Road. This is another excellent place to turn back, providing a total distance trekked of 20 km. A picnic table is there, and a garbage can, bicycle racks, and trailhead kiosk with a map. A bronze plaque declares this the Harold H. Dent Rest Area, commemorating an Ontario Provincial Police officer murdered at the Navan train station in 1940.

The pathway continues, crossing McKinnons Creek 500 m later. Some of Navan's houses should be visible to the left, but with urban sprawl devouring land all around Ottawa, new houses are springing up all around this section. The trail begins a rare turn, this time very gradually to the left. Trim Road is crossed at 11.2 km.

The remaining 1.5 km is my favourite section on the entire Pathway Link. Initially, the trail is elevated a few metres above the surrounding land, Navan to the left, farmland to the right. By 12 km, it has moved into a forested area where there are low embankments above it. In May, shortly before the leaves fully open, these woods are carpeted with a variety of wildflowers, including both white and purple trilliums. It is an exceptionally colourful and magical spot, particularly after a long Canadian winter. Bear Creek is crossed at 12.2 km; there is even a bench here. Shortly after, a signed snowmobile trail branches left into the forest.

12.7 km The pathway reaches wide and busy Frank Kenney Road. It continues another 9.6 km to connect to the Prescott-Russell Recreational Path, but I recommend turning back and retracing your route to Anderson Road.

Mer Bleue Bog

One of the largest bogs in Southern Ontario, Mer Bleue is a provincial conservation area and an internationally significant wetland protected under the United Nations' Ramsar Convention on Wetlands. This 33.43 km^2 area is home to a variety of rare creatures, including the spotted turtle and Fletcher's dragonfly, an insect known only in a handful of sites worldwide.

Situated in an ancient channel of the Ottawa River, more than half of the bog is a raised boreal peat dome of sphagnum bog, an ecological community usually found much further north in Canada.

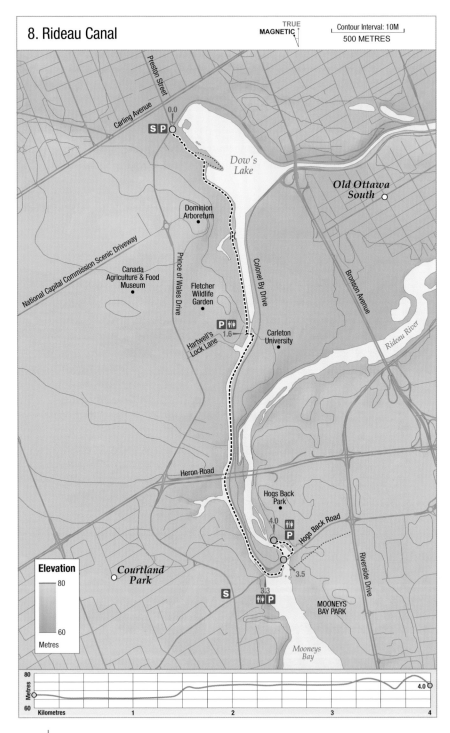

8. Rideau Canal

TRUE
MAGNETIC

Contour Interval: 10M
500 METRES

Preston Street

Carling Avenue

S P

0.0

Dow's Lake

Old Ottawa South

Dominion Arboretum

National Capital Commission Scenic Driveway

Canada Agriculture & Food Museum

Prince of Wales Drive

Fletcher Wildlife Garden

Colonel By Drive

Bronson Avenue

Rideau River

P

1.6

Hartwell's Lock Lane

Carleton University

Heron Road

Hogs Back Park

4.0

P

Hogs Back Road

Riverside Drive

3.5

Elevation

80

60

Metres

Courtland Park

S

3.3

P

MOONEYS BAY PARK

Mooneys Bay

80

Metres

4.0

60

Kilometres   1   2   3   4

8. Rideau Canal

Distance: 8 km return
Type: linear
Difficulty: 2
Ascent/descent: 55 m
Hiking time: 2+ hrs
Trail conditions: asphalt, natural surface

Cellphone coverage: excellent
Uses: walking, biking*, inline skating*, snowshoeing, cross-country skiing
Facilities: benches, garbage cans, interpretive panels, outhouses, picnic tables
Hazards: high usage, ticks

Finding the trailhead: From Highway 417 east, take exit 121A onto Bronson Avenue. After 500 m, turn right onto Carling Avenue. Follow it for 750 m, then turn left onto Preston Street. A pay parking area is on right; the entrance is on Prince of Wales Drive. The trail begins on the east side of Prince of Wales, at the intersection with Preston.

Several OC Transpo Routes stop at Carling Avenue and Preston Street, about 150 m from the trailhead.

Trailhead: 45°23'45.6" N, 75°42'24.6" W

Introduction: The Rideau Canal is one of the defining physical characteristics of the city of Ottawa. Designed as a secure military supply route, the canal has become one of the city's premier recreational facilities, its banks being a popular location for walkers, runners, and cyclists. In winter, the Rideau Canal is transformed into one of the longest, and most heavily used, ice skating rinks in the world.

Anywhere along the canal is a scenic place to walk, but the section between Dow's Lake and Hogs Back Falls is my favourite section within the urban core. Dow's Lake, its pavilion with its restaurants, its canoe and bike rental facilities, is a popular site; the Dominion Arboretum and Central Experimental Farm offer a wide possibility of enticing side-trip explorations; and Hogs Back Falls offers one of the most dramatic natural views available in the city.

This is an excellent weekend walking option, particularly early in the day. Expect a considerable number of cyclists, especially on the eastern bank of the navigation channel. Be cautious making any changes of direction.

Route description: Begin on the Rideau Canal Western Pathway, just across the intersection of Preston Street and Prince of Wales Drive. There is a large trailhead kiosk, with map, located here, and map brochures might be available. Your route begins by passing directly in front of HMCS *Carleton*, the home of the Canadian Forces Naval Reserve in Ottawa—so close to the main building that you squeeze between its front doors and two commemorative cannon pointing toward Dow's Lake.

The wide track of the Pathway, bisected by a bright yellow lane line, is asphalt surfaced, with carefully tended lawns beyond its edges. Just past HMCS *Carleton* is the first of many junctions. Keep on the asphalt pathway – although the narrow crushed-stone path that leads to the tip of a point of land and probably the best view of Dow's Lake is a nice diversion.

Benches are everywhere, too numerous to mention, and almost all facing the water. After passing a small wetland, the attractive and well-maintained grounds of the Dominium Arboretum begin to the right. At 500 m, there is a series of interpretive panels about the Arboretum and the nearby Experimental Farm – with more benches. There is also a panel that names this section the Rideau Canal Promenade.

The paved track curves gradually right, Dow's Lake narrowing into the navigation channel. At 800 m, a signed side trail branches right into the Arboretum, but you continue straight, where it says that a museum is 1.8 km distant. An attractive bridge crosses a small creek 100 m later, with a small pond bordered by large willows to the right.

Your route soon is moving parallel to the water, canal to the left and a long line of pine and spruce trees, many of them with donation plaques attached, on your right.

The pathway remains straight, though several side trails branch right. Carleton University's towers are to the left. At 1.4 km there is a major trail junction, where there are more interpretive posts. Keep left and climb a small hill.

1.6 km Arrive at Hartwells Lock, a delightful spot with benches, picnic tables, and scads of interpretive panels describing both the Rideau Canal's history and its current uses. It's also the end of the Promenade, and a very busy place during the summer, with recreational boats passing through and Parks Canada staff operating the locks.

Cross the canal here, on the narrow wooden walkway – fortunately railed – located on top of the lock gates. Cyclists must dismount to get across, and it is too narrow for wheelchairs. On the far side there is another map station; you are now on the Rideau Canal Eastern Pathway. A sign states that Parliament is 6.9 km to the left. Hogs Back Falls, however, is 1.7 km away on the right.

This next section, so close to Carleton University, can be exuberantly busy during the school year. Hundreds of university students use it to commute, and lighting and many benches are there. For 1.5 km, the trail runs flush to the stone wall bordering the Rideau Canal, with busy Colonel By Drive only a few metres to the left.

The far bank is thickly wooded, with occasional small streams feeding into the canal. About 600 m from Hartwells, a lighted crosswalk on your left is the last opportunity to turn into Carleton University, and 300 m further the pathway passes underneath the massive bridges of Heron Road. Stairwells connect to their sidewalks above. Watch for the golden dome of St. John the Baptist Ukrainian Catholic National Shrine peeking through the trees on the right.

3.3 km The pathway reaches Hogs Back Lock Station. Across the canal is a small field with picnic tables, garbage cans, washrooms, and benches: an attractive spot to stop. Just a few metres beyond that are a shopping centre, restaurants, and a ubiquitous Tim Hortons. Continuing, the trail passes beneath Hogs Back Road through a small tunnel and emerges onto Mooneys Bay, an artificial lake.

On your right is the Rideau Canoe Club. Ahead, and to the left, you can see the Mooneys Bay Park and beach. The path curves left, splitting: follow alongside the lake shore past benches, a viewing platform, and an interpretive panel, then underneath Hogs Back Road once again.

3.5 km The path emerges at lively Hogs Back Falls, at the west end of the dam that created Mooneys Bay. There are walkways on both sides of the falls, providing excellent views of the swirling waters, and interpretive signs explain both the geology and the construction challenges of damming the Rideau. Walk down the bare rock, which has a railing, directly ahead of you for no more than 200 m for the best views.

Return to the tunnel mouth. Take the walkway on the top of the dam to reach Hogs Back Park, where there is a lookout and numerous benches where you may sit and contemplate the power and beauty of the waterfall. There is also a canteen, and washrooms. When ready, retrace your route back to Dow's Lake.

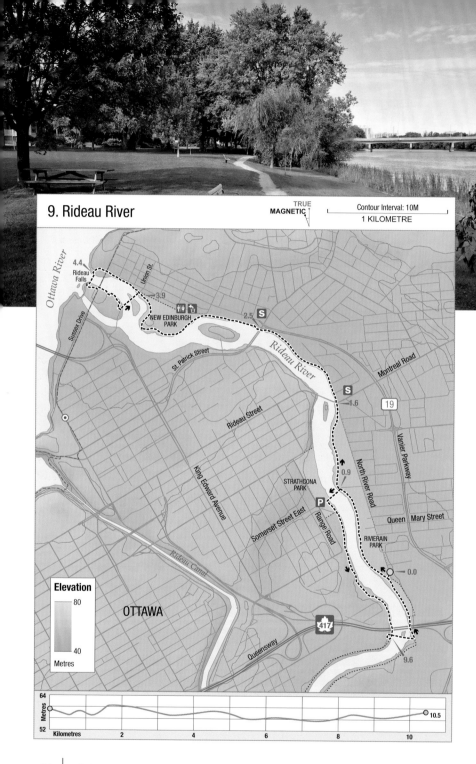

9. Rideau River

TRUE
MAGNETIC

Contour Interval: 10M
1 KILOMETRE

4.4
Rideau
Falls

Ottawa River

Union St.

3.9

NEW EDINBURGH
PARK

2.5 **S**

St. Patrick Street

Rideau River

Montreal Road

S

Rideau Street

1.6

19

Vanier Parkway

King Edward Avenue

0.9

STRATHCONA
PARK

Somerset Street East

P

North River Road

Queen Mary Street

RIVIERAIN
PARK

0.0

Range Road

Sussex Drive

Rideau Canal

Elevation

80

OTTAWA

417

40

Metres

Queensway

9.6

64

Metres

52

Kilometres   2   4   6   8   10

10.5

9. Rideau River

Distance: 10.5 km return
Type: linear with side loops
Difficulty: 2
Ascent/descent: 18 m
Hiking time: 2.5+ hrs
Trail conditions: asphalt, crushed stone
Cellphone coverage: excellent

Uses: walking, biking*, inline skating*, snowshoeing, cross-country skiing
Facilities: benches, drinking water, garbage cans, interpretive panels, picnic tables, washrooms
Hazards: high usage, road crossings, ticks

Finding the trailhead: Take exit 117 off Highway 417 and continue on the Vanier Parkway. Follow it for 650 m if you are coming from the east, or 1.2 km if coming from the west, then turn left onto Queen Mary Street. In 300 m, turn left onto North River Road. Continue to its end, about 400 m further. Park on the road.

Trailhead: 45°25'14.6" N, 75°39'51.2" W

Introduction: The Rideau River cuts through the middle of Ottawa, and for much of its length it is lined by a superb path system. This route is so attractive that it is among the busiest in the city, particularly on warm summer evenings and during the morning and evening commute. Hikers need to stay on their side of the path, as cyclists are numerous and frequently travelling quite fast.

Walking anywhere along the river's pathways is worthwhile, but I have selected a route that begins near Highway 417, then follows the eastern bank of the Rideau all the way to its confluence with the Ottawa River at scenic Rideau Falls, only a few hundred metres from the official residences of both the Prime Minister and the Governor General. This route also includes a visit to some of Ottawa's lesser-known memorials.

Places to stop and picnic are found in many areas along this route, including lovely Strathcona Park, on the west bank of the Rideau River. There are also a number of restaurants found quite close to this pathway.

Route description: From near the end of North River Road, a short track connects to the Rideau Eastern River Pathway, on the right. This is a broad open area of meticulously trimmed lawns interspersed with tall, leafy trees. Turn right at the pathway, where a sign states that it is 4.1 km to Rideau Falls.

The wide asphalt track follows the course of the Rideau River, which is often hidden by thick vegetation growing on its bank. Benches and garbage cans are liberally distributed along the route.

At 500 m, a connecting trail toward Queen Mary Street branches right, and there is a bronze plaque honouring local poet Benjamin Sulte, part of the Poet's Pathway commemorative system. About 300 m later, a shallow spot along the river creates a modest cataract, and a gathering spot for ducks.

900 m The gently curving path reaches an often hectic four-way junction. To the right is the Rideau Sports Centre, where there is a restaurant. On the left is the Adàwe Crossing pedestrian and cycling bridge. Continue straight, with the path now squeezed into a narrow space between tennis courts and water for the next hundred or so metres.

The river is shallow and slow moving, framed by bulrushes, and often busy with waterfowl, including mergansers and grebes as well as mallards and Canada geese. At 1.1 km, a gravel path branches right, into Riverain Park, and 100 m beyond that an asphalt pathway does as well. Keep straight (left), unless you want to use the playgrounds there.

1.6 km The parkland ends when the trail reaches the busy signalized intersection of Montreal Road and North River Road. Cross, and continue on the pathway, which now is immediately alongside the road. Fortunately, green-space – Kingsview Park – resumes 300 m further, and the trail curves left, away from the street. Numerous high-rise buildings are visible across the river, but this section has some pleasant shade, and the houses along North River Road are attractive single residences.

2.5 km This route reaches another busy intersection, St. Patrick Street and the Vanier Parkway. This time, however, keep left and follow the pathway beneath the bridge to the junction on the opposite side, where a sign states that 1.7 km remains to Rideau Falls.

For the next section, there is a choice of route. The asphalt pathway continues, but to its left is a crushed-stone track, something that walkers might prefer. In any case, they parallel and reconnect in New Edinburgh Park at Stanley Avenue at 3 km. Washrooms and drinking water are available inside the park's nearby field house.

The crushed-stone pathway continues, curving left to remain near the river. There are excellent viewing sites along here, about 300 m from the field house near some tennis courts, and about 300 m after that where it appears as if a ridge once crossed. This is also an off-leash dog area, and can be extremely busy with frolicking canines.

At 3.9 km, the crushed-stone trail reconnects to asphalt pathway; keep left to reach Union Street less than 100 m later. This lovely short section, shaded by some magnificent hardwoods, is quite close to Stanley Street, until it reaches Sussex Drive at 4.3 km.

Several impressive buildings are nearby, with Rideau Hall and the Prime Minister's residence a short distance along the sidewalk to your right. However, cross the road and pass through an entrance gate for the Canadian Geographic Society. Continue straight, turning left at their building.

4.4 km You reach the Rideau Falls, where there is a conveniently located restaurant. The view from here, across the Ottawa River, is quite attractive – as is the waterfall. Cross on a walkway above the waterfall onto Green Island. On the opposite bank is a park with a number of interesting memorials, such as a monument to the Mackenzie-Papineau Battalion, which fought in the Spanish Civil War.

Keep left, close to the river, and return to Sussex Drive. Cross, and head directly toward the large building (Diefenbaker Building). There is a sidewalk with a white rail fence to the left of the parking entrance. Follow it; when it reaches the building there is a walkway that works around the structure to emerge at its far side at a picnic area. From there, walk up to the road – Union Street – turn left, and cross the white-painted steel bridge to return to the Rideau River Eastern Pathway at 5.2 km.

Retrace your route the 3 km back to the Adàwe Crossing. Turn right, and cross the Rideau River. You will arrive in Strathcona Park at the parking area at the end of Somerset Street East. Some of the most attractive sections of this park are to the right, and worth exploring. However, today turn left.

Huge old trees line the wide path, which is situated well above the water, and within 150 m it passes into a wooded area, where a forested hillside on the right insulates you somewhat from the apartment building, and other residences, above. Around 250 m later it emerges at the end of Range Road, where there is a wading pool and playground area with changing rooms, open only in the summer.

Trees give way to grassy fields that run right into the river, with the large playing area of Robinson Field to the right. The trail curves left around housing to squeeze into the narrow space between them and the river. After that, there is a city works area on your right – then busy, noisy Highway 417.

The pathway crosses beneath it, where it reaches a former railway bridge, now the Rideau River Pedestrian/Cycling bridge, at 9.6 km. Cross, and on the other side turn left again. The pathway runs underneath the Queensway once more. From here, less than 500 m remains to return to North River Road, where you started.

10. Rideau River Nature Trail

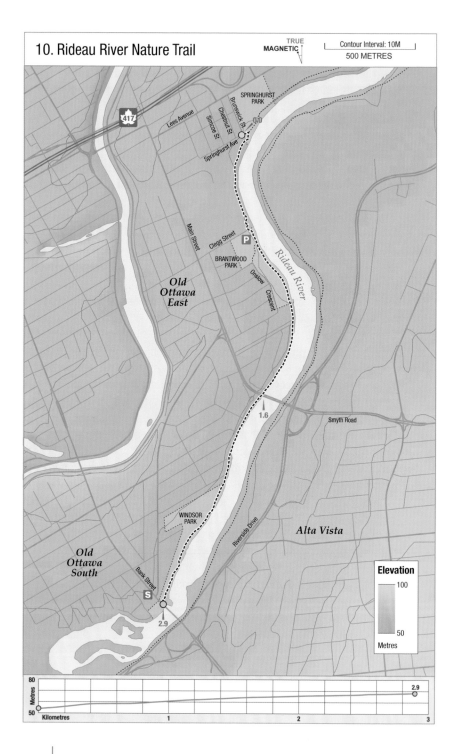

TRUE
MAGNETIC

Contour Interval: 10M

500 METRES

417

Lees Avenue

Chestnut St

Simcoe St

Brunswick St

Springhurst Ave

SPRINGHURST PARK

2.0

Rideau River

Main Street

Clegg Street

BRANTWOOD PARK

Onslow Crescent

P

Old Ottawa East

1.6

Smyth Road

WINDSOR PARK

Riverside Drive

Alta Vista

Old Ottawa South

Bank Street

S

2.9

Elevation

100

50

Metres

80

Metres

50

Kilometres

1

2

3

2.9

10. Rideau River Nature Trail

Distance: 5.8 km return
Type: linear
Difficulty: 1
Ascent/descent: 5 m
Hiking time: 1.5+ hrs
Trail conditions: asphalt, natural surface

Cellphone coverage: excellent
Uses: walking, biking*, snowshoeing, cross-country skiing
Facilities: benches, garbage cans, interpretive panels, picnic tables
Hazards: road crossings, ticks

Finding the trailhead: From the east: take exit 118 off Highway 417. Turn right onto Lees Avenue and follow it for 1.2 km. Turn left onto Chestnut Street, then left again in 250 m onto Springhurst Avenue. Park on the street. Begin the walk at the junction of Springhurst and Brunswick Streets, 100 m further.

From the west: take exit 118 off Highway 417. Turn right onto Lees Avenue, then left in 50 m at Simcoe Street. In 250 m turn left onto Springhurst Avenue. Begin the walk at the junction of Springhurst and Brunswick Streets, 150 m further. Park on the street.

Trailhead: 45°24'44.3" N, 75°40'23.6" W

Introduction: While most of the east bank of the Rideau River through Ottawa is parkland, the western bank has extensive areas of urban development, among which are a number of small parks. So I was delighted to discover a city pathway that follows the river through this area. It passes through several neighbourhoods, often extremely close to private homes and occasionally incorporating short sections of quiet streets, and is agreeably informal when compared to the highly systematized consistency of the National Capital Commission's pathways.

I chose the section between Highway 417 and Bank Street, an area that provides a pleasant distance for a family outing or an after-supper stroll, but which avoids the busy area near the University of Ottawa Lees Campus. Continue 1 km in that direction to link up with this book's Rideau River route. Beyond Bank Street, an unmaintained but well-used track continues as far as Brewer Park, Bronson Avenue, and Carleton University.

The trailhead is 750 m from the Lees O-Train Station, and buses on routes 5 and 6 stop at Bank Street.

Route description: A paved path begins at the corner of Springhurst and Brunswick Streets and quickly connects to the main trail. Basketball courts and a playground are to the left, while on the right is still more parkland. Directly ahead is the Rideau River, and there are benches and an interpretive

panel in sight. In fact, there are so many benches along this route that I cannot mention them all.

At the main trail, turn right. In 2019, the next few hundred metres were busy with the transformation of some of the former grounds of St. Pauls University into a new residential area. The path is well defined but a bit rough – wood chips mostly – until all the construction is complete. At 250 m there is a very attractive lookout with railings and benches overlooking the river, to the left. There is another at 550 m, about at the end of the new development, at the corner of Telmon Street and Scholastic Drive.

The paved pathway resumes, snaking down a small hill to arrive at the parking area for Brantwood Park at the end of Clegg Street. The pathway parallels the river; to the right are tennis courts and a broad mown area with scattered trees, benches, and other park paraphernalia.

At 750 m, the route splits, with the asphalt track curving right to end on Onslow Crescent. Continue straight, on a dirt track worn into the grass. Except for the occasional willow, nothing lies between the path and the water. The narrow footpath continues through the park, with many facilities to the right. Only one interpretive panel is on the left, and you might notice very occasional Rideau River Nature Trail markers on trees.

Leaving the field, the track enters a short – 100 m – section of forest, shaded beneath some impressively tall, thick maple trees. It emerges onto Brantwood Drive, where you continue straight, walking to the left of this quiet street, until popping back into the trees at 1.2 km, where there is another interpretive panel, this one on riparian habitat.

For the next 300 m, the trail follows a broad dirt track quite closely behind a row of homes, but with excellent views of the river to the left. This is a very lovely section. But the footpath soon intersects Rideau Garden Drive, where the well-trodden path continues in the grass to the left of the asphalt.

1.6 km The route passes underneath Smyth Road and its bridge across the Rideau River. A plaque, facing back towards the direction from which you came, welcomes walkers to Old Ottawa East. Once past, the trail enters Brighton Beach Park. Rideau River Drive is to the right, less than 10 m across a lawn, though shaded by a row of very tall trees.

This is another tranquil section, with barely obstructed views of the river and a selection of picnic tables and benches from which to choose. At 2 km, the trail reaches another street; once again continue straight, on the grass on its left. When it resumes off-road again, 100 m further, it becomes a wide, asphalt-surfaced pathway.

This next open area is Windsor Park, which features more tennis courts and side trails to adjacent streets. About 2.5 km, a crushed-stone pathway branches left into some trees and closer to the water. Either route is fine, as they reconnect quite soon.

The asphalt trail stays in the open, passing quite close to a large, older apartment building, and other homes, then squeezing past the Windsor Park Flood Control Dyke and Pumping Station.

2.9 km The path reaches Bank Street, at the end of its bridge across the Rideau River and at an OC Transpo stop. A wide variety of businesses and restaurants are to the right, and the Billings Bridge Shopping Centre is to the left, across the river.

Just before reaching Bank Street, the trail splits, with the left branch going beneath the bridge. On the far side is a plaque honouring Linda Thom, an Ottawa native who won an Olympic gold medal in shooting in 1984. This small park is named for her.

Retrace the route to return to Springhurst Park.

11. Carbide Wilson Ruins

Gatineau Park

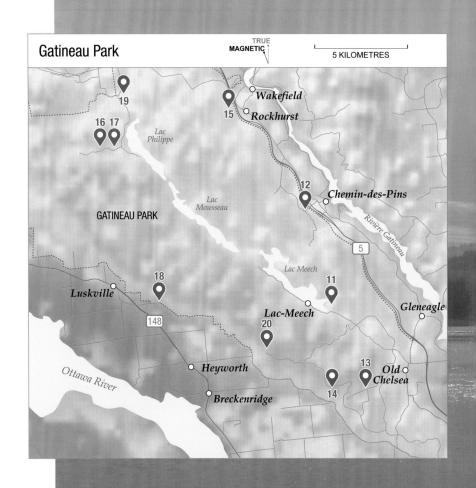

Gatineau Park

TRUE
MAGNETIC

5 KILOMETRES

19

Wakefield

16 17

15 Rockhurst

Lac
Philippe

12 Chemin-des-Pins

Lac
Mousseau

GATINEAU PARK

Rivière Gatineau

5

Lac Meech

18

11

Luskville

Lac-Meech

Gleneagle

148

20

13 Old
Chelsea

Ottawa River

Heyworth

14

Breckenridge

National Capital Commission

The National Capital Commission was created in 1959 to "create pride and unity through Canada's Capital Region." The Commission manages public federal buildings like the Houses of Parliament and administers the Greenbelt, Capital Pathway, and Gatineau Park. These three areas consist of more than 450 km of managed trails available for public use, one of the largest recreational trail networks of any city in North America.

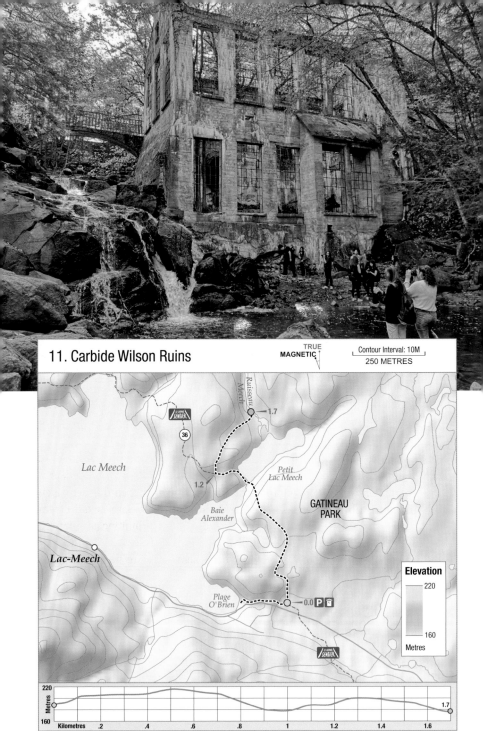

11. Carbide Wilson Ruins

TRUE
MAGNETIC

Contour Interval: 10M
250 METRES

Ruisseau Meech

1.7

36

1.2

Lac Meech

Petit Lac Meech

GATINEAU PARK

Baie Alexander

Lac-Meech

Plage O'Brien

0.0 P

Elevation

220

160

Metres

1.7

220

Metres

160

Kilometres   .2   .4   .6   .8   1   1.2   1.4   1.6

1.7

11. Carbide Wilson Ruins

Distance: 3.5 km return. The side trail to Plage O'Brien adds an extra 700 m return.
Type: linear
Difficulty: 1
Ascent/descent: 139 m
Hiking time: 1+ hrs
Trail conditions: compacted earth, crushed stone, natural surface

Cellphone coverage: good, except in the ravine around the Carbide Wilson Ruins
Uses: walking, biking*, cross-country skiing
Facilities: benches, garbage cans, interpretive panels, outhouses, picnic tables
Hazards: high usage, ticks, wildlife

Finding the trailhead: From the Macdonald-Cartier Bridge, follow Autoroute 5 for 12 km, then take exit 12. Turn left onto Chemin Old Chelsea, which will become Chemin du Lac Meech. Continue for 6.1 km, then turn right into parking area P11. (There is a fee to use this parking area most of the year.)

Trailhead: 45°31'37.4" N, 75°51'52.0" W

Introduction: Lac Meech (Meech Lake) is known to one generation of Canadians because of the proposed constitutional amendments that came from a conference held in the Wilson House, which is located on Lac Meech. But Thomas "Carbide" Wilson, the original owner of Wilson House, is better known to recreationalists because of the nearby remains of a fertilizer plant that he constructed in the early 1900s.

The Carbide Wilson Ruins have long been a favourite destination of hikers, but only in recent years has an official trail been opened there. This is part of a multi-year program in Gatineau Park to expand their trail network by incorporating many of the most popular unofficial footpaths, while closing some others, and thereby protecting sensitive plants by limiting human traffic through the forest.

This is a fairly short hike, but it has a significant amount of elevation change. In addition, the terrain around the ruins is rocky, often slippery, and features some steep-sided slopes. Families should enjoy this, but watch children carefully around the ruins.

Dogs are permitted on leash most of the year, but in winter they are not allowed on these trails.

Trail 36 is part of both The Great Trail (Trans Canada) and the National Hiking Trail.

Route description: From the trailhead kiosk, which features a map, follow Trail 36 – also known as the Discovery Trail – across the entrance road to Wilson

Canadian Inventor

Thomas Wilson (1860-1915) discovered how to produce calcium carbide, which had a wide variety of industrial uses at the time. He sold the U.S. patent to his process, but kept it in forty other countries and amassed considerable wealth.

In 1909 he purchased 186 ha of land in what is now Gatineau Park, and built his own power generating station, dam, and the first phosphorous acid condensation plant in the world. Unfortunately, his finances collapsed, the property was seized, and the power station, dam, and plant were not maintained.

Today's Carbide Wilson Ruins constitute a fascinating remnant of Canada's industrial and entrepreneurial history.

House and, for the first 200 m, uphill. The wide path stays close to the road initially, before curving right and passing some large rocky outcroppings. Expect to have plenty of company along this section, especially on weekends. The surrounding forest is mostly hardwoods, providing overhead shade in summer and a blaze of colour in the autumn.

At 750 m, the path descends fairly steeply, delivering you to a large, wide bridge 150 m later. To your right is Petit Lac Meech (Little Meech Lake); to the left, Baie Alexander (Alexander Bay) and Lac Meech. On the opposite side of this bridge are several interpretive panels, and a short side trail to a better viewing spot on the main lake.

Trail 36 continues straight, narrowing as it works between the pond and a rocky hillside on the left. Once past the pond, an informal footpath branches right; ignore that.

1.2 km Arrive at the junction of Trail 36 and the path to the ruins, on the right. This is well signed and also notes that bicycles are not to be used on the next section of this route.

The path continues to be quite wide, but it is quite rough at points. Wheelchairs and baby carriages, which might have been able to traverse Trail 36, will not likely be able to manage this section of path, particularly once it begins to descend, at 1.5 km.

Incidentally, once the trail descends, cell reception is lost until you return to this spot.

1.7 km After a steep 200 m drop, the trail reaches the ruins. Although the formal pathway ends here, people wander all around and through the large stone remains. To the right are the remains of the former dam. Directly ahead, a small cataract tumbles over a large jumble of boulders and exposed, smooth rock. On the opposite bank of Ruisseau Meech (Meech Brook) are still more structures, and below the buildings is a narrow, steep-sided ravine. Several interpretive panels tell the site's story.

This is a charming, attractive location, and most of the year it is easy to cross the creek. In the autumn it is particularly photogenic, and a popular destination for just about everybody.

When you are finished exploring, retrace the 1.7 km back to the parking lot. Once there, turn right, past the kiosk and outhouses, and head toward Plage O'Brien (O'Brien Beach). The crushed-stone pathway climbs at first, and there is a fence on the left, but it soon descends to reach the sandy beach just 400 m from P11.

Even in the fall, when almost no one swims, numerous picnic tables are scattered about the small open area, which enjoys a magnificent view up Lac Meech. Unless you are in a rush, this is the perfect place to relax and enjoy a snack after the relatively short hike to the Carbide Wilson Ruins.

If you do this walk without including Plage O'Brien, the hike is about 3.5 km.

12. Caverne Lusk (Lusk Cave)

TRUE
MAGNETIC

Contour Interval: 10M

1 KILOMETRE

0.0 P

73

Plage Parent

Petit lac
Renaud

55

Lac
Philippe

73

Elevation

360

180

Metres

11.2

Plage
Smith

54

3.0

50

54

7.3

Lusk Cabin Lac Lusk

Caverne
Lusk

6.1

7.7

350
Metres
150

Kilometres   2   4   6   8   10   12

12.7

12. Caverne Lusk (Lusk Cave)

Distance: 12.7 km
Type: loop
Difficulty: 4 (elevation)
Ascent/descent: 270 m
Hiking time: 3+ hrs
Trail conditions: compacted earth, crushed stone, natural surface

Cellphone coverage: generally good, though poor near Lac Lusk and around Caverne Lusk
Uses: walking, biking*, snowshoeing*, cross-country skiing*
Facilities: benches, garbage cans, interpretive panels, outhouse, picnic tables, shelters
Hazards: poison ivy, ticks, wildlife

Finding the trailhead: From the Macdonald-Cartier Bridge, follow Autoroute 5 for 30 km to exit 28. At the roundabout, in 500 m, take the fourth exit onto Route 366. Keep right on Route 366 at the next roundabout. Follow Route 366 for 7.5 km, then turn left onto Chemin du Lac-Philippe. Continue for 4.5 km, then turn left into Plage Parent (Parent Beach). The parking area is 350 m further and the trail begins in its southwest corner.

There is a fee to enter this section of the park (most of the year).

Trailhead: 45°36'18.2" N, 76°00'36.7" W

Introduction: Caves are uncommon in the Canadian Shield, but Caverne Lusk (Lusk Cave) is one of these sites and is a popular destination. Expect many people near the caves. However, the route I selected avoids the most frequently travelled route, which follows Trail 50 alongside the shoreline of Lac Philippe (Philippe Lake).

In winter, most of this route is available for cross-country skiing, except for the short section from Trail 54 to the caves, which is closed to protect hibernating bats in the caves. In addition, the road to Plage Parent is closed. The winter start for both cross-country skiing and snowshoeing is that used in Snowshoe Trail 73 (p. 122).

This is a challenging route, both because of its distance and elevation change. Newer hikers, or those with children, should consider undertaking just the section to Lusk Cabin and return – about 7 km – or use Trail 50 to access the caverns.

Route description: From the parking area, where there are garbage cans and a trailhead kiosk with map, follow the wide, crushed-stone pathway to the left of the kiosk, then turn right at the junction 50 m later. This path crosses a tiny brook, then climbs to reach a paved road at 250 m.

Continue straight – even though there is a sign saying that Caverne Lusk is to the left – crossing this road and keeping on the grass to the left of the road heading uphill. You should soon sight a Trail 55 marker, and Petit lac Renaud (Little Renaud Lake) is visible to the left.

Trail 55 uses this road, where the asphalt ends at about 400 m and which is only used by campers and park maintenance staff. Tall hardwoods bordering it provide a fair amount of shade, though not an overhead canopy. Group camp-site entrances branch off on the right.

At 700 m, turn onto Trail 54 as it splits left; a sign states that Lusk Cabin is 2.8 km. This is a lovely route, wide and with a good treadway. Tall, attractive trees provide shade, changing to pine and hemlock lining the rocky hillsides once the climb begins. About 300 m from the junction, a wide bridge crosses a little creek, and an informal path on the right leads up to the large Renaud Shelter.

The path now climbs, occasionally steeply, following and crossing another tiny stream several times. Numerous wet areas, meadows, and occasional ponds – depending upon how wet it has been – can be glimpsed as the trail climbs the hillside. At 2.5 km, there is a larger pool, garnished with a beaver lodge, on the right.

3 km Trail 54 reaches a signed junction, indicating that Caverne Lusk is to the left, along a footpath. Continue straight, along the wide track toward Lusk Cabin, 500 m distant. This may be booked for an overnight stay only during the winter, but at other times of the year it is a wonderful destination by itself. This sturdy structure sits on a gentle grass slope facing Lac Lusk, and it features benches, a picnic table, and an outhouse. Even in winter, it is open as a day-use shelter between 10:00 a.m. and 4:00 p.m.

Retrace the 500 m back to the junction, and turn right – also Trail 54. Bicycling is not permitted; from the width of a woods road it narrows into a meandering footpath. In 600 m it reaches the edge of Lac Lusk (Lusk Lake), though nowhere near Lusk Cabin, and works its way along the edge of the water for several hundred metres under a lovely pine canopy, although traversing several wet areas.

Once it turns away from Lac Lusk, at 4.9 km, a fairly steady climb resumes to 5.6 km – the highest elevation on this route. For 200 m, the path descends. It then makes a 90° left turn and rises briefly before resuming its descent, sometimes steeply, entering a glade of towering maples bordered by a steep hill to your left.

6.1 km The trail reaches the junction with Sentier de la Caverne Lusk/Lusk Cave Trail. Continue straight, the trail now generally downhill and quite rugged, crossing numerous wet areas, many with boardwalks. This footpath is

Caverne Lusk (Lusk Cave)

In the past ice age, a mountain of ice two kilometres high covered Eastern Ontario and Western Quebec. As this began to melt, about 12,500 years ago, water trapped beneath the ice sheet exerted tremendous pressure on the rocks below. Softer rocks, such as the marble found near Caverne Lusk, dissolved more quickly. In the Caverne Lusk, this became an underground watercourse as the stream scoured its way through the more easily eroded marble.

The cave is split into two sections, both open to those who wish to explore. The water in the first (upper) portion is only ankle-deep, while in the lower section it is waist-high and a brief immersion is required to exit.

much wider, testament to its heavy usage, and expect to encounter groups of chattering people along this section. At 7.3 km, Trail 54 reaches the junction to Caverne Lusk, where you turn right and find the first interpretive panel.

The path is wider now, with stairs to assist the climb. The combination of informal paths, directional signs, interpretive panels, and cave entrances is a bit too complicated to describe. However, the main route is well defined, so walkers are unlikely to become misplaced. The trail ends at the top of the first grotto, about 400 m from the junction.

Once the caves have been viewed, it is time to return. Retrace the 500 m to the main trail. If you are getting tired, turn right and walk down the hill to connect with Trail 50 at the tip of Lac Philippe. Follow this wide, easy track back alongside the water to Plage Parent.

Otherwise, turn left and retrace Trail 54 uphill to its junction with the Sentier de la Caverne, reaching it at about 9.3 km. Turn right; the signpost states that it is 2 km to the Lac Philippe campground.

Although another 400 m of climb are required on the snaking footpath, still beneath a splendid hardwood canopy, the route soon descends, rapidly and steeply. It skirts a small wet area 500 m later then passes beneath some massive pine trees. It crosses a tiny outflow – unbridged – then continues to descend, except to climb one small ridge.

11.2 km Sentier de la Caverne emerges from the forest onto wide Trail 50 opposite campsites 339 and 340. To the left is a parking area; head toward that, but once at the parking lot, turn right onto the asphalt pathway toward Plage Smith (Smith Beach). Barely 100 m further and there is a change house; turn left, and, keeping this structure on the right, follow the footpath past it. This intersects another footpath at the shore of Lac Philippe; turn left again.

Follow this scenic shoreline path back to Plage Parent. (You might notice Snowshoe Trail 73 markers; follow those.) There are numerous side routes, as the campground is to the left. Remain as close to the water as possible until, crossing a small bridge, the footpath emerges onto Plage Parent, about 12.4 km, where there are picnic tables, a playground, beach volleyball nets, and a change house with washrooms.

Turn left and follow the asphalt road past the change house. It curves right, climbs, then reverts to a crushed-stone track. About 300 m from the beach, it reaches a junction. Turn right, and retrace the 50 m back to the trailhead.

Sugar Maple

Although more than one dozen varieties of maple grow around Ottawa, none is valued more than the sugar maple, which makes up much of the hardwoods of the region. Growing as high as 35 m, and festooned with its iconic pointed leaves, the sugar maple is one of the most colourful trees in the fall, and in the spring it is the major source of sap for making maple syrup.

A long-lived tree common in mature forests, extensive sugar maple stands are found in many of the region's parks and protected areas wherever soil conditions permit.

13. Chute de Luskville (Luskville Falls)

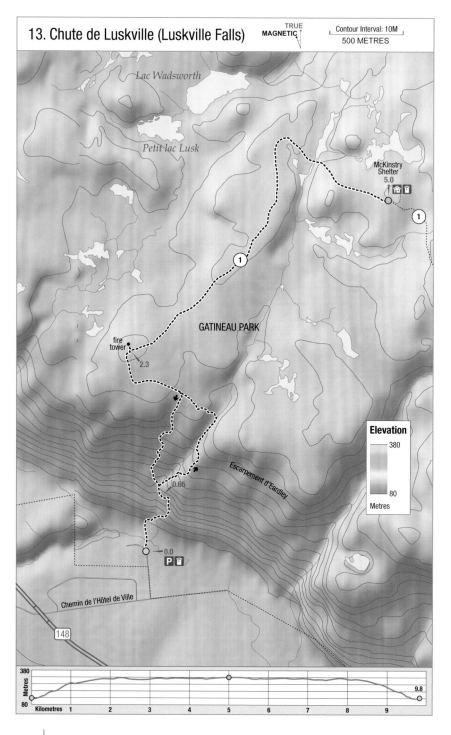

TRUE
MAGNETIC

Contour Interval: 10M
500 METRES

Lac Wadsworth

Petit lac Lusk

McKinstry
Shelter
5.0

①

GATINEAU PARK

fire
tower
2.3

Escarpement d'Eardley

Elevation
380

80

Metres

0.65

0.0
P

Chemin de l'Hôtel de Ville

148

380
Metres
80
Kilometres   1   2   3   4   5   6   7   8   9

9.8

13. Chute de Luskville (Luskville Falls)

Distance: 9.8 km return
Type: linear
Difficulty: 4 (rugged terrain)
Ascent/descent: 372 m
Hiking time: 3+ hrs
Trail conditions: compacted earth, natural surface
Cellphone coverage: good throughout

Uses: walking, biking*, cross-country skiing*
Facilities: benches, garbage cans, interpretive panels, outhouses, picnic tables
Hazards: cliffs, poison ivy, rugged terrain, ticks, wildlife

Finding the trailhead: From the Macdonald-Cartier Bridge, take exit 1, keeping left at the fork to Boulevard Maisonneuve/Gatineau Centre-Ville. Once on Boulevard Maisonneuve, turn right in 600 m onto Boulevard des Allumettières. At the next three roundabouts, over 2.2 km, continue straight (second exit) on Boulevard des Allumettières/Route148. From the third roundabout, continue straight another 11 km, then turn right onto Route 148. Follow it for 18 km, then turn right onto Chemin de l'Hôtel de Ville. In 750 m, turn left; the parking area is 400 m further.

Trailhead: 45°31'57.8" N, 75°59'37.2" W

Introduction: This trail is for those who like to climb — or, perhaps, those who enjoy gasping for breath and speaking in very short sentences. In less than 2.5 km, this path rises nearly 290 m, much of it over rocky, rough terrain. Few other routes in this book are so steep or so rugged. It is definitely not for everyone, but I loved it!

However, the path highlights one of the prettiest waterfalls in the region, certainly the nicest in Gatineau Park. Further, the main cataract is only 350 m from the trailhead and does not require any serious effort to reach. And for those who do not wish to make the steep climb to the fire tower, the trailhead is a lovely picnic area, well shaded and with open play space for children.

In the first edition, I ended this route at the fire tower, which unsurprisingly is at the highest elevation reached. That was a rather short, albeit challenging, hike. I decided to extend this route to the McKinstry Shelter, which doubles the distance but is an easy stroll after the climb. However, there are no further views, so most people turn back at the fire tower.

Biking and cross-country skiing are only possible on the section between the fire tower and McKinstry Shelter. The first section of this route is closed in winter.

Route description: The path begins near the entrance to the picnic area. There is a trailhead kiosk, with a map, a large interpretive display, and a sign indicating that it is 350 m to the waterfall and 2.5 km to the fire tower. It heads down a set of stairs, crosses a small bridge, and up another set of stairs on the far side. The pathway initially is crushed stone, but soon it becomes mostly bare rock. At 200 m, the trail turns sharply right, and does climb a little, but at 300 m there is an interpretive panel at the base of a vertical rock face: Chute de Luskville (Luskville Falls).

From here, the ascent is steep and immediate, very rocky and rugged, the route signed either by blue on the trees or white arrows painted on the rocks. The trail separates from the stream, passing alongside imposing rock faces. At 450 m, there is an interpretive panel on the left, on an open rock overlooking the farmland around Luskville. Fortunately, tall hardwoods shade most of your scramble.

650 m The route reconnects with the creek at a junction. Keep right, where a sign indicates that the Pontiac Lookout is a further 500 m and the fire tower 1.8 km. For another 100 m, the route parallels the creek, then it turns away to climb possibly the steepest section yet. Fortunately, many stone steps assist your ascent. As you climb, more and more large pine trees may be found on the slope, sprouting between the oak on the thin soil.

An interpretive panel at the lookout, once you eventually drag yourself there, explains both the succession of tree species and the namesake of this lookout. (Resting a moment here might not be the worst option.)

From here, the trail curves left, and actually descends slightly to return to the stream. For several hundred metres you follow the quite narrow brook through the thick vegetation, climbing almost gently by comparison with your earlier exertions. At 1.4 km, the path turns left and crosses the brook, without a bridge.

As you pass into woods increasingly dominated by pine, the rocks become covered by their needles, the path widening and the climb becoming less steep. About 300 m from the creek is another interpretive panel, and just beyond that another trail junction; keep straight/right. Closer to the summit Jack pines appear, and the route crosses more areas of large, bare rock.

⚲ 2.3 km The path emerges from the forest, where there is another interpretive panel and the fire tower. There is no longer a view here, as the vegetation has been permitted to grow back, and the fire tower is enclosed by a high steel fence.

However, Ridge Road/Trail 1 connects here. The signpost indicates that the McKinstry Shelter is 2.5 km away. Follow wide Trail 1, which resembles a forestry road. There is little shade on this track, and no side paths. Nor is there any particular view, as the trail follows the top of the escarpment. However, despite the rolling terrain, it is very easy walking compared with the ascent from Luskville, and a pleasant stroll through a forest.

⚲ 5 km Arrive at McKinstry Shelter, which is to the left. Outside is a picnic table and outhouse; inside are several tables and a wood stove. A signpost indicates that it is 9.5 km further to P12 on Lac Meech (Meech Lake). This is a fine place to stop and have lunch or a snack. When you are ready, retrace Trail 1 back to the fire tower.

At the interpretive panel, at 7.9 km, turn left onto the footpath you climbed and begin your descent. After 500 m, turn right when you reach the junction. This route is slightly shorter, and it works down the hillside on the west side of the creek. It descends constantly and features no grand lookout like Pontiac, but there are a few views along the way. It reconnects at the first junction, 650 m from the picnic area, where the brook must be crossed, again without a bridge.

Whatever route you choose, be prepared to rest as often during the descent as you did in the climb. Going downhill can be very difficult for the knees. In any case, the picnic ground at the trailhead, well shaded and with quite a few tables, is a good spot to relax and stretch after this strenuous climb.

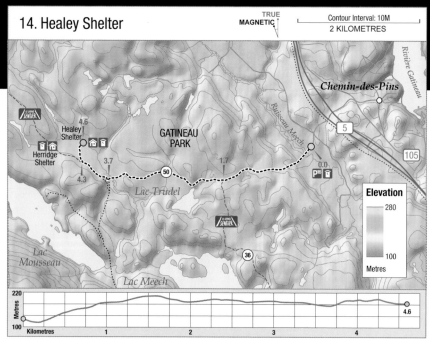

14. Healey Shelter

TRUE
MAGNETIC

Contour Interval: 10M
2 KILOMETRES

Rivière Gatineau

Chemin-des-Pins

5

105

LE GRAND SENTIER

4.6
Healey
Shelter

GATINEAU
PARK

Ruisseau Meech

Herridge
Shelter

3.7

4.3

1.7

0.0

P16

Lac Trudel

Elevation

280

LE GRAND SENTIER

Lac
Mousseau

36

100

Metres

Lac Meech

220

Metres

100

Kilometres

4.6

1

2

3

4

14. Healey Shelter

Distance: 9.2 km return
Type: linear
Difficulty: 2
Ascent/descent: 217 m
Hiking time: 2.5+ hrs
Trail conditions: compacted earth
Cellphone coverage: generally good, but some dead zones in the few low areas

Uses: walking, biking, cross-country skiing
Facilities: benches, garbage cans, interpretive panels, outhouses, picnic tables
Hazards: poison ivy, ticks, wildlife

Finding the trailhead: From the Macdonald-Cartier Bridge, follow Autoroute 5 for 22 km to exit 21. Turn right, for 150 m, then left onto Route 105. Turn left at Chemin Pine in 700 m. Keep left at the stop sign at 900 m; parking area P16 is on the left in about 200 m.

Trailhead: 45°34'19.9" N, 75°53'08.3" W

Introduction: Healey Shelter is located on the former homestead of Irish immigrants Edward and Bridget Healey, who came to this area in 1863, attempting to farm the thin soil of the Gatineau Hills. Gatineau Park designed the shelter to resemble their house, externally, at least.

Healey Shelter is now a year-round destination for thousands of outdoor enthusiasts. It is also a popular destination for nighttime hikers. On several evenings I have joined groups sharing a meal by candlelight after dark at Healey. Sometimes it is so busy there is no room!

In spring, white trilliums are very common, making this a wonderful blossom sighting walk as well. Because of the many hardwoods, this is an excellent fall colours hike. In winter, Healey Shelter can be accessed by cross-country ski, winter bicycle, and snowshoe trails, and it is well positioned to be accessed from park trailheads in Wakefield, Lac Phillippe (Philippe Lake), and Plage O'Brien (O'Brien Beach). The route from P16 is the shortest, and often the least busy.

Be aware, the first 2 km, mostly uphill, make the start somewhat daunting if you have been inactive all winter, so this is not a good hike for novices.

Route description: Trail 50 is a continuation of a former settler road, so it is wide and almost completely free of potholes and tree roots. Except for a very brief dip at the start, to cross the bridge over Ruisseau Meech (Meech Creek), the 1 km is uphill as you cross the fields by the trailhead and enter the forest, which is mixed hardwoods and softwoods. The first – nearly – level section is

National Hiking Trail

Long before there was The Great Trail (previously known as the Trans Canada Trail), the volunteers of Hike Canada decided to create a footpath crossing the country. Spurred by the opening of the 700 km Bruce Trail in Ontario in 1967, hikers from across the country formed a national association and in 1971 declared their intent to create a cross-Canada hiking trail.

Since then, slowly but surely, more and more pieces have been designated as a section of the National Hiking Trail, and by 2017 the total completed stood at 3,800 km.

very brief, however, and the path climbs again, continuing uphill until reaching the junction with Trail 36.

1.7 km At this important junction, a sign directs you right, indicating that Healey Shelter is 3 km further. If you head left, expect a long 7 km in the wrong direction before you reach P11 at Plage O'Brien. Your route, which thankfully finally drops downhill somewhat, is now part of both The Great Trail (Trans Canada) and the National Hiking Trail. You should notice the signs for each affixed to some trees.

Small Lac Trudel (Trudel Lake) appears on the left about 500 m later. Just beyond that, after a short climb, is a Great Trail Discovery Panel about ruffed grouse. The terrain becomes more rolling through here, with many small hills surrounding the path. In May, before leaves provide too much shade, expect to see clusters of white and purple trillium from the edge of the pathway as far as you can see. Continue through the forest for an additional 1 km, then you cross a small creek on an unrailed bridge.

3.7 km Almost immediately after the creek is a signed junction, which directs you right toward both the Healey and Herridge Shelters. After climbing a short, but steep, hill, there is another junction 200 m further; keep right here also. Another Discovery Panel is found here, describing the pileated woodpecker. (Both left-hand paths here are not routes open to the public.)

Though still climbing slightly, the wide path feels nearly level by comparison. At 4.3 km, it branches. To reach Healey, turn right. The trail heads downhill, soon moving into an area of former fields. Curving right, Healey Shelter comes into view, situated at the edge of the treeline. If you wish to also visit Herridge Shelter, keep straight/left where the trail branches; Herridge is only a few hundred metres further.

4.6 km Healey Shelter is an excellent destination for lunch or to enjoy a snack. Benches and picnic tables have been placed outside — and there are also both "his" and "hers" outhouses. Inside the shelter there is a wood stove, and many more tables. The building contains two levels and features an interpretive panel that outlines the history of the house and the property. Firewood, should you need it, may be found out back.

Camping is not permitted, but about 6.5 km beyond Herridge Shelter is the Lac Philippe campground should you decide you want to spend an evening in the park. It is also about 10 km to P17 near Wakefield if you want to drop a car at either end and make Healey Shelter a stop in a long hike.

Otherwise, when you are finished your visit to Healey, retrace the route to return to P16.

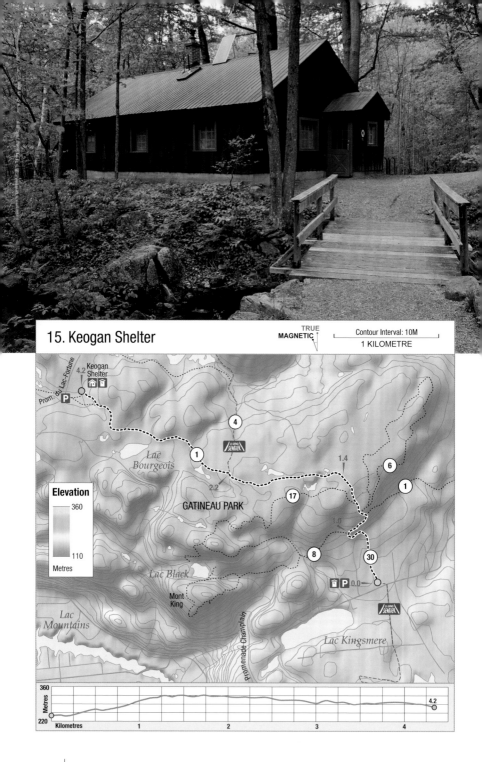

15. Keogan Shelter

TRUE
MAGNETIC

Contour Interval: 10M
1 KILOMETRE

Keogan Shelter
4.2
Prom. du Lac-Fortune
P

4

1
Lac Bourgeois

1.4

6
1

2.2

17

Elevation
360

GATINEAU PARK

1.0

110
Metres

8
30

Lac Black
0.0

Mont King

Lac Mountains

Promenade Champlain

Lac Kingsmere

360
Metres
220
Kilometres   1   2   3   4

4.2

15. Keogan Shelter

Distance: 8.4 km return
Type: linear
Difficulty: 3
Ascent/descent: 211 m
Hiking time: 2.5+ hrs
Trail conditions: compacted earth
Cellphone coverage: good for the first 1.4 km, then spotty or non-existent

for the remainder of the route
Uses: walking, biking, cross-country skiing
Facilities: benches, garbage cans, interpretive panels, outhouse, picnic tables
Hazards: poison ivy, ticks, wildlife

Finding the trailhead: From the Macdonald-Cartier Bridge, follow Autoroute 5 for 12 km to exit 12 for Old Chelsea. Turn left onto Chemin Old Chelsea and continue straight through the community, then turn left onto Chemin Kingsmere in 1.1 km. Follow it for 3 km into Kingsmere; turn right into P7.

Trailhead: 45°29'27.4" N, 75°50'31.7" W

Introduction: Much of the route to Keogan Shelter from P7 follows Trail 1, the Ridge Road, and the spine of Gatineau Park's trail network. Originally a settlement road, Trail 1 has been widened and improved so that it is easily walkable, if a little hilly at times. Keogan Shelter, one of the larger such structures in the park, is an excellent location for a picnic, either as a destination or simply as a convenient waypoint for a longer bike ride or cross-country ski along busy Trail 1.

This is a pleasant forest walk and suitable for most average hikers. However, because it climbs more than 100 m in its first 1.4 km, I have ranked it as slightly more challenging than its distance would otherwise warrant. Once past this initial ascent, the rest of the walk should be quite easy. The only viewpoint is at Wattsford's Lookout, very early along the route.

Both The Great Trail (Trans Canada) and the National Hiking Trail follow portions of this route, and their signage may be found along with that of Gatineau Park.

Route description: From P7, where there are garbage cans, an outhouse, and a trailhead kiosk with a map, wide and solid Trail 30 climbs almost straight from the parking area. It heads up through high, lush forest, including some magnificent pine, and passes several old, moss-covered stone walls. At 500 m, it curves left and descends slightly: enjoy this short break!

About 200 m, it arrives at the junction with Trail 8. Keep right on Trail 30 as it curves through 180° and resumes climbing.

1 km Trail 30 connects to Trail 1/Ridge Road and ends. On the right is Wattsford's Lookout, which boasts a distant view of Ottawa-Gatineau's higher buildings and features both a bench and a Great Trail interpretive panel.

Turn left onto Trail 1; among the many directional signs at this junction is one stating that Keogan Shelter is 3.5 km distant. The uphill slog resumes, passing Skyline Trail (Trail 6) to the right and Trail 17 to the left in the next 150 m. Finally, at about 1.4 km, the Ridge Road crests and levels. Cellphone reception is lost shortly afterwards.

About 200 m further, Trail 1 briefly emerges from the trees to cross between two marshy ponds that are usually dry in the summer. From here the path continues mostly level, though undulating slightly, until about 1.9 km when there is a distinct downhill.

2.2 km At the junction with Trail 4, there is a Great Trail interpretive panel about the black-capped chickadee. Trail 4 (the National Hiking Trail and The Great Trail) branches right; continue straight on Trail 1.

Most of this route passes through thick stands of hardwood trees. In summer, their verdant foliage enshrouds the pathway, and sunlight passing through them suffuses everything with a greenish tinge. Views are few, except ahead and behind along the channel cut by the trail, and few sounds penetrate the Ridge Road's leafy blanket but for birdsong and the wind. In fall, like most of Gatineau Park, these same trees are transformed into an implausibly colourful quilt.

Generally speaking, the remainder of the distance to Keogan is downhill, but this area is replete with small knolls and sloping hillsides, so the path occasionally includes some small climbs. At 3.4 km, the path almost touches the edge of small Lac Bourgeois, which has some open water.

After passing through another wet area about 400 m further, the trail makes its final climb, 10 m over the following 100 m. Shortly after it crests, there is a Gatineau Park interpretive panel which explains that Trail 1 was originally a settlement track cleared by Irish settlers in the 1830s and 1840s.

4.2 km Less than 200 m beyond the interpretive plaque, the side trail to Keogan branches right from the Ridge Road. Paved Promenade du Lac-Fortune is little more than 250 m directly ahead, but turn right and finish the remaining 200 m to Keogan Shelter.

This is a rather large building, situated beside small Ruisseau Fortune (Fortune Creek). Outside are bicycle racks, picnic tables, and two outhouses. A bridge traverses the small watercourse, but for much of the year the stream can easily be stepped over. Inside are a wood stove, information panels, and at least a dozen picnic tables.

Because of its proximity to the road, this is another popular picnic spot, especially in the spring when one is looking for an escape from mosquitoes! But it is probably even more used in winter, when cross-country skiers warm themselves. Approaching it after dark and seeing the glow of candles through its windows and the smoke curling up from its chimney is quite delightful.

After your visit, retrace Trail 1 and Trail 30 back to the start at P7.

The Great Trail

The most ambitious trail project ever attempted worldwide, The Great Trail (known until 2017 as the Trans Canada Trail) set the goal to be a connected recreational pathway winding through every province and territory, connecting the Atlantic to the Pacific to the Arctic Oceans. Its core uses include walking, bicycling, cross-country skiing, horseback riding, snowmobiling, canoeing, and kayaking, although the individual sections of the trail permit different uses.

The Ottawa area claims significant portions of the trail, particularly through Gatineau Park and along the National Capital pathways. Several sections are profiled in *The Best of The Great Trail, Volume 1.*

16. Lac Brown (Brown Lake)

TRUE
MAGNETIC

Contour Interval: 10M
1 KILOMETRE

Rivière Gatineau

Wakefield

53

0.5

366

0.0

P17

52

GATINEAU
PARK

Rockhurst

5

105

Elevation

220

2.4

57

3.0
Lac Brown
Cabin

90

52

Metres

*Lac
Brown*

190

Metres

140

Kilometres   1   2   3

16. Lac Brown (Brown Lake)

Distance: 6 km return
Type: linear
Difficulty: 2
Ascent/descent: 111 m
Hiking time: 1.5+ hrs
Trail conditions: compacted earth, crushed stone, natural surface

Cellphone coverage: excellent
Uses: walking, biking*, cross-country skiing
Facilities: garbage cans, interpretive panels, outhouse, picnic tables
Hazards: poison ivy, ticks, wildlife

Finding the trailhead: From the Macdonald-Cartier Bridge, follow Autoroute 5 for 30 km to exit 28. At the roundabout, 500 m later, take the fourth exit onto Route 366. At the next roundabout, 110 m further, stay right on Route 366. Turn left into parking area P17 in 160 m.

Trailhead: 45°37'42.4" N, 75°56'24.2" W

Introduction: This relatively short hike should be quite easy for most, but, like almost all routes in Gatineau Park, it does include a fair amount of elevation change. Nevertheless, the wide, well-surfaced pathway somewhat alleviates the climbing, and it does end on a downhill slope, which is always nice. Spring and fall are my favourite times for this walk, the former because of its wildflowers, and the latter because of the glorious colours of the leaves.

Trails 52, 53, and 57 permit biking in the warm months, but they allow only cross-country skiing in the winter. Snowshoe Trail 72 connects P17 to Lac Brown (Brown Lake), but it follows a different route than the one I have profiled.

Nearby rustic Wakefield is a popular tourist destination and worth a visit. Its Black Sheep Inn is nationally known for its outstanding evening musical offerings. (Don't be deceived by its rough appearance, outside or in.) The final resting place of Prime Minister Lester B. Pearson may be found in the local cemetery.

Route description: In the large parking area there is an outhouse, along with garbage cans, and a trailhead kiosk with a map. This is usually a busy spot, with walkers but especially bicyclists beginning their recreation here. In winter, snowshoe, winter cycling, and cross-country ski routes start from here.

The path, Trail 53, is a wide, crushed-stone track that cuts across an unmown grass-covered field. Initially this route is in the open, completely without shade. At 300 m, about the time that the trail enters the forest, a sign states that Lac Brown is 3 km distant, and shortly after that there is an interpretive panel, which explains that the wide, road-like pathway was originally the Chemin Kennedy, constructed by Irish settlers to connect the communities of Wakefield and Masham.

📍 **500 m** The path arrives at a four-way junction, which is well signed. Trail 53, which also now becomes part of The Great Trail (Trans Canada), continues straight. To the right, Trail 52 heads into the community of Wakefield. Turn left onto what is also Trail 52, which is part of the National Hiking Trail and Le Sentier national au Québec.

Trail 52 is wide and is shaded beneath a marvellous canopy of hardwoods as it climbs, at times rather steeply, for the next 500 m. As you ascend, the vegetation will gradually change to spruce and pine, but almost always these are tall enough to shelter the path.

There is a brief section of level ground, perhaps 100 m, with low hills on either side, before the climb resumes, reaching the highest point of this hike, more than 55 m above P17, at 1.2 km. At roughly the same point, Trail 52 curves left, then begins an almost non-stop descent —except for some level stretches— to Lac Brown. ("Level" is a relative term, as the ground undulates, but doesn't climb or drop more than a metre each time.)

Trail 52 is reasonably well signed, with the number inside a blue square. Any white over red markers indicate the route of the Sentier national au Québec. Regrettably, a number of unofficial mountain bike trails cross Trail 52, particularly shortly before and after it makes its turn. These are unsigned, and users of them tend to erupt unexpectedly from the trees to dart across 52.

The forest is quite attractive, as the route gradually descends. Watch for the remains of an old stone fence on your right, at about 1.5 km. The path even makes a few little twists and turns, descending gradually until you cross a little brook at about 2 km.

Shortly after, the trail emerges into a somewhat more open area, an overgrown field. Low hills are visible ahead, and a few apple trees can be spotted in the chest-high vegetation grown up in the former fields. The route gently descends to cross another, somewhat larger creek about 350 m later.

2.4 km Arrive at the signed junction of Trails 52 and 57. Turn left, onto Trail 57. The path remains wide and easy to follow, though now mostly without shade and with a broad swampy area visible to the right. Only 600 m remains, with the trail gradually curving right. Trail 57 ends at an open field; a snowshoe trail emerges from the trees on the left to connect here as well.

Directly ahead is an open area bordering the large swampy area – Lac Brown is actually out of sight – and housing a large cabin. A sign states that the Lac Brown Cabin is paid accommodation, and asks that the privacy of the occupants be respected.

This is your destination and – assuming that the cabin is unoccupied – there is an outhouse, and picnic tables are available where you may relax before you return along the route you hiked in. If people have stayed at the cabin overnight, depart leaving them undisturbed.

17. Lac Taylor (Taylor Lake)

TRUE
MAGNETIC

Contour Interval: 10M
1 KILOMETRE

Elevation

380

180

Metres

GATINEAU PARK

13.1

55

14.4

50

Chemin du Lac-Philippe

15.1

Lac Philippe

Lac
Taylor

Lac
de la
Vase

56

4.0

5.2

2.9

55

Lac
Renaud

Renaud
Shelter

P
0.0

54

6.2

350

Metres

150

Kilometres 2   4   6   8   10   12   14   16

17. Lac Taylor (Taylor Lake)

Distance: 16 km
Type: loop
Difficulty: 5 (distance, elevation)
Ascent/descent: 277 m
Hiking time: 4+ hrs
Trail conditions: compacted earth, crushed stone
Cellphone coverage: good until Lac Taylor, no reception on most of Trails 55 or 56 after leaving the camping area
Uses: walking, biking*, cross-country skiing
Facilities: benches, garbage cans, interpretive panels, outhouses, picnic tables
Hazards: poison ivy, ticks, wildlife

Finding the trailhead: From the Macdonald-Cartier Bridge, follow Autoroute 5 for 30 km to exit 28. At the roundabout, in 500 m, take the fourth exit onto Route 366. Keep right on Route 366 at the next roundabout. Follow Route 366 for 7.5 km, then turn left onto Chemin du Lac-Philippe. Continue for 4.5 km, then turn left into Plage Parent (Parent Beach). The parking area is 350 m further and the trail begins in its southwest corner.

There is a fee to enter this section of the park (most of the year).

Trailhead: 45°36'18.2" N, 76°00'36.7" W

Introduction: Gatineau Park is enormously popular, and this means that the trails closest to the cities are often far busier than I prefer. Trails 55 and 56, starting far from the urban areas and heading toward the park's more remote campsites, are somewhat overlooked parts of the park's trail system. Even so, expect to see others on your walk, particularly around Lac Taylor (Taylor Lake). As always, if you prefer solitude, pick weekdays and/or early mornings.

The trail conditions are generally very good, as most of the track is either a dirt road currently used to access the campsites or former roads with compacted surfaces. However, the extended climb beyond Lac Taylor on Trail 56 will make this a challenge for most. Skipping this section and remaining on Trail 55 exclusively will provide a much shorter – about 9.5 km – and less strenuous experience.

In winter, most of this route is available for cross-country skiing, but the road to Plage Parent (Parent Beach) is closed. The winter start is the same as Snowshoe Trail 73 (p. 122).

Route description: From the parking area, where there are garbage cans and a trailhead kiosk with map, follow the wide, crushed-stone pathway to the left of the kiosk, then turn right at the junction 100 m later. This path crosses a tiny brook, then climbs to reach a paved road junction at 250 m.

Continue straight, crossing this road, and keeping on the grass to the left of the road heading uphill. You should soon sight a Trail 55 marker, and the asphalt ends at about 400 m. Petit lac Renaud (Little Renaud Lake) is visible to the left.

Trail 55 shares this road, which is only used by campers and park maintenance staff. The tall trees bordering it provide a fair amount of shade, though not a complete overhead canopy. Group campsite entrances branch off on the right, and at 700 m Trail 54 splits left; continue straight. Little more than 200 m further, there is a side path to the left to the impressive new Renaud Shelter. With its picnic tables, firepits, outhouse, and quite attractive building—with lots of windows for sunlight—this is worth a short side trip, even if you don't tarry.

Less than 100 m beyond the shelter, and Group Campsite 3, Trail 55 reaches Lac Renaud (Renaud Lake), and for the next 600 m it works its way around the water. At one point the road splits; keep to the left branch. A bench facing the lake permits views of it and the surrounding hills. At 1.7 km, just beyond the end of the lake, there is a small parking area with a mown path through the grass to a viewing platform—though this is nearly obscured by rapidly growing vegetation.

After Lac Renaud, Trail 55 works over the rolling terrain, narrows, and becomes shaded by trees on the ridge close to the left.

2.9 km At the end of a large parking area, Trail 55 and Trail 56 connect. Lac Taylor is visible directly ahead, as are markers indicating the location of campsites, and there is a trailhead kiosk with a map at the junction. Turn left onto Trail 56. Almost immediately, on the right, Gatineau Park's Ohomisi Yurt can be seen.

Trail 56 is still used as a road, but there is very little traffic. There are several exits to the right to clusters of campsites, while an imposing-looking ridge usually borders on the left. At 3.7 km, an unmarked footpath, on the left, is an informal trail to tiny, and lovely, Lac Clair (Clair Lake). Anyone wishing a swim might want to explore this 800 m (return) side trip.

Nearly 300 m further, an outhouse sits beside the trail.

At 4.1 km, the trail reaches the end of Lac Taylor, where a wooden gate bars further vehicle travel. Trail 56 curves left and begins a fairly steep ascent, which continues for 800 m until it reaches small Lac de la Vase (de la Vase Lake). The treadway is in fairly decent shape, though there are some erosion runnels deep enough to constitute a hazard for cyclists.

After reaching this lake, which is on the right, Trail 56 continues to gradually climb, and more grass covers the treadway while branches from bordering trees constrict the passage.

5.2 km Just beyond the end of Lac de la Vase, there is a signed junction. Turn left, toward the lookout, and climb the 1 km to the trail's end, where a bench sits on a large bare rock, with a view to the south. Candidly, this lookout isn't one of the park's best as it mostly offers views of trees, but in the fall these are quite colourful. In addition, this was an industrial site, and some remains, such as a storage container, can be found among the trees bordering the former road.

This is the highest point of this route, and a reasonable spot to rest and have a snack. Afterwards, retrace the 3.3 km on Trail 56 back to the junction with Trail 55. By this point, you will have walked 9.5 km.

At this junction, continue straight/left onto Trail 55 as it follows the other shore of Lac Taylor. I enjoyed this section quite a bit, as it passes very close to the water and many of the campsites. The road is used by vehicles, but it is quite narrow and winding, so be attentive. About 700 m from the junction, Taylor Yurt is on the right, and 150 m further the campsites end and a wooden gate blocks further vehicle access.

From here, the trail heads into thick forest, with a slightly rougher treadway. The terrain is generally rolling as it works between rocky knolls, except for one steep downhill at 10.6 km. At 11.4 km, at what appears to have once been a junction, Trail 55 turns 90° right, and a large wetland can be seen on the right shortly afterwards. About 700 m further, the route turns even more sharply right, then drops briefly into a soggy area between two tiny ponds.

13.1 km After a series of small hills, and after the treadway has become almost completely grass covered, Trail 55 arrives at an unsigned junction, where there is a bench. Turn right, again sharply. Both routes look as if they are former roads. About 350 m later another route branches left; keep straight. And at the next one, 200 m further, keep right.

Trail 55 begins to curve, first left, then right, then left again. Keep on the most well-defined track and watch for route markers: the number 55 inside a green circle. At 14.4 km, it reaches a signed junction. Trail 51 heads left, while Trail 55 makes another 90° turn right.

From here it is an uphill, but straightforward, walk for 500 m to Group Campsite 1, where there are picnic tables, benches, and an outhouse. Trail 55 then heads downhill to Chemin du Lac-Philippe at 15.1 km.

This is an asphalt road, but with a wide grass strip on both sides. It is also signed as Trail 50, and a section of The Great Trail (Trans Canada). Turn right, and follow this for 750 m, ignoring signs to Plage Parent. Just past the registration building for the campsite, you will reach the road to Lac Taylor and the path back to the trailhead. Turn left, and retrace the first 250 m of this route.

18. Mont King (King Mountain)

Escarpement d'Eardley (Eardley Escarpment)

The most prominent geographical feature of Gatineau Park, the Escarpement d'Eardley towers 300 m above the Ottawa Valley and sits like a defensive wall facing the city of Gatineau. This volcanic rock face is a southern extension of the Canadian Shield, and during the last ice age it formed the northern boundary of the great Champlain Sea, which covered most of Eastern Ontario.

The top of the escarpment affords magnificent views over the Ottawa Valley, and the many trails and lookouts found there are among Gatineau Park's busiest, especially during the fall when the hardwoods that cover its slopes change colour.

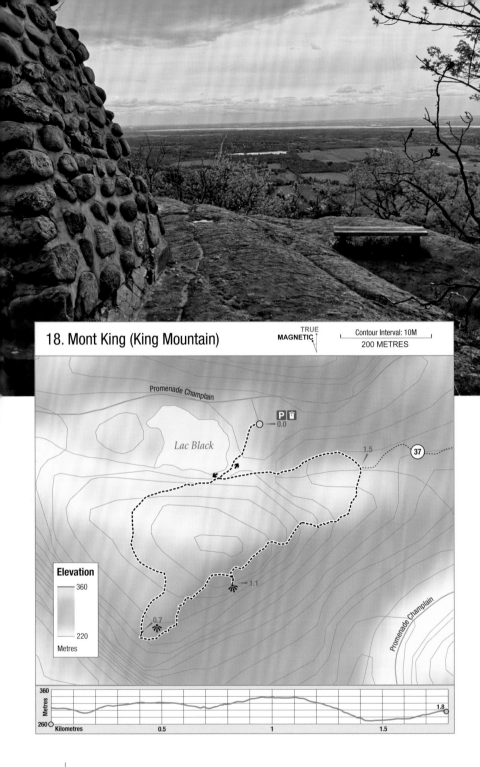

18. Mont King (King Mountain)

TRUE
MAGNETIC

Contour Interval: 10M
200 METRES

Promenade Champlain

P

0.0

Lac Black

1.5

37

Elevation

360

220

Metres

1.1

0.7

Promenade Champlain

360
Metres
260

Kilometres   0.5   1   1.5

1.8

18. Mont King (King Mountain)

Distance: 1.8 km
Type: loop
Difficulty: 1
Ascent/descent: 93 m
Hiking time: 1+ hrs
Trail conditions: compacted earth, crushed stone, natural surface

Cellphone coverage: excellent
Uses: walking
Facilities: benches, garbage cans, interpretive panels, outhouse, picnic tables
Hazards: cliffs. high usage, poison ivy, ticks, wildlife

Finding the trailhead: From the Macdonald-Cartier Bridge, follow Autoroute 5 for 12 km to exit 12 for Old Chelsea. Turn left onto Chemin Old Chelsea and continue through the community. At 1.1 km, it becomes Chemin du Lac Meech. Follow it for 3.8 km; turn left onto Chemin Dunlop, then right in 350 m onto Promenade du Lac-Fortune. Follow it for 4 km, then turn left onto Promenade Champlain. The parking area and trailhead are on the right in 2.9 km. Please note that this road is closed to traffic in winter.

Trailhead: 45°29'31.3" N, 75°51'43.0" W

Introduction: The 1.8 km Mont King (King Mountain) Trail loop is one of the most popular trails in Gatineau Park, because in a relatively short distance it provides expansive and largely unobstructed views of the Ottawa Valley from the edge of the Escarpement d'Eardley (Eardley Escarpment). It also features some of the park's most elaborate boardwalks and stair systems, significantly mitigating the not-insignificant amount of climbing required on this short path. The Mont King Trail also features an elaborate system of interpretive panels, describing both the topography and the flora found along the route. There is even a brief history of Gatineau Park thrown in.

Mont King Trail is also constantly busy, so expect that you might need to share the trail with walkers of a wide variety of fitness and experience levels.

In the first edition of *Hiking Trails of Ottawa*, I began this hike from P7 on Chemin Kingsmere, which provided a 6.5 km round trip. However, that seemed to please neither novices – too challenging – nor experienced walkers. So, still wishing to include this route, I decided to focus on the short loop from its parking area on Promenade Champlain, which is how most people access it.

Dogs are not permitted, even on leash, on the Mont King Trail.

Route description: There is a pleasant picnic area next to the fairly large parking area. Tables, bicycle parking, garbage cans, interpretive panels, outhouses, and a trailhead kiosk are all within sight. Follow the crushed-stone pathway through the picnic area, past the kiosk, and downhill on a staircase to a trail junction at 150 m.

Continue straight/right, and up the first climb. On the right, small Lac Black (Black Lake) nearly touches the path. However, you now face the most daunting section of the walk. As you do, several interpretive panels explain – almost teasing your sore leg muscles – that you are about to climb to the southern edge of the Canadian Shield, the lip of the Escarpement d'Eardley, more than 300 m above the floor of the Ottawa Valley.

Fortunately, this steepest section is relatively short, and you are assisted by stone stairs built into the path. It is also shaded under towering hemlocks, and the conveniently spaced interpretive panels permit you to pretend to find them absorbing while you actually pause to catch your breath.

But the effort is worthwhile, even though the climb continues beyond the final set of stairs. Leaving the softwoods overlooking Lac Black, the trail meanders through groves of red and white oak before reaching the high point at 550 m. From there, it actually descends – more than you climbed from the parking lot – to reach a bare rock perched on the edge of Mont King (King Mountain) with views in almost every direction, at 700 m.

Directly beneath sits Lac Mountains (Mountains Lake), just outside the park's boundaries, and farmland stretches away like a dappled carpet toward the broad silver ribbon of the Ottawa River in the distance. There is even a bench so that you may tarry and enjoy the view.

This panorama might be worth the climb by itself, but more remains. The trail curves left, and for the next several hundred metres scampers over the bare slope of the mountain, climbing again, but not as aggressively. It also detours occasionally into forested folds between rocky spurs. The views are magnificent, particularly later in the day when the sun is behind you. Even the towers of Ottawa can be sighted, peeking over the hills to the southeast. Frequent interpretive panels provide context.

1.1 km The final viewpoint features a massive stone cairn, fronted with a bronze plaque, marking a National Heritage Site: the position of the first triangulation station of the Geodetic Survey of Canada, erected in July 1905. Before satellite navigation, detailed surveys could only be conducted with the assistance of stations where the exact latitude and longitude were precisely calculated. This was the first of many such locations established in Canada.

From here the trail begins to move away from the crest, and after 300 m of additional excellent views, begins to descend down the reverse side of Mont King. It is often quite steep, but there are multiple sets of stairs that make it easier. One interpretive panel, pointing out bear claw scars on flanking trees, often generates nervous comments.

1.5 km After a descent of nearly 50 m, the path reaches, at its lowest point, a junction with Trail 37, which leads back toward P7 and Chemin Kingsmere. Turn left and begin to climb again. The trail now works between two rocky knolls, with wetter ground to the left. But the treadway is wide and surfaced in crushed stone. More interpretive panels remain before the loop is completed at the edge of Lac Black.

Turn right, and retrace the 150 m back to the parking area.

19. Snowshoe Trail 73

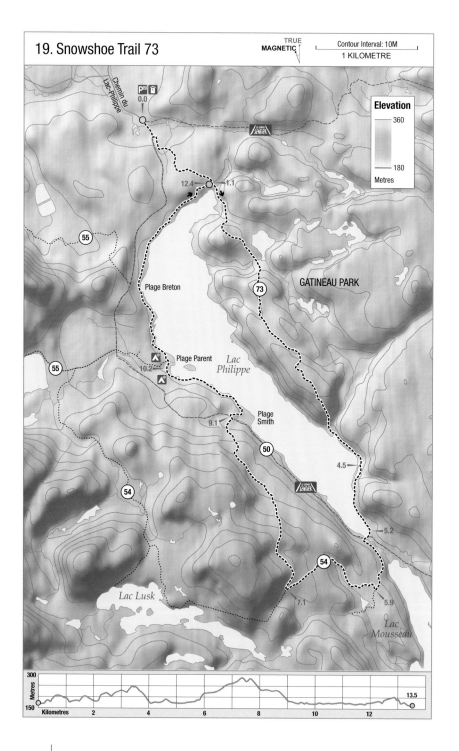

TRUE
MAGNETIC

Contour Interval: 10M
1 KILOMETRE

Elevation
360
180
Metres

0.0

12.4   1.1

55

Plage Breton

73   GATINEAU PARK

55

Plage Parent

10.2

Lac Philippe

Plage Smith

9.1

50

4.5

54

5.2

54

5.9

Lac Mousseau

7.1

Lac Lusk

300
Metres
150
Kilometres   2   4   6   8   10   12

13.5

19. Snowshoe Trail 73

Distance: 13.5 km
Type: loop
Difficulty: 4 (rugged terrain)
Ascent/descent: 450 m
Hiking time: 4+ hrs
Trail conditions: natural surface (snow and ice)

Cellphone coverage: several dead zones when you are behind hills
Uses: snowshoeing
Facilities: benches, firepits, garbage cans, outhouses
Hazards: wildlife

Finding the trailhead: From the Macdonald-Cartier Bridge, follow Autoroute 5 for 32.6 km to exit 28. Turn left onto Highway 366, and continue for 7.5 km, then turn left onto Chemin du Lac-Philippe. Trailhead P19 is on the left in 2.4 km. The National Capital Commission charges a fee for the use of all snowshoe trails in Gatineau Park.

Trailhead: 45°37'28.1" N, 76°00'36.9" W

Introduction: Because of recent equipment improvements, snowshoeing has been rapidly growing in popularity in Canada. And with more than 60 km of signed snowshoe track, Gatineau Park provides a wide variety of options, both for the beginner and the more experienced outdoors enthusiast. In 2019-20, the park offered sixteen separate trails accessed from eight different starting locations, with snowshoe rentals available at its Visitor Centre for those wishing to try it out.

I selected Trail 73, one of the park's more challenging routes, because of its scenery—it offers superb views of Lac Philippe (Philippe Lake) at several points—and its route: it accesses part of Gatineau Park that has no summer/fall trails. Because of its length, challenging terrain, and the time required to complete it, I recommend Trail 73 only for experienced winter hikers, and I rated it one level higher than its distance would warrant.

Route description: From the P19 trailhead, Snowshoe Trail 73 starts on Chemin du Lac-Philippe, which is also used for cross-country skiing. (Please do not walk in or on the groomed ski track.) Head past the gate for 200 m, until a blue snowshoe trail sign directs you left and off the road.

Passing an old cedar barn, the track parallels the road, in a clearing, for nearly 200 m before turning left again and into the forest. Most of the nearby trees are hardwoods, so in the winter extended views of the surrounding terrain are possible—revealing how hilly it is!

The path initially drops downhill to a small creek and an unrailed bridge, before climbing a surprisingly steep hillside. The exact route might be difficult

to follow if you are the first walker of the day; watch the trees for blue snowshoe trail signs. After an invigorating meander over the uneven ground, the following descent leads to a junction within sight of the north end of Lac Philippe.

1.1 km At this junction, several signs point to the right toward yurts, winter tenting areas, and Rest Area 2. To the left, the only sign states that Rest Area 1 is 3 km distant (a slight underestimation). Head that way.

The path continues to descend, now through a belt of conifers, but in less than 100 m it crosses another little bridge over the outflow from a nearby pond. Shortly after this, the trail emerges into a hilly landscape dominated by hardwood trees, now entirely without leaves. The rugged terrain of the Laurentides (Laurentian Mountains), with many rocky outcroppings, is fully exposed to your view.

For the first 300 m, Lac Philippe is visible to the right. However, as it climbs the next hill, the route curves away from the water and for the next 2 km works up and down several knolls, often in shallow ravines with higher ground on both sides. (Expect limited cellphone reception in some of these ravines.)

At about 3.5 km, you reach the highest point on this section, and over the next 600 m the trail descends 75 m until it returns to lake level, just before crossing another small creek. The route now follows the shoreline of Lac Philippe, sometimes almost dipping into the water.

4.5 km As the trail curves around a tiny, sheltered cove, you reach Rest Area 1, on the right, where there are benches, a firepit, and a good supply of wood. On a busy weekend you will often find other trekkers pausing, the fire crackling away: a welcome respite to warm fingers and toes.

Continuing on, the path widens to look like an old road, and within sight of the rest area is the stone foundation of a former cottage. For the next 700 m, this former laneway is the route, and it stays quite close to the water. As it nears the end of long, slender Lac Philippe, the path once again narrows to a footpath and kisses the edge of the water.

5.2 km Emerging from the trees, Trail 73 intersects with the wide cross-country ski Trail 50. Turn right, crossing the clearing; on the far side – in about 100 m – your route heads back into the forest, now sharing with all-season Trail 54, which is also open for back-country skiing.

The real climb begins here, with 100+ m of elevation gain over the next 2 km. Initially curving left, the trail provides good views of Lac Mousseau (Harrington Lake), the next in the chain of large lakes in the centre of Gatineau Park. (Lac Meech follows Lac Mousseau.) After about 300 m, the path curves right and climbs more steeply, including one long staircase – which might be snow covered, of course.

At 5.9 km, you reach the junction with the path that leads to the Caverne Lusk (Lusk Cavern) – closed in winter so not to disturb hibernating bats. Trail 73 turns sharply right and continues to ascend the deeply incised hillside, often passing between higher knolls. Because it does this, there are several wet areas along this section – fine when snow covered, but icy when not and very soggy if there is a thaw.

7.1 km In the middle of one of these wet areas sits a junction sign. Trail 54 continues straight; stay on Trail 73, which turns sharply right and ascends the final hill, reaching this trail's highest point about 200 m later. Unfortunately, no panoramic view rewards your effort, as a slightly lower hill lies between here and Lac Philippe.

After another 300+ m of uneven ground, including passing next to a small pond where the path can be flooded, the long descent back to lake level begins after crossing a narrow, unbridged brook. A quite pretty section follows, an area that in winter is almost always shaded by the steeper slopes on the left. Although there are short, nearly level stretches, it is mostly distinctly down-hill. At 8.7 km, the path turns sharply right and completes its descent.

9.1 km Trail 73 emerges from the forest to reconnect with wide Trail 50, near an area that is a picnic ground (before the snow arrives). Turn left, where there is a parking area (in summer). Once there, turn right toward Plage Smith (Smith

Beach), but just before you reach it the lake signs direct you left, alongside a changing house/washroom (locked in winter). A footpath leads toward the water, where you make another left turn. Fortunately, this busy 200 m is well signed.

Now a footpath alongside Lac Philippe, Trail 73 becomes easy to follow. To the left are summer campsites and picnic grounds, with their service roads often parallel to your path. Side tracks are frequent, as are several signs that direct toward winter campsites and yurts. Watch carefully for the blue trail markers, but if in doubt keep as close as possible to the water.

10.2 km You arrive at Rest Area 2, which, because it is also a summer picnic area, is much more elaborate than the rustic Rest Area 1. It features picnic tables with an overhead roof (but no walls). With its excellent views of Lac Philippe, this is a fine location to rest and eat lunch, especially if a fire has been lit.

The next 1.4 km is easy to follow, as your route traverses Plages Parent et Breton (Parent and Breton Beaches) and the boat rental. The shuttered buildings and stacked picnic tables look strange to anyone familiar with these busy summer areas. Paths connecting to parking areas are frequent, but watch for the blue signs and stay close to Lac Philippe.

At the far end of Plage Breton (Breton Beach), the trail re-enters the forest and becomes a narrow footpath once again. It remains near the water, but rougher ground forces it to climb slightly and move away a little.

12.4 km Returning to the first junction you encountered, you complete the loop. Turn left and retrace the final 1.1 km to trailhead P19.

Laurentian Highlands

The rugged hills of Gatineau Park look like a different world from the flatlands of the city of Ottawa. They are, in fact, part of the Canadian Shield, a portion of that landmass called the Laurentian Highlands that extends from the Gatineau and Ottawa Rivers in the west to beyond the Saguenay River in the east.

Unlike the sedimentary lowlands of Eastern Ontario, the Laurentian Highlands are composed of frequent intrusions of tough igneous and metamorphic rocks. Many south-facing escarpments give the area a mountainous appearance, and its rolling terrain is full of lakes surrounded by hills ranging in elevation from 400 to 800 m.

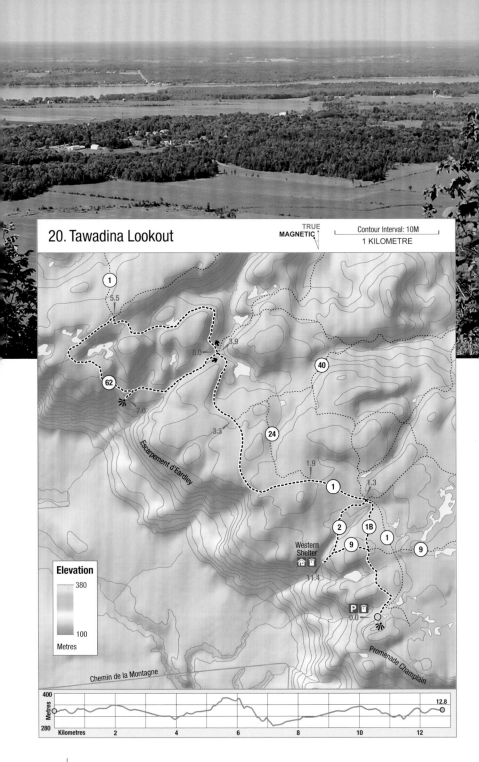

20. Tawadina Lookout

TRUE
MAGNETIC

Contour Interval: 10M
1 KILOMETRE

Escarpement d'Eardley

Western Shelter

Promenade Champlain

Chemin de la Montagne

Elevation
380

100
Metres

5.5
3.9
8.0
62
7.0
3.3
24
40
1.9
1
1.3
2
1B
1
9
11.4
9
0.0

400
Metres
280
Kilometres   2   4   6   8   10   12
12.8

20. Tawadina Lookout

Distance: 12.8 km
Type: loop
Difficulty: 3
Ascent/descent: 302 m
Hiking time: 3+ hrs
Trail conditions: compacted earth, natural surface
Cellphone coverage: reliable only on the lookouts or near the edge of the escarpment; no reception in any low areas
Uses: walking, biking*, snowshoeing*, cross-country skiing*
Facilities: benches, garbage cans, outhouses, picnic tables
Hazards: cliffs, poison ivy, ticks, wildlife

Finding the trailhead: From the Macdonald-Cartier Bridge, follow Autoroute 5 for 12 km to exit 12 for Old Chelsea. Turn left onto Chemin Old Chelsea and continue through the community. At 1.1 km the road becomes Chemin du Lac Meech. Follow it for 3.8 km, then turn left onto Chemin Dunlop, then right in 350 m onto Promenade du Lac-Fortune. Follow it for 4 km; turn right onto Promenade Champlain. A parking area is at the end of the road in 2.3 km; the trailhead is at the far end of the parking area.
Note: This road is closed to vehicle traffic in winter.

Trailhead: 45°30'34.1" N, 75°54'38.8" W

Introduction: The view from the Tawadina Lookout is one of the finest in Gatineau Park, and it can be accessed only by a fairly arduous hike. In the first edition of *Hiking Trails of Ottawa*, I profiled the most common method of reaching Tawadina, via the Sentier du Loup. However, this trail is now so heavily used that its parking lot is frequently filled early in the day, and once that lot is full no one else can hike it.

Fortunately, there is another way to reach Tawadina, and that is by beginning at the Champlain Lookout and hiking most of the way on the Ridge Road/Trail 1. I consider this just as pleasant – and almost as challenging – as the Sentier du Loup, with the added benefit that it is far less busy.

Trail 1 is similar to an old forestry road, wide and with few rocks or tree roots. Nevertheless, though easy to walk, there is considerable elevation change. Novices and those with children should just do the loop that includes Western Shelter, about 3.3 km.

In winter, Trail 1 can only be used for cross-country-skiing, while Trail 62 is snowshoe only.

Route description: This route begins on the opposite side of the parking area – where there are garbage cans and outhouses – from the Champlain

Lookout. A trailhead kiosk, including a map, sits beside what appears to be a continuation of the road, though crushed stone rather than asphalt. Just 100 m along this road, further vehicle access is blocked by a wooden gate, on the other side of which is a trail junction; turn left onto Trail 1B.

This track still resembles a road, but it appears far less used than the Ridge Road. As the trail descends to cross a little brook, at about 550 m, there are even some erosion runnels in the treadway. The trees surrounding the pathway are mostly tall hardwood and provide excellent shade.

The first of many trail junctions is with Trail 9, at 750 m; continue straight. After this, 1B narrows somewhat, and more exposed rock appears in the treadway. The path descends to cross the end of a small pond, about 450 m later, before curving left and climbing to connect to Trail 2, McClusky Road, only a few steps from a multi-trail junction.

1.3 km Trail 1B ends, reconnecting with Trail 1, where there is a bench. Turn left onto Trail 1, heading in the direction of McKinstry Shelter. The next section is not the most attractive. The wide, gravel track is without shade and can be quite busy with cyclists, requiring walkers to take extra care not to make any sudden turns or changes in direction. It also climbs.

At 1.9 km, Trail 24 branches right; keep straight/left. Shortly after that a long downhill begins. There is even overhead shade again. About 600 m further, there is a bench and lookout, with a reasonably good view of the Ottawa River and farmland, to the left.

After another short rise, the pathway resumes its descent. This section is quite pleasant, with several low vertical rock walls facing the trail. At 3.3 km, Trail 24 connects again, on the right; again, keep straight/left. Shortly after that, a large pond – in the summer it is a meadow – can be seen on the right.

Trail 1 first connects to Trail 62 at 3.9 km. Those wishing to avoid most of this route's climb to reach Tawadina should turn left here, as at this point it is only 1 km to the lookout along Trail 62. Otherwise, continue straight on the Ridge Road.

What follows is what I promised, an almost unrelieved ascent of nearly 75 m to the next junction with Trail 62, but on a pathway curving around several hills and meadows, and bordered by gorgeous woodlands.

5.5 km In the steepest climb thus far, and just after the tightest turn, Trail 1 reaches the second junction with the Sentier du Loup/Trail 62. Watch to the right for the signpost, and there is a bench here as well. (On a hot summer's day, it might be needed!)

Turn left onto the slender footpath of Trail 62, which is littered with rocks and tree roots. This runs along a ridge with more mixed forest and lower ground to the left. About 400 m from the junction, it works alongside an

attractive pond/meadow, crossing its outflow, and at 6.1 km it turns sharply left and drops off this ridge.

Back into hardwoods, the footpath meanders through the forest, occasionally climbing little rocky outcrops, but generally descending – a very pleasant section. It crosses a small creek at 6.7 km, and 200 m further it reaches the turnoff to the Tawadina Lookout.

7 km Tawadina Lookout is a massive area of bare rock facing southwest, providing a broad vista from the edge of the Escarpement d'Eardley (Eardley Escarpment). Even though it is often busy with people, there is usually ample room to find a spot to sit and have a snack.

Returning to the main trail, turn right. Trail 62 descends to a boardwalk in 200 m. Once across, the path becomes wider and better surfaced, and it continues that way back to the junction with Trail 1 at 8 km. Turn right, and return the 2.7 km back to the junction with Trail 1B.

Once there, turn right onto Trail 2, and follow this wide track toward Western Shelter. This has lovely shade and is in excellent condition. Watch for old stone walls, the remains of former homesteads. It crosses a little brook about 400 m along and reaches a junction with Trail 9, 200 m further; keep straight.

At 11.4 km, Trail 2 ends at the Western Shelter, which also provides a bit of a view. There is an outhouse here, benches, and picnic tables – another pleasant location for a brief rest.

When ready, return the 200 m to the junction with Trail 9 and turn right. In 400 m this connects to Trail 1B. Turn right again; only 750 m remains back to the trailhead at Champlain Lookout.

30. Véloroute des Draveurs

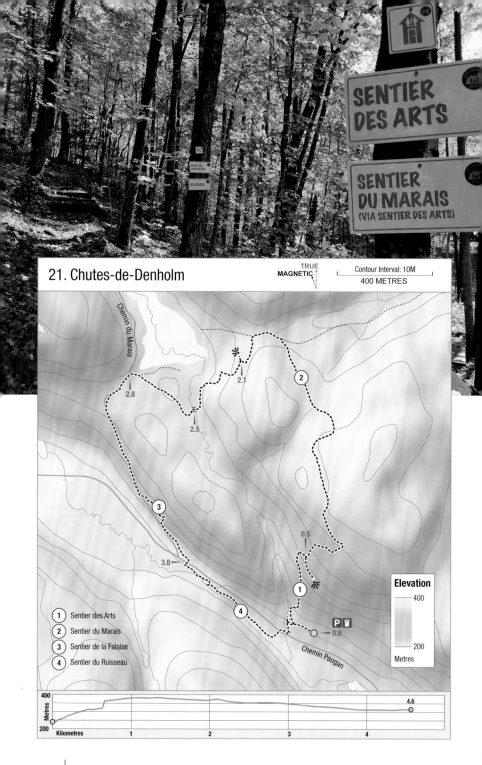

21. Chutes-de-Denholm

TRUE
MAGNETIC

Contour Interval: 10M
400 METRES

Chemin du Marais

2.8

2.5

2.1

2

3

3.8

0.5

1

4

P 🚻
0.0

Chemin Paugan

Elevation

400

200

Metres

1 Sentier des Arts
2 Sentier du Marais
3 Sentier de la Falaise
4 Sentier du Ruisseau

400

Metres

200

Kilometres   1   2   3   4

4.6

21. Chutes-de-Denholm

Distance: 4.6 km
Type: loop
Difficulty: 2
Ascent/descent: 171 m
Hiking time: 1.5+ hrs
Trail conditions: natural surface
Cellphone coverage: only available at higher elevations on the Chemin Paugan side of the hill

Uses: walking, ATV*, snowshoeing
Facilities: benches, garbage cans, interpretive panels, outhouses, picnic tables
Hazards: cliffs, hunting, motorized use, road crossing, ticks, wildlife

Finding the trailhead: From the Macdonald-Cartier Bridge, take exit 2 off Autoroute 5 for Autoroute 50. In 2.6 km, take exit 138 for Route 307/Rue Saint-Louis, in the direction of Cantley. Follow Route 307 for 42 km, then turn left onto Chemin des Voyageurs. In 2.9 km, turn left onto Chemin Paugan. Continue for 3.9 km; the parking area and trailhead are on the right.

Trailhead: 45°48'09.3" N, 75°47'18.1" W

Introduction: The Parc des chutes de Denholm is a municipal facility where the trails were originally built by volunteers, and this not-for-profit group still does most of the maintenance except in the trailhead parking lot. Their trail is a relatively short loop that begins near the waterfall, but it climbs the steep hillside to a pair of viewing platforms before descending to finish alongside a bubbling brook. The route is extremely well signed, with benches, interpretive panels (mostly in French), and other amenities. And I truly enjoy the works by local artists that may be found along the Sentier des Arts.

The climb required might be a challenge for beginners and children, so I wouldn't recommend this as their very first trail to try. After a few of the easier routes in the city and the Greenbelt – once you have decided that you enjoy hiking and are ready for something more – try this one, particularly once the leaves have turned colour in the fall. The area is fairly remote, so pack your lunch.

This trail is closed during hunting season, usually mid-October to mid-November.

Route description: In the parking area is a trailhead kiosk with map, outhouses, and lots of signage. To the right is an ominously steep hill, heavily forested with tall hardwoods, but the path begins level heading toward the waterfall. In less than 100 m, it arrives at a junction, where there is a bench; turn right onto the Sentier des Arts. As promised, a variety of artworks, all using the natural materials found in the area, may be found adjacent to the footpath. Small plaques identify the artists and their work.

The climb begins immediately, steeply up the hillside with a view of the creek to the left. At 150 m, the narrow footpath curves right, moving away from the cataract and ravine. Lots of hiker signs mark the route, and there are benches along the way. Several interesting interpretive panels describing the landscape and the flora are affixed to trees, and provide an excellent excuse to stop and briefly rest. I needed that, because the ascent is 82 m in less than 400 m.

📍 **500 m** The Sentier des Arts reaches a junction with the Sentier du Marais, where there is a map. Turn right, and in 100 m – thankfully, slightly downhill – the Sentier des Arts ends at a lookout, where there is a picnic table along with a very nice rock carving created by an Inuit artist.

Return to the junction, continuing straight/right on the Sentier du Marais. For the next 350 m the path climbs, but more gradually. It passes through slopes of mostly hardwoods, with additional interpretive panels on occasion. By 1.1 km, the path levels, although higher ground rises on both sides. About 100 m further there is even one interpretive panel in English, because it quotes Jane Goodall.

The ground is undulating, with plenty of low rises, so the path gradually curves left with little ups and down, but generally descending. Cell reception is lost as the trail works behind the hilltops. At 1.8 km, the trail reaches a forest road, which is used by ATVs, and another interpretive panel – one of many. Turn left and follow this wide track for about 150 m, until the Sentier du Marais branches left. This is well signed, and there is another map.

📍 **2.1 km** Passing another interpretive panel, the trail arrives at the lookout, a wooden platform with benches on the hillside overlooking a large marsh. From here, the footpath drops quite rapidly and steadily, and there are many more softwoods among the trees around you. In about 150 m, the path makes a sharp left turn sharing a track with vehicles, and maybe 50 m later turns right and onto a footpath; watch carefully for trail markers during this descent. Another English interpretive panel – a Helen Keller quote – is found during the final descent to the brook.

At 2.5 km, the path reaches a sturdy metal bridge. Cross, and on the opposite bank the trail soon becomes a wide track, possibly used by motorized vehicles. (An abandoned van rusting in the forest proves that people certainly

once drove here.) This dirt-surfaced road connects to the gravelled Chemin du Marais at 2.8 km, where there is another trail map. Turn left and follow this road downhill for 600 m to the junction with the Sentier de la Falaise, and turn left here.

This narrow footpath has some of the most difficult walking of the entire route. It is not suitable for small children, as it works alongside the steep hillside and several vertical rock faces, but it makes for very interesting viewing. From this footpath the Chemin du Marais can almost always be seen. At 3.8 km, the Sentier de la Falaise reaches the paved Chemin Paugan. Cross, where there is a map, and begin the Sentier du Ruisseau.

The rocky path descends to the brook, turns left, and traces its way alongside. This is another pretty section, with higher ground left and right and the brook gurgling boisterously. The walking is challenging here, too. After a short 500 m, the trail turns left, soon after a bench in a spot labelled as a place of silence, and returns to the Chemin Paugan at one end of a bridge.

Turn right and cross this bridge, then left onto a footpath. The waterfall is visible directly ahead, and as you head toward it, reach the junction to the trail exit. Advance and view the waterfall, then return to this junction, turn left, and walk the 100 m back to the trailhead.

22. Cycloparc PPJ

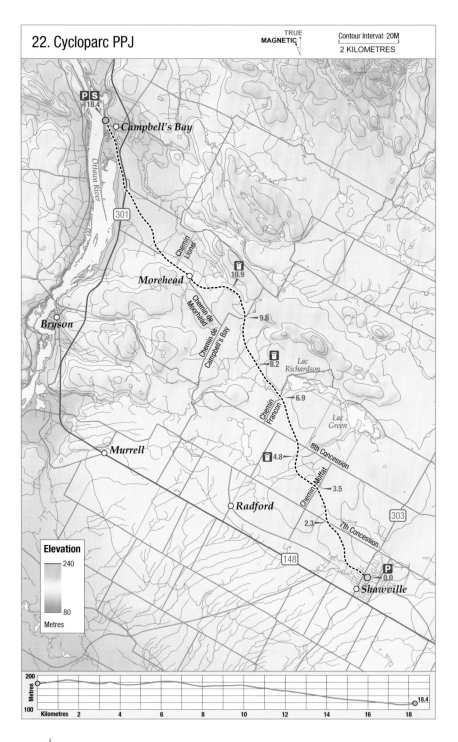

22. Cycloparc PPJ

Distance: 36.8 km return
Type: linear
Difficulty: 5 (distance)
Ascent/descent: 155 m
Hiking time: 10+ hrs
Trail conditions: asphalt, crushed stone

Cellphone coverage: excellent
Uses: walking, biking, snowmobiling
Facilities: benches, garbage cans, interpretive panels, outhouses, picnic tables
Hazards: hunting, poison ivy, road crossings, ticks, wildlife

Finding the trailhead: From the Macdonald-Cartier Bridge, take exit 1, keeping left at the fork to Boulevard Maisonneuve/Gatineau Centre-Ville. Once on Boulevard Maisonneuve, turn right in 600 m onto Boulevard des Allumettières. At the next three roundabouts, over 2.2 km, continue straight (second exit) on Boulevard des Allumettières/Route 148. From the third roundabout, continue straight another 11 km, then turn right onto Route 148. Follow it for 61 km, then turn right onto Rue Centre/Route 303. In 750 m, turn right onto Rue Railroad. The parking area is on the left in 150 m.

Trailhead: 45°36'18.9" N, 76°29'17.5" W

Introduction: The Cycloparc PPJ is a 92 km recreational trail located entirely within the Municipalité de Pontiac. This essentially rural community, fewer than 15,000 people spread over an area of 13,848 km², has developed a tremendous off-road walking and cycling resource. The Cycloparc follows the route of the abandoned Pontiac Pacific Junction Railway – nicknamed locally as the "Push, Pull, and Jerk."

The Cycloparc may have been designed with cycling in mind – it is part of Quebec's famous Route verte – but its gentle route, wetlands, and pastoral setting make it ideal for those who want a brisk ramble without encountering any calf-burning, knee-destroying hills.

This particular section is best walked over two days. There is a campground in Campbell's Bay beside the Ottawa River.

Route description: The parking area sits in a large, open field with the Shawville Fairgrounds to the right. Head left, on the asphalt-surfaced pathway, where there are benches, garbage cans, and a bike rack. At Route 303/Rue Centre, at 150 m, gates lie across the trail. There is also a kiosk listing local businesses and showing a map of the Cycloparc PPJ. In addition to the local signs, there are markers for La Route verte, the province-spanning cycling network. This is a section of Route 1.

This former rail bed is raised and dry, and usually tree lined. Markers at each kilometre indicate your progress along a trail that is as straight as the railway could make it over the low, level ground, and there are signs at each road crossing indicating the road's name and the distance to the next community. Although you do spend considerable time passing through forest, overall this route is very pastoral.

At 750 m, after passing through a narrow gate, the asphalt ends, and the trail surface becomes crushed stone. With Shawville left behind, the trail passes through alternating cultivated fields and forest. When it crosses the dirt-surfaced 7th Concession, at 2.3 km, you might notice that there are signs warning vehicle traffic of the trail crossing.

A large area of wetland follows, with marsh on both sides of the trail, continuing almost to Chemin Moffat, which the pathway reaches at 3.5 km. (The sign here says it is 14.6 km to Fort-Coulonge; in fact, it is that distance to Campbell's Bay.)

Where there are cultivated fields near the pathway, as near this spot, there is often a crossing used by farm machinery. This equipment also sometimes uses the trail, which can damage the treadway.

4.8 km The path arrives at the first picnic area, a pleasant shaded section, with a table, bench, garbage can, bike rack, and an outhouse. It is also post 9 (of 12) of a virtual tour of the railroad available for downloading on your phone. Finally, this is an excellent location for casual day hikers to have a snack then return to Shawville.

The next road crossing, 8th Concession, is only 500 m further, after which the trail is lower than the ground on either side for a considerable distance. This is pretty much all cultivated fields as well, almost as far as Chemin Francon, at 6.9 km.

Beyond this, the area moves into thick vegetation, with higher than usual hillsides bordering the pathway. After 700 m, this rougher section ends, and the trail settles into a long straightaway, soon bordered on the right by a large wetland.

8.2 km Halte (Rest Area) 10 sits on a small hill on the right, surrounded by marsh. If the mosquitoes aren't too bad, this is a pretty place to pause for a snack. There is also an interpretive panel (in French only). The wetlands, sometimes on the left as well, continue almost to the Km 27 marker before the pathway returns to cultivated fields.

At 9.8 km, gravel-surfaced Chemin de Campbell's Bay is crossed, after which the pathway begins to noticeably descend, and the trail moves into an area of thick hardwoods, with sloping ground on both sides. It also begins a long curve to the left to follow the contour of the terrain. This might have been my favourite section of this route.

10.9 km The next rest area is somewhat less attractive. It appeared newly built, but it is unshaded and has no view. Continuing, glimpses through the trees to the right are possible, showing how much higher this area is. By the Km 29

marker, the path emerges from the forest and there are lovely views of the pastoral valley to the right.

Around 12.3 km, Chemin de Moorhead starts running parallel on the left and very close to the trail. When it crosses Chemin Lionel, about 700 m later, it is only a few steps away. They continue close for another 700 m, when the Cycloparc curves right, still descending. By 14.5 km, the trail fully emerges from tree cover and continues with cultivated fields, sometimes tended to the edge of the pathway, on both sides.

It is entirely pastoral until 15.8 km, when the trail passes Campbell's Bay Ciment, on the left, then crosses underneath Highway 148, 100 m later. From here the route feels quite isolated. It curves right and is actually running parallel and quite close to the Ottawa River, but the river is rarely visible through the thick vegetation. As it is quite a bit lower than Route 148, no houses can be seen.

So the path works through this sheltered woodland until passing through another gate and emerging, quite abruptly, into the community of Campbell's Bay at 17.6 km. The trail crosses a small bridge and then enters into a large open area. The businesses lining Rue Front are on the right, while a restaurant and recreation area are to the left.

18.4 km Stopping anywhere is fine, but I continued to Halte (Rest Area) 8, which is on the trail, with a lovely view overlooking the Ottawa River. However, it is still Quebec on the opposite side: Île du Grand Calumet. Retrace your route to return to Shawville.

Wild Turkey

One of the newest wildlife residents in Ontario and Quebec, the wild turkey, is actually returning to where it once was common. Having almost vanished across North America because of deforestation and unregulated hunting, turkeys have been reintroduced in many regions of the continent — and populations have grown quickly. Turkeys congregate on the ground in flocks as large as two hundred, especially in the winter.

In Eastern Canada, wild turkeys spread north from New York State and rapidly expanded their range throughout Ontario and Quebec. By 2005, the local population was considered secure enough to permit regular hunting in the spring during breeding season. Turkeys are the largest game bird in North America.

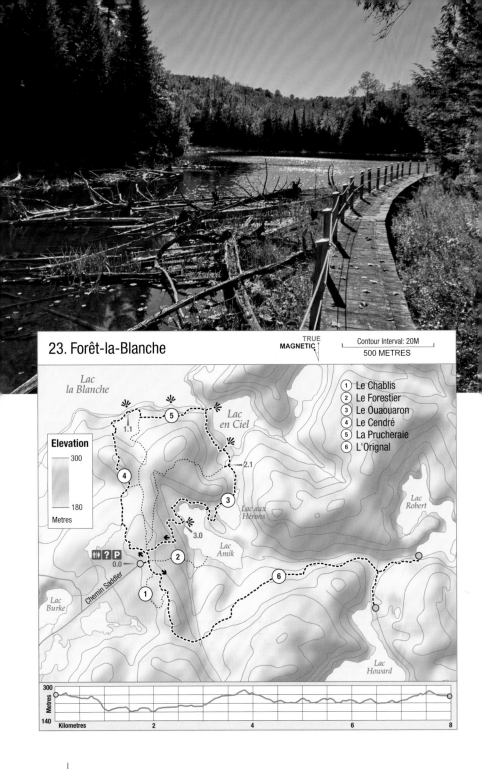

23. Forêt-la-Blanche

TRUE
MAGNETIC

Contour Interval: 20M
500 METRES

Lac
la Blanche

Lac
en Ciel

1 Le Chablis
2 Le Forestier
3 Le Ouaouaron
4 Le Cendré
5 La Prucheraie
6 L'Orignal

Elevation

300

180

Metres

1.1

5

4

2.1

3

Lac aux
Hérons

Lac
Robert

3.0

Lac
Amik

2

0.0

6

Chemin Saddler

1

Lac
Burke

Lac
Howard

300

Metres

140

Kilometres

2

4

6

8

23. Forêt-la-Blanche

Distance: 8 km
Type: loop
Difficulty: 2
Ascent/descent: 292 m
Hiking time: 2+ hrs
Trail conditions: compacted earth, natural surface
Cellphone coverage: possibly at parking area only, not elsewhere
Uses: walking, snowshoeing, cross-country skiing
Facilities: benches, garbage cans, interpretive panels, outhouses, picnic tables
Hazards: ticks, wildlife

Finding the trailhead: From the Macdonald-Cartier Bridge, follow Autoroute 5 for 1.1 km to exit 2, then turn right onto Highway 50. Follow Autoroute 50 for 38 km to exit 174. Turn left at Chemin Doherty/Route 309. At the roundabout in 650 m, turn right onto Route 315. Follow it for 14 km, then turn right onto Chemin Saddler (dirt). Continue for 2 km to the parking lot. An access fee is payable at the interpretation centre — or at the collection box by the trailhead when the centre is closed.

Trailhead: 45°42'35.9" N, 75°17'41.1" W

Introduction: The Réserve écologique de la Forêt-la-Blanche was officially established in 2008 to protect the great diversity of plant life found in the Outaouais region. Within its 2,000 ha, several rare stands of old-growth forests, including some of the last sites in Quebec with trees more than four hundred years old, and a number of endangered plants, such as ginseng, may be found. Trails are open daily, year-round, 10:00 a.m. to 5:00 p.m. Dogs are not permitted on the trails.

Forêt-la-Blanche is good for novices and families, yet also worthwhile for more experienced trekkers. Because of the significant climbing required, newer hikers will probably find the 3.4 km loop sufficient. This also has by far the best viewing opportunities and amenities. Trail 6, L'Orignal, is more remote, longer, and only reaches two smaller lakes.

Route description: From the parking lot, a signed path leads to the interpretation centre, where you pay your entry fees. Next to this building is a large trailhead pavilion, which includes a map of the path network. Begin on trail 4, Le Cendre. From the pavilion, turn left, passing under a wooden gateway labelled Départ des Sentiers and keeping to the left-hand route on the wide, crushed-stone trail. There is a bench, and the first of many interpretive panels: eastern white pine. Within 10 m is a second trail junction; turn left, onto trail 4.

The treadway becomes a natural, packed-earth surface, and it quickly becomes apparent that in this hilly area the route will almost always be going up or down. In addition to the many text panels, you will sight occasional numbered posts. Also interpretive in purpose, these are explained by a brochure available at the centre.

Le Cendre descends to a viewing platform overlooking a significant wet area, at 350 m. Lush hardwoods cloak the path as it winds over small bridges and reaches another junction 250 m further; keep left. After a short climb, the trail steeply descends toward Lac la Blanche, visible ahead through the vegetation. Several elaborate stair systems make the descent easier, including the appropriately named Le Grand Escalier, which even has a picnic table and bench partway. On wet days the metal mesh covering each step, preventing slipping, will be appreciated.

Descending this hill, hardwoods give way to a high canopy of hemlocks, cedars, and other softwoods, and the air temperature on this north-facing slope is often several degrees lower.

📍 **1.1 km** A wooden platform, with picnic table, bench, map, and interpretive signage, provides a lookout into Lac la Blanche. Beneath a thick softwood canopy, this is a very tranquil spot. From here, the trail soon climbs away from the lake, to the junction with Trail 5, La Prucheraie, 100 m further.

Turn left onto Trail 5, which begins 10-15 m above lake level, reaches another viewing platform, then descends to Lac la Blanche at the mouth of a tiny creek draining into it. Another bench and interpretive panel are here. Trail 5 follows the creek, and at 1.6 km it reaches a side path to an attractive viewing platform overlooking small, hill-enclosed Lac en Ciel.

From here, La Prucheraie becomes more challenging, narrowing and climbing for the next 400 m before dropping down to another viewing area on the lake. It then crosses a small bridge.

2.1 km After another short, steep climb, Trail 5 connects to Trail 3, Le Ouaouaron. Turn right, and walk the 15 m to a viewing platform overlooking a small waterfall. Then return to this junction and continue toward Lac aux Hérons.

Trail 3 follows the creek, which is on the right until crossing on a sturdy, unrailed bridge 100 m later. Less than 50 m further, where there is a Lac aux Hérons sign, a 200 m long boardwalk begins and traces the edge of the lake, offering gorgeous views.

After a short curving section in the forest, Trail 3 reaches Lac Amik, and works its way on the right shore, including another long section of elevated boardwalk.

3 km Just before leaving Lac Amik, Trail 3 reaches a final viewing platform overlooking the water and many steep hills. The remaining 400 m is almost all climb, the trail switching back and forth up the hillside, with frequent assists from stairs and occasional benches for resting, until it returns to the Départ des Sentiers gateway.

For most, the 3.4 km loop will be sufficient. For others, Trail 6, L'Orignal, might be an interesting addition. This begins in the opposite direction of the other walk, keeping left at the two junctions with Trail 1 found in the first 250 m. After the second, the trail soon changes character, and a sign at 350 m warns that this is an unmaintained backcountry trail. This means thicker vegetation in the treadway, and fewer bridges or boardwalks. There is little signage, but the route follows an old forest road so it should be easy to follow, and there are several interpretive panels.

After 1.8 km, it reaches a signed junction: left to Lac Robert, 250 m further, and right to Lac Howard, about 200 m. Both routes end at the shore of placid lakes, hugged by steep, tree-covered hills. No sounds disturb the tranquillity, and either makes a pleasant site for a quiet lunch.

Retrace your route back to the Départ des Sentiers. Adding this 4.6 km to the loop will provide a total hike of 8 km.

24. La Route des Zingues

TRUE
MAGNETIC

Contour Interval: 20M
1 KILOMETRE

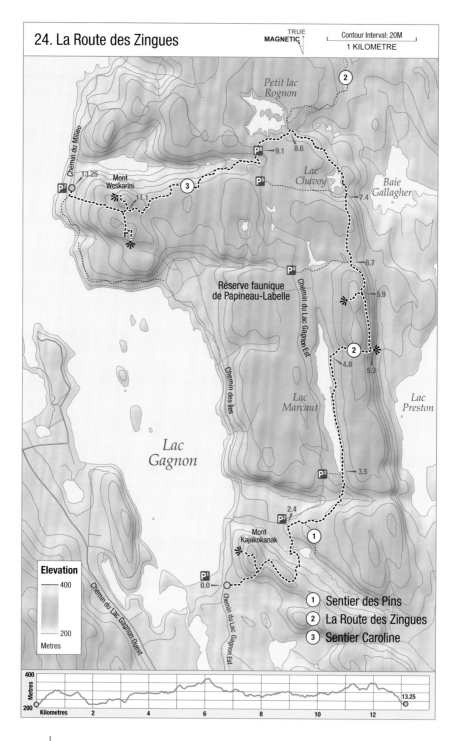

Petit lac
Rognon

2

Chemin du Milieu

13.25

P⁷

Mont
Weskarini

3

11.1

P⁶ 9.1 8.6

P⁵

Lac
Chavoy

Baie
Gallagher

7.4

6.7

P⁴

Réserve faunique
de Papineau-Labelle

Chemin du Lac Gagnon Est

5.9

2

4.8

5.3

Chemin des Îles

Lac
Marcaut

Lac
Preston

Lac
Gagnon

P³ 3.5

2.4

P²

Mont
Kajakokanak

1

Elevation

400

200

Metres

P¹
0.0

Chemin du Lac Gagnon Ouest

Chemin du Lac Gagnon Est

1 Sentier des Pins
2 La Route des Zingues
3 Sentier Caroline

400
Metres
200

Kilometres   2   4   6   8   10   12

13.25

24. La Route des Zingues

Distance: 26.5 km return
Type: linear
Difficulty: 5 (distance, navigation, remoteness, rugged terrain)
Ascent/descent: 919 m
Hiking time: 7+ hrs
Trail conditions: natural surface

Cellphone coverage: good except from the junction to P5 until P6
Uses: walking, snowshoeing
Facilities: benches
Hazards: cliffs, hunting, poison ivy, ticks, wildlife

Finding the trailhead: From the Macdonald-Cartier Bridge, follow Autoroute 5 for 1.1 km to exit 2, then turn right onto Autoroute 50. Follow Autoroute 50 for 51 km to exit 187, then turn right onto Route 317 toward Ripon. In 25 km, turn right onto Rue Boucher/Route 317. Continue to end of Route 317 in 7.1 km, then turn left onto Route 321. In Duhamel, in 26 km, turn right onto Chemin du Lac Gagnon/Rue Principale, staying left in 2.2 km to remain on Chemin du Lac Gagnon Ouest. Turn right onto Chemin du Lac Gagnon Est (dirt) in 1.1 km. Continue for 3.2 km; the trailhead and a small parking area are on the right.

Trailhead: 46°04'11.1" N, 75°05'30.5" W (start); 46°06'26.2"N, 75°06'51.2" W (finish)

Introduction: La Route des Zingues, an allusion to the Route to the Indies, the finding of which was the dream of the early European explorers, is a challenging footpath inside the Réserve faunique de Papineau-Labelle that is a section of the Sentier national au Québec. It was opened in 2011.

This is the most challenging route in the second edition, but it is also one of my favourites. This is definitely for experienced hikers only, and it may be considered something to aspire to, a future goal. I chose to begin this route at P1, but exit about two-thirds of the way through and finish on the Sentier Caroline. A second car can be left at the Sentier Caroline trailhead, P7, or at P6, which the Sentier Caroline passes.

All the parking areas, except for P7, are located on Chemin du Lac Gagnon Est. Exit to one of these in case of emergency – or if you just want an easier and shorter return to P1.

Dogs are not permitted on this trail at any time. Sections of this route are closed during hunting season.

Route description: The small parking area fits about six cars. A map panel explains that this is actually Parc Pimatina, a 32 ha conservation area owned by the Municipalité de Duhamel. The first portion of this hike will be on its trails.

As this is part of the Sentier national au Québec, the route is signed with its distinctive white over red rectangles (rather like the Polish flag). Junctions are well marked with text signage, and side trails have white over orange markers. There are also kilometre indicators, starting from P1, but these do not include the distance of the side trails.

Within 50 m, the slender footpath begins its climb up the slopes of Mont Kajakokanak. This is Canadian Shield terrain, rocky and studded with steep hills. At 400 m, the first junction, turn left to reach the viewing platform near the mountain's peak. This has benches, an interpretive panel (in French), and a lovely view of Lac Gagnon.

Return to the main trail, which meanders behind the hardwood-draped mountain, dropping down to cross a brook at a small lake at 2.1 km. A tall rock face rises from the far side of this pond.

2.4 km The path reaches the first junction to an exit: P2 is less than 200 m directly ahead. Turn right 90° onto the Sentier des Pins. Climbing again, this trail reaches the clearly marked junction with La Route des Zingues, where there is a map, 200 m later. Turn left and follow the red and white markers through the thick forest, which now features more softwood. At 2.9 km, the path passes a large glacial erratic boulder.

From the junction, the trail climbs a little, but then descends slightly into a ravine, crossing a brook at 3.1 km. Less than 100 m further, it crosses again, at the base of a waterfall. Curving left, the path follows this creek uphill to its source, Lac Marcaut.

3.5 km At the start of long, slender Lac Marcaut is a junction to P3, about 400 m left. Keep straight, following the path as it works alongside this pretty body of water. There is a lovely viewing area on a spit of bare rock, sheltered by white pine, at 4.3 km.

Shortly after, the path climbs to pass above a rock face before returning to water level. At 4.8 km, it turns right, toward the col du Trou-Malin, climbing into a narrow passage between two ridges through striking hardwoods. About 300 m later, at the high point, where the path skirts between tall rock faces, there is a sign indicating "la faille tombée" (the fallen fault), and a small cave. From the pass, picking over the stony ground, the trail descends to a viewpoint at 5.3 km. Large Lac Preston, to the right, is still nearly 100 m lower.

The path turns left, working parallel to the ridgeline, on some of the easiest walking of the entire route. At 5.9 km is the turnoff to "le rocher de Sisyphe" – check your Greek mythology – another lookout. Turn left, over the hill's crest, to a bench and interpretive panel perched beside a massive boulder. Lac Gagnon is visible in the distance, as are all the peaks that this trail will eventually ascend.

Returning to the main trail, turn left. It quickly begins to descend, heading into another narrow gully between knolls.

6.7 km At its lowest level, the footpath connects to an 800 m exit trail to P4. Continue straight; after a short climb, the next section descends overall, and although easy walking, the footpath is far less distinct than it was earlier, possibly indicating less use.

7.4 km The next junction, partway down a moderately steep hillside, is decorated with a number of signs. P5 is 1 km left; continue straight toward Petit lac Rognon, 1.4 km further. Working around tiny Lac Chavoy, the path reaches a designated lookout 200 m later, then crosses the creek draining the pond – quite an attractive spot.

The following section was some of the most challenging thus far, working along a hillside with lots of rocks intruding into the undulating treadway. An attractive area, it also feels remote and coincidently has been without cell reception since the junction to P5. It also passes alongside "le mur à mousse" (the moss wall).

8.6 km The trail arrives at the junction to P6, where there is a warning sign stating that this is the final road access for La Route des Zingues, which continues for another 10 km. Lac Rognon is 100 m further, should you wish to have a look; otherwise, turn left toward Mont Weskarini.

I really enjoyed this next section, which was mostly softwoods and liberally decorated – on May 31 – with painted trillium. At 9.1 km, the trail reaches small P6, where there is a map. Cross the dirt road and continue on the Sentier Caroline. In about 100 m this connects to a path from P5 and turns sharply right.

Over the next section, the trail passes through a rare stand of mature trees, some four hundred years old. Once it leaves these giants, the young trees seem mere scrubs. Over the next 1 km, the footpath was sometimes challenging to follow, and only those with good navigation skills will be comfortable.

11.1 km The junction to Mont Weskarini branches right, a 200 m push to a panoramic viewpoint, perhaps the best on this route. And less than 100 m further on Sentier Caroline is the junction to viewpoint La tuque. For some reason I found the 500 m trek to this spot particularly challenging, but it also offers

fine views of Lac Gagnon looking south.

If you include both side trails, then only 650 m downhill remains from the La tuque junction to the road: Chemin du Mileau. P7 is to the right, 75 m further.

Either end your hike here, or retrace the route back to P1.

Eastern Larch

Also known as tamarack, Alaska larch, and American larch, the eastern larch is the forest's most distinctive conifer. Every fall, it sheds all its needles, which turn bright golden before they drop, and in the spring it blossoms in miniscule purple flowers.

One of the first species to grow alongside bogs and other wetlands, the larch is one of the dominant tree species of the Acadian forest. First Nations peoples used its roots to sew birchbark strips into their canoes, while the bark had medicinal uses. Some claim that the larch's gummy sap, when chewed, is as sweet as maple sugar.

25. Mont Morissette

TRUE
MAGNETIC

Contour Interval: 10M
500 METRES

Elevation
— 400

— 170
Metres

Chemin Saint Jacques

Chemin de la Tour

Mont
Morissette

1.9

1.1

1.5

2

1

Lac
Morissette

0.0 P

5.4

5.8

Chemin du Lac Long

Lac
à Laurier

Lac
Dénommé

450

Metres

250

Kilometres

2

4

6

6.4

25. Mont Morissette

Distance: 6.4 km
Type: loop
Difficulty: 2
Ascent/descent: 258 m
Hiking time: 2+ hrs
Trail conditions: natural surface
Cellphone coverage: good at higher elevations, several dead zones when lower, including at the trailhead
Uses: walking, snowshoeing
Facilities: benches, garbage cans, interpretive panels, outhouses, picnic tables
Hazards: ticks, wildlife

Finding the trailhead: From the Macdonald-Cartier Bridge, follow Autoroute 5 for 34 km, then turn right onto Route 105/Route 366. In 1 km, turn left at the signalized intersection onto QC-105. Follow it for 58 km to Gracefield, then turn left onto Rue Saint Eugène (which quickly changes to Chemin de Blue Sea). In 12 km, turn left onto Rue du Pont. (The road soon changes its name to Chemin du Lac Long.) The trailhead parking area is on the right in 6.4 km.

Trailhead: 46°13'10.3" N, 76°05'58.8" W

Introduction: Situated on 589 ha of gorgeous Laurentian hillscape high above Lac Blue Sea, and with more than 13 km of superb hiking paths, Mont Morissette is an excellent hiking destination on its own merits. However, with the opening of its 18 m observation tower in 2013, perched atop its 400 m summit, Mont Morissette has become a destination not to be missed.

The park's trail network is organized so that it can be hiked as two independent loops. I have profiled Trails 1 and 2, which includes the observation tower and most of the footpath on the north side of Chemin du Lac Long. Trail 3, which begins across the road from the parking area, is a 7 km loop around the peak on the south side of this road, but it offers no similarly grand viewpoint.

While the entire loop will be too challenging for young children, a visit to the top of the observation tower should be possible, although even this is a significant climb. It is possible to drive and park at the base of the tower. Those wishing to save the best – the tower – for last should hike this route in reverse.

Route description: From the landscaped parking area, where one can find a map, picnic tables, and garbage cans, cross a tiny bridge and enter the forest on a winding footpath. Less than 50 m later, this reaches a junction between Trails 1 and 2, where there is an outhouse. Turn left onto Trail 1, and immediately you begin to climb.

The well-defined track is clearly marked, with bright white rectangles sporting an orange hiker symbol. Trail 1, in particular, has these in abundance, so it

is rare that the next one ahead cannot be seen. The hillside is covered in mixed forest, with hardwoods dominating.

At about 300 m there is a short concrete staircase – but no sign of a former dwelling – and at 500 m, near the first respite from the steady ascent, is a map. The trail turns right and works along the slope for about 100 m, slightly descending, before curving left and climbing again. After 200 m of fairly steep ascent, it turns left and provides another short break. Turning right, the trail makes its final push to the summit, reaching the Chemin de la Tour, where there is another map, at slightly more than 1 km. Turn right, and follow the road the remaining distance to the summit.

1.1 km Arrive at the base of the observation tower. This is an extensively developed area, with a large parking lot, picnic tables, an outhouse, many interpretive panels, and a pavilion with maps of both the trail system and the nearby area posted. There are actually two towers: the original fire tower, non-operational and one of the few remaining in Quebec, and the new observation tower, which is considerably higher.

The observation tower is impressive, with several intermediate platforms in addition to its highest. There are interpretive panels on each level, and those at the top name the various landmarks visible. The first time I visited, a red-tailed hawk circled quite close to the tower several times.

To continue, turn left when back at the bottom of the tower, descending on what appears to be an old road. In about 100 m, the footpath branches right, heading toward another signed Point de vue. The trail works over the uneven terrain, always nudging up or down, but definitely downhill overall.

1.5 km Trail 1 arrives at a shelter, to the left of which is a viewing platform with an excellent view of Lac Blue Sea and terrain to the south. The shelter has a map beside its entrance, and a wood stove inside. It is intended for four-season use. Outside is a picnic table and outhouse near the hut, shaded beneath tall, mature hardwoods. Only 400 m further than the tower, this is a much more tranquil setting for a snack.

Continuing beyond the shelter, Trail 1 curves left, climbing gradually as it works back along the mountain. At 1.9 km, it reaches the junction with Trail 2, and the last chance to not undertake the entire loop. Turn right onto Trail 2, where a few metres later an ATV track crosses the path, and there is another map.

Working gently downhill, nearly level at times, the well-defined footpath meanders through the woods, with rocks and tree roots a constant tripping hazard. It crosses another road-like clearing about 200 m further, but that appears not to be used by vehicle traffic. At about 2.3 km the downhill gradient increases, dropping distinctly for the next 500 m.

After crossing a tiny bridge at 2.9 km, the trail climbs onto a rocky ridge and into an old-growth forest, signed: Prucheraie. Toward the end of this stand of old hemlocks, at about 3.4 km, is another map. The winding path that follows is difficult to describe, but easy to follow thanks to the signage. It works down the slope, then back up, running along or between several ridges of rock.

5.4 km The path reaches the edge of a pond, which is a lovely sight with Mont Morissette rising behind it. A careful examination of the hillside should reveal the viewpoint at the shelter. About 200 m further, at the end of this wetland, is the sign Étang des Castors, marking a beaver pond, and there are plank bridges spanning its outflow.

At about 5.8 km, Trail 2 crosses an old road; about 200 m further find a map, where Trail 3 connects from the left. Continue straight, reaching the junction by the outhouse only 350 m later. Turn left to return to the trailhead.

26. Parcours Louis-Joseph-Papineau

TRUE
MAGNETIC

Contour Interval: 20M
2 KILOMETRES

Saint-André-Avellin

317

Saint-Sixte

P 🚻 S ?

0.0

321

10.9

P 3.9

10.1

7.8

Rang Saint-Louis

Elevation

300

160

Metres

250
Metres
50

Kilometres

2

4

6

8

10

10.9

26. Parcours Louis-Joseph-Papineau

Distance: 21.8 km return
Type: linear
Difficulty: 5 (distance)
Ascent/descent: 491 m
Hiking time: 6+ hrs
Trail conditions: crushed stone
Cellphone coverage: good throughout

Uses: walking, biking, snowshoeing, cross-country skiing
Facilities: benches, garbage cans, interpretive panels, picnic tables
Hazards: hunting, road crossing, ticks, wildlife

Finding the trailhead: From the Macdonald-Cartier Bridge, follow Autoroute 5 to exit 2 and turn right onto Autoroute 50. Continue on Autoroute 50 for 69 km to exit 205. Turn right onto Côte des Cascades, then turn left onto Route 321, 300 m later. Continue for 8.2 km to Saint-André-Avellin. The entrance to the parking area is a dirt lane on the left immediately past a bar at 35 Rue Principale. The trailhead is at end of a lane about 50 m from Route 321.

Trailhead: 45°43'13.1" N, 75°03'29.0" W

Introduction: How often can you hike and also view artwork? Rarely, so for that reason this trail is quite special. The MRC de Papineau should be congratulated for demonstrating that a trail can be more than just a path through the forest. Sadly, many of the pieces that I admired so much in 2010 have not survived, either because of the elements or the work of vandals. Nevertheless, some remain, and they add immeasurably to the hiking experience.

As this is a linear pathway, those interested in a shorter walk can choose to return at any point along the way rather than complete the full distance. However, for all but experienced hikers, I recommend turning back at the SAJO. After this the trail becomes much more challenging.

Route description: The path begins at the welcome centre for the Club de ski de fond des Montagnes Blanches, where one finds an outhouse, bike racks, and a bench. The wide trail, covered in crushed stone, features numerous signs, including a map, in the first 300 m. (All signage is in French only.)

Numerous side trails branch off, part of the cross-country ski network, but the main route is easy to follow as it climbs steadily for the first 1.1 km, passing a gate, several houses to the right, and the first piece of art, on the left. At the top are a picnic table and another map of the ski trails.

Gently descending, the trail passes a gazebo, 200 m later, and more sculptures. It winds sinuously around a couple of knolls, the vegetation overhead quite thick. Climbing again, the trail emerges from the forest at 2 km to a small

field with a bench and a bicycle rack. Descending again, it crosses a bridge 400 m later, after which it climbs again.

For the next 700 m the route is wide and flat, forest on the right, pasture to the left, passing another bench and picnic table along the way. At 3.2 km, there is a short, steep hill, where about 25 m up are the remnants of La Bibliothèque Minérale, a stone library constructed of various rock types found in the region. It was, and is still, my favourite artwork on the route.

This hill climbs another 100 m – there is a bench at the top – then descends equally steeply, emerging into broad fields, which are cleared right up to the edge of the trail.

3.9 km The Parcours reaches Rang Saint-Louis, where there are gates and lots of regulatory signs. There is also a small parking area, and the Km 4 marker. Once across, the route passes several houses and continues between fields toward a wooded hilltop. Just before the trees, 500 m from the road, it turns left and skirts around this hill following the edge of the forest, but in the open.

Some surviving artworks can be found just after the Km 5 signpost, and 400 m later the trail turns 90° left to skirt a large gravel pit. At 5.6 km, the path crosses the pit entrance, then immediately turns sharply right. Another large field must be crossed, with the pit on the right, until you reach the forest, where there is a bench, and the path turns left again.

For the next 1.6 km, the path passes through dense forest, small wetlands, rolling terrain, steep hills – and one high rock face – on its wide, crushed-stone route. There are occasional side trails, and even a hunting/snowmobile cabin, but the area feels remote.

7.8 km Quite abruptly the path emerges from the forest at the edge of a sports field: the SAJO youth camp. For the next several hundred metres, the trail passes through what is sometimes a very active spot. Sport equipment is everywhere, including a zip line, archery butts, and a teepee. The Parcours soon runs parallel to a dirt road, camp buildings on the left, and the camp's own trails branching right heading uphill.

This is a good place to head back, because beyond the SAJO the trail becomes both more physically and navigationally challenging. After nearly 700 m alongside the road, the pathway turns right and begins a steep climb into a quite lovely wooded hollow known as La Vallée-des-Ours (Valley of the Bears). At 8.8 km, it turns left through 180° and descends back out again.

From here, in 2019, the route became a little difficult to follow, as it reaches two poorly signed junctions with roads that look too similar to the pathway. After that, it climbs its biggest hill, which sports deep erosion runnels and encroaching vegetation. It almost appeared abandoned.

10.1 km For those who continue, the path reaches a dilapidated but scenic viewpoint overlooking Route 317 and the rural hamlet of Saint-Sixte. The scenic view should compensate for the difficult climb, and I recommend that most turn back here.

Since 2010, work has been undertaken to complete the trail to Saint-Sixte, but for some reason beyond this lookout much of it is overgrown – although crushed stone can be found for a considerable distance further. Experienced hikers only should continue along this overgrown route. More climbing is required, but not too much, and it does pass some charming beaver ponds – and even an interpretive panel! After 750 m, an indistinct footpath branches left, onto a large area of bare rock. This is by far the best viewpoint available. Just beyond this the Parcours has been submerged by the waters of a beaver pond.

At whatever point your hike ends, retrace your route to return to Saint-André-Avellin.

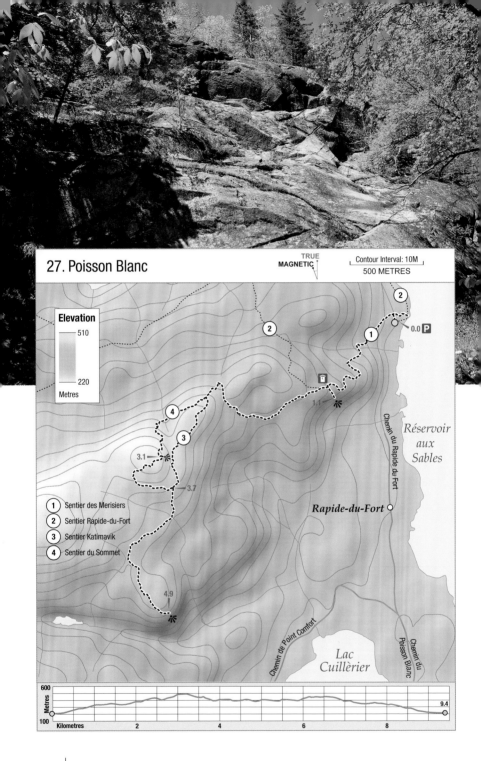

27. Poisson Blanc

TRUE
MAGNETIC

Contour Interval: 10M
500 METRES

Elevation

510

220

Metres

1 Sentier des Merisiers
2 Sentier Rapide-du-Fort
3 Sentier Katimavik
4 Sentier du Sommet

2

1

0.0 P

1.1

3.1

3.7

4.9

Réservoir
aux
Sables

Rapide-du-Fort

Chemin du Rapide du Fort

Chemin de Point Comfort

Chemin du
Poisson Blanc

Lac
Cuillèrier

27. Poisson Blanc

Distance: 9.4 km return
Type: linear
Difficulty: 4 (rugged terrain)
Ascent/descent: 620 m
Hiking time: 3+ hrs
Trail conditions: natural surface
Cellphone coverage: good on hilltops, some dead spots in ravines
Uses: walking, snowshoeing
Facilities: benches, garbage cans, interpretive panels, outhouses, picnic tables
Hazards: cliffs, rugged terrain, ticks, wildlife

Finding the trailhead: From the Macdonald-Cartier Bridge, follow Autoroute 5 for 1.1 km to exit 2, then turn right onto Autoroute 50. Follow Autoroute 50 for 38 km to exit 174. Turn left onto Route 309 N, and follow it for 73 km to Notre-Dame-du-Laus; turn left onto Chemin de Val Ombreuse, then right in 180 m onto Chemin du Poisson Blanc. In 8.8 km, keep right on Chemin du Rapide du Fort (dirt). The trailhead and parking are on the left in 1.9 km.

Trailhead: 46°08'21.1" N, 75°41'05.5" W

Introduction: This is another excellent hiking trail that has been built since the first edition of *Hiking Trails of Ottawa* was published. Parc Régional du Poisson Blanc was officially created in 2008, and it took several years to develop their trails. More are planned: I hiked this route in June 2019, and later that month the park opened the 9 km (return) Sentier Desjardins nearby.

This route ascends imposing Montagne du Diable, more than 250 m above the Réservoir aux Sables. The Sentier du Sommet, which climbs to this route's highest point, is considerably more challenging than the main Sentier Katimavik – including a few places where hands as well as feet are required. Novices should content themselves with the 2.6 km (return) Sentier des Merisiers, which reaches a quite good lookout and a lovely beach.

Camping is available in the park, with some sites quite close to this trail, and there are many island campsites for canoeists.

Route description: There is a fine trailhead pavilion at the parking area, which shelters a picnic table and mounts a large map of the park. Start by walking along a continuation of the road; in less than 100 m there is a well-signed junction, marked with large blue signs and another map. Turn left, onto the Sentier des Merisiers.

Beginning on a wide footpath, it soon begins to climb through the shading hardwoods. At about 300 m, after crossing the first of three short bridges, the trail works through the mouth of a ravine before making a short, steep climb. At 600 m, it makes a sharp left turn and eases briefly. Then, curving right, then left, then right again, the path pushes up to a junction at 1 km. Turn left to reach the lookout (belvédère).

1.1 km The path arrives at a roofed viewing platform, which has benches and a picnic table and sits on a large projecting rock face. An outhouse is nearby. The vista, facing south, is huge, extending over several lakes and the broad valley. This is a worthwhile destination on its own.

Returning to the junction, which has a map, turn left onto the Sentier Rapide-du-Fort. Its junction with Sentier Katimavik is 200 m further, along what appears to be an old woods road. En route, several large boulders, glacial erratics, can be seen among the trees.

The junction is well marked, including another map. Turn left, onto a footpath. It is signed with blue diamond markers, a hiker in white in the middle. This immediately becomes rougher walking, as it works along a sloping hillside. Little more than 100 m from a junction, there is a rope to assist on a short, steep descent. Creek crossings now are unbridged, though stones have been placed to assist.

The path continues to climb, sometimes over stony ground, other times with water draining into it when it is between two knolls. At least twice more there are rope assists before it reaches the next junction, at 2.3 km.

If the previous kilometre wasn't intimidating, keep straight/right; you will love the Sentier du sommet. (Otherwise, turn left and continue on Katimavik.) Sommet begins with another roped stretch, but then actually becomes easier walking, even descending – although with another rope assist.

At 2.7 km, the path crosses a tiny trickle in a gorge, then begins – with another rope – the final ascent to the summit. The next 200 m are quite challenging, including scrambling up a low rock wall (rope again!). At the top of that particular climb, a sign says that only 100 m remain to the summit, and the walking is relatively easy.

3.1 km Arrive at the lookout, a broad expanse of bare rock facing east, but with pretty good visibility north and south as well. Lunch here might be in order, to permit any quavering limbs some respite, or just to enjoy the broad panorama a few minutes longer.

Return from the viewpoint to the main trail, where there are directional signs and a map. Turn left, towards the posted Point de vue, which is 1.6 km

further. This portion of the trail is far less distinct, hinting that people generally hike to the summit, then return the same way. In fact, this portion is much easier, requiring neither scrambling over rock walls nor rope assists.

At 3.7 km, the Sentier du sommet ends, reconnecting with Katimavik at a different junction. Turn right towards the posted Point de vue. The first 150 m descends to a small creek, then the path works across the hardwood-draped slopes, generally climbing but with a few dips, for another 800 m before dropping quite sharply for the remainder of this route.

4.9 km The Point de vue is a large flat rock, facing south and overlooking Lac du Poisson Blanc and its dozens of small islands. Some shade is provided by a mix of pine and hardwoods. This is another tranquil site worthy of an extended stop.

To return, retrace your route, except follow Sentier Katimavik instead of the Sentier du sommet. After 4.2 km, you will be back at the first junction with the Sentier des Merisiers. Continue downhill another 100 m to reach a picnic area beside the water. Have another snack, maybe a swim, then return the 150 m to the trailhead.

Sentier national au Québec

Since 1984, volunteers have been quietly working to create a footpath across Quebec, connecting to New Brunswick and Ontario. In 2012, they reached the 1,000 km milestone with the opening of new sections in the Lanaudière and Capitale-Nationale regions.

The Sentier national au Québec is a true hiking path, built for foot traffic only, and the various sections are some of the best hiking available in the province. Usually well maintained and signed with the characteristic white and red marker, they are also frequently remote and rugged. Expect to work up a sweat when you hike the Sentier national.

White Pine

At the time of Confederation, lumber was the most important resource of Eastern Canada. Workers felled the mature forests, then floated the logs down rivers during the spring flood where they could be milled into lumber, then shipped to the United States and Great Britain.

The queen of the forest was the majestic white pine. Living up to four hundred years and towering more than 50 m, the white pine was highly desired for its use in ships' masts. White pines prefer well-drained soil and cool, humid climates, but can also grow in boggy areas and rocky highlands. They are one of three pine species native to the region, and can be distinguished by their bundle of five needles together. They retain their needles and green colour throughout the year.

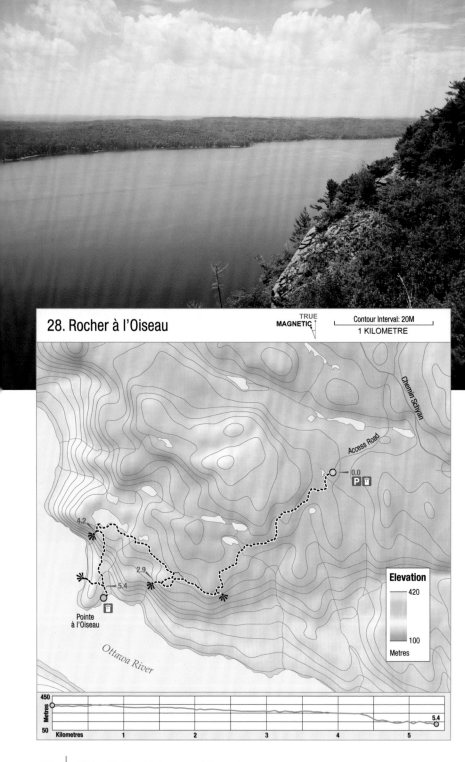

28. Rocher à l'Oiseau

TRUE
MAGNETIC

Contour Interval: 20M
1 KILOMETRE

Chemin Schyan

Access Road

0.0
P

4.2

2.9

5.4

Pointe
à l'Oiseau

Ottawa River

Elevation
420

100
Metres

28. Rocher à l'Oiseau

Distance: 10.8 km return
Type: linear
Difficulty: 3
Ascent/descent: 422 m
Hiking time: 3+ hrs
Trail conditions: natural surface
Cellphone coverage: none at trailhead; good at Rocher à l'Oiseau and high on the river-facing slope
Uses: walking, horseback riding, snowshoeing, cross-country skiing
Facilities: interpretive panels, outhouses, picnic tables
Hazards: cliffs, hunting, rugged terrain, ticks, wildlife

Finding the trailhead: From the Macdonald-Cartier Bridge, take exit 1, keeping left at the fork to Boulevard Maisonneuve/Gatineau Centre-Ville. Once on Boulevard Maisonneuve, turn right in 600 m onto Boulevard des Allumettières. At the next three roundabouts, over 2.2 km, continue straight (2nd exit) on Boulevard des Allumettières/Route 148. From the third roundabout, continue straight another 11 km, then turn right onto Route 148. Follow it for 119 km, then turn right onto Chemin de Chapeau Waltham. The road name changes to Chemin de Chapeau Sheenboro and then Rue Sheen. Turn right onto Chemin de la Montagne in 30 km, then left in 3.3 km onto Chemin Schyan (dirt). Continue for 6.2 km, then turn left onto the Sentier du Rocher-à-l'Oiseau access road, which ends in 1.3 km. There is an entry fee, payable at the ZEC St-Patrice office.

Trailhead: 46°02'24.4" N, 77°16'39.4" W

Introduction: Rocher à l'Oiseau has been a destination from long before European settlement. Its 150+ m sheer rock face springs straight out of the Ottawa River, something seen nowhere else along the river's course. Various Anishinaabe legends are associated with the Rocher, and their pictographs on its sides are considered the most important rock art site in Quebec.

Boaters have always viewed it from the water, but in 2010 a new hiking trail permitted easy access to the top of the rock, while a somewhat more challenging section descends to the Ottawa River. Because of its scenic magnificence and anthropological/historical importance, I included this trail in *Hiking Trails of Ottawa* despite its considerable distance from the National Capital Region.

The hike to the top of the Rocher and return is about 8 km and should be comfortable for most novice hikers, though I wouldn't recommend this as their first outing! Those uncomfortable driving narrow, rocky lanes might prefer to park on the Chemin Schyan and hike the 1.3 km to the official trailhead.

Route description: At the small parking area there is an outhouse along with a large sign with a map. The wide footpath descends to cross a railed bridge, then moves into quite hilly terrain. The forest is a mixture of hardwoods and softwoods, with a number of tall white pine trees scattered about. Because of the many small rocky knolls, the path – aptly named La Fôret / Forest Trail / Nôpimi Mîkâns – curves and winds around them, and small bridges are provided to cross the many patches of wet ground between the hills.

For the first 700 m, the rolling route tends uphill, but after that it descends overall – with a few obvious short exceptions. About 900 m, the pass skirts a long rock face, to the right, with the Km 1 sign and an interpretive sign – trilingual: French, English, and Anishinaabe – and just beyond, a large boulder.

About 400 m further a bridge with railings spans a small creek, after which there is a particularly pleasant stretch of hardwood forest. This entire route is shaded. The Km 2 sign also indicates that 2 km remains to the lookout.

After a short 100 m descent, a side path to the first viewpoint branches left. Scampering up onto the large, bare rock, the viewer obtains the first glimpses of the Ottawa River – although the surrounding vegetation has grown up and is partly obscuring.

The main trail curves right, even climbing a little before reaching a junction 350 m later to another lookout, on the left in 250 m. Head toward it; there is a second junction 300 m further indicating the lookout is 50 m to the left.

2.9 km Arrive at the edge of a cliff – with no railing – to find an interpretive panel and a panoramic vista high above the Ottawa River. Few structures can be seen, but looking right Chalk River Laboratories, home to operating nuclear reactors from 1945 to 2018, is clearly visible.

Returning to the junction, turn left and rejoin the main trail 200 m later. Turn left again, and in 350 m the trail passes the Km 3 sign. (Including both lookouts, add another 500+ m.) The up-and-down becomes more pronounced as the trail works over some rocky ridges. About 100 m further there is a small pond to the right, and at 3.8 km the path crosses a small creek to arrive beside a lovely small lake.

The next 350 m is easy strolling, and the almost level path meanders alongside this charming tarn. Tall pines shelter the route, and at 4.1 km it arrives at a picnic table and interpretive panel – and a great spot for a swim. (I did.) But

that is for the return. Rocher à l'Oiseau is so close, almost in sight. Turn sharply left and hurry along the footpath.

4.2 km Arrive at the top of Rocher à l'Oiseau, where there are two interpretive panels, and an expansive vista looking west and south. A considerable amount of bare rock is available to descend to for a look around. There are few grander views available in the Ottawa Valley.

The Ascension Trail continues, deceptively level for 100 m, before steeply dropping over the rocky hillside; a rope offers assistance. About 100 m of elevation is lost in the following 300 m. This section is the most challenging along this route. Please remember that it must be climbed on the return.

At 4.9 km, the Point Trail branches right, heading toward another lookout, but at water level. Definitely do this, even though it cruelly starts by climbing up about 20 m before dropping down to a gorgeous location, which provides an exceptional view of Rocher à l'Oiseau from below. Two more of the first-rate interpretive panels are located here.

5.4 km Return to the main trail and turn right. Barely 100 m remains to a sandy, sheltered beach, where there are picnic tables and an outhouse. In summer, this is a popular picnic location with cottagers who boat here. (One group kindly offered my friend and me a cold beer: we gratefully – almost reverentially – accepted.)

Retrace your route, which will be only about 5 km without the side trails, to return to the trailhead. And don't forget your swim; it will feel amazing after the climb back up.

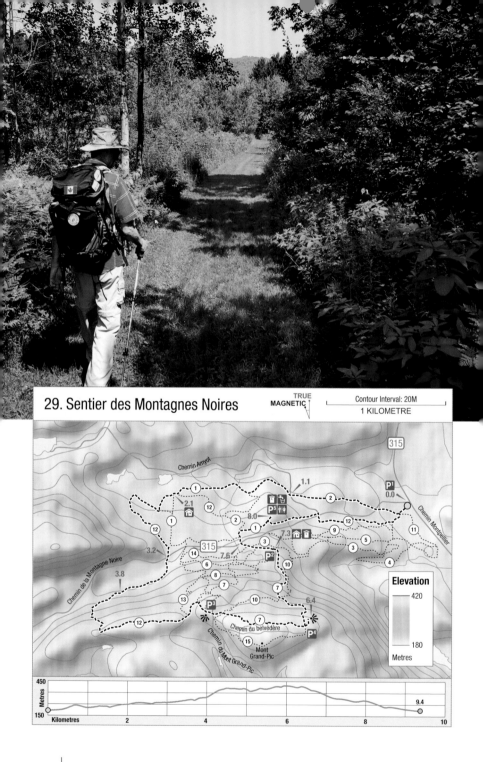

29. Sentier des Montagnes Noires

TRUE
MAGNETIC

Contour Interval: 20M
1 KILOMETRE

Chemin Amyot

315

P¹
0.0

1.1

2.1

8.0

7.3

7.6

315

3.2

3.8

Chemin de la Montagne Noire

6.4

P³

P²

P⁴

P⁵

Chemin du belvédère

Chemin du Mont Grand-Pic

Mont Grand-Pic

Chemin Montpellier

Elevation

420

180

Metres

450

Metres

150

9.4

Kilometres   2   4   6   8   10

29. Sentier des Montagnes Noires

Distance: 9.4 km return
Type: loop
Difficulty: 3
Ascent/descent: 300 m
Hiking time: 2.5+ hrs
Trail conditions: compacted earth, natural surface

Cellphone coverage: excellent
Uses: walking, biking*, snowshoeing, cross-country skiing
Facilities: benches, garbage cans, interpretive panels, outhouses, picnic tables
Hazards: road crossings, ticks, wildlife

Finding the trailhead: From the Macdonald-Cartier Bridge, follow Autoroute 5 for 1.1 km to exit 2, then turn right onto Autoroute 50. Follow Autoroute 50 for 51 km to exit 187, then turn right onto Route 317 toward Ripon. In 25 km, turn left onto Chemin de Montpelier. In 4.7 km, turn left onto Chemin de la Montagne Noire (dirt). Park on the left at trailhead P1. A fee is required. It can be paid at the trailhead.

Trailhead: 45°48'32.5" N, 75°08'50.4" W

Introduction: Parc des Montagnes Noires de Ripon's delightful system of trails has been considerably upgraded in recent years, including the addition of an observation tower in 2019. Between its two viewpoints, there are panoramic views of the hills in all directions; on a clear day the ski hill of Mont Tremblant, more than 70 km distant, can be seen. There is a small camping area within the park, and the White Birch refuge is available for up to six people, summer and winter.

New trails have been added, including one in 2019, so this route is different from that found in the first edition of *Hiking Trails of Ottawa*. With this maze of pathways it is easy to turn onto the wrong path, but signage is usually quite clear, so watch for the trail numbers. If you see the wrong one, backtrack to the previous junction.

This should be enjoyable as a day hike and picnic for lone hikers or families, as many options of varying length and difficulty are available.

Route description: On the large map displayed in P1, you will see that every trail segment is numbered, and that points of interest are letter-coded. The uses permitted on each trail segment are listed, as is the distance and difficulty rating.

Begin following a wide, grass-surface pathway, reaching the Trail 2 junction in 75 m from P1; turn right. Climbing gradually, this crosses Chemin de la Montaigne Noire at 300 m. The grass surface ends when the trail enters an area of tall maple, private property signs on both sides, with the blue tubing for maple-sap collection visible on the right.

After a short – and very welcome – downhill section, Trail 2 crosses Chemin Amyot at 1.1 km. The trail curves right just across the road; note the toboggan field on the left. It re-enters forest, climbing gently but keeping a pine-covered summit to the left. About 350 m later it reaches a junction with Trail 1. Continue straight/right on Trail 1, climbing on a former woods road, with higher ground on the left and a deep gully to the right.

At 2.1 km, Trail 12 connects on the left. Stay on Trail 1, crossing a small brook and reaching Refuge Trappeur less than 100 m further. A picnic table is outside – but so are the mosquitoes! Continue straight/right; 150 m later there is a junction with Trail 12 – this was new in 2019.

Turn right onto Trail 12, a footpath through dense forest that descends to a small bridge before curving left and climbing again. This is a pleasant, remote section, although with more rocks and tree roots intruding into the treadway. This path also contains more small elevation changes, as it works over the undulating terrain. It reaches an open area just before (almost) reconnecting with Trail 1 at 3.2 km. But Trail 12 immediately turns right, crossing Chemin de la Montagne Noire about 50 m later.

Trail 12 curves right and begins a steeper ascent on a slender track grubbed into the hillside. Several puncheons assist crossing tiny wet areas in the first few hundred metres. At 3.8 km, the route begins switchbacking up the slope in 500 m of relatively steep climb. After that it turns left, working along a ridge for the next 600 m. It still climbs, but much more gently, and even with some occasional downhill sections. The thick hardwoods provide no views, although there is a small lake to the right.

After a short, distinct downhill, the trail reached an area, at 5 km, where in 2019 there was some construction. The pathway was widened into a dirt road, which continued as it climbed. In 350 m, Trail 7 crosses; turn right onto Trail 7 and follow it to the observation tower, just 100 m distant.

The tower wasn't completed when I visited in 2019 – neither July nor October – but it promises to provide wonderful views south and west. Trail 7 follows the access road to P3 on Chemin du Mont Grand-Pic, which it crosses at about 5.4 km. This is a lovely path, beneath gorgeous forest and encountering some large rock features, because it is almost at the summit of Mont Grand-Pic. Bicycle/ski Trail 10 branches left 200 m from the road.

After a pleasant ramble, passing some interpretive panels and crossing several large rocks, Trail 10 reaches a junction. P4 is on the right, where there is an outhouse. Continue straight/left, with a wide path curving left to a lookout.

6.4 km Reach the belvédère (lookout), an impressive structure that includes a covered table, three other picnic tables, a garbage can, and several excellent interpretive panels, as well as expansive views north and east. This is a fine location for a break.

After, return to Trail 7, turning right and descending Mont Grand-Pic, crossing Trail 10 along the way, to reach Chemin du Mont Grand-Pic, Refuge Le Rustique, and large P2, at 7.3 km.

From here, it gets a bit complicated, because many trails converge. Cross the road, and head left, still on now wide Trail 7. Several other trails connect, but continue straight until this path crosses Chemin de la Montagne Noire, 300 m further. This path soon links with Trail 1; continue straight/right on Trail 1 as it curves right, reaches a junction with Trail 2, then passes the group camping area and another refuge.

8 km If you managed all that successfully, Trail 1 arrives at P5 and the new Chalet Stéphane Richer, where there are picnic tables, an outhouse, and a trailhead kiosk with map outside, and washrooms and drinking water indoors, available whenever the building, which is the administrative centre of the park, is open.

From here, on the road side of the chalet, pick up Trail 12, which resumes and heads downhill. After 350 m, this pleasant footpath first crosses Chemin Amyot, then Chemin de la Montagne Noire. Working along a slope, the road visible to the left for some time, at 9.1 km, Trail 12 briefly connects to mountain bike Trail 9 – for only about 10 m. From here Trail 12 ends 100 m later on Trail 5. Turn left and return to P1, only 300 m further.

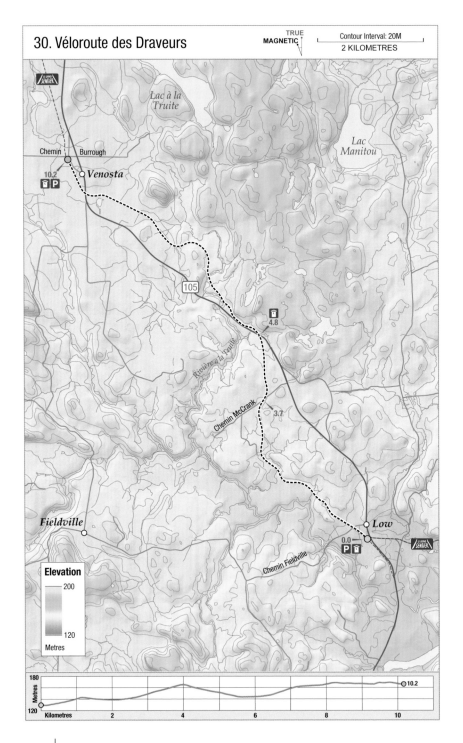

30. Véloroute des Draveurs

TRUE
MAGNETIC

Contour Interval: 20M
2 KILOMETRES

Lac à la
Truite

Lac
Manitou

Chemin   Burrough

10.2

Venosta

105

4.8

Rivière à la Truite

Chemin McCrank   3.7

Fieldville

Low

0.0

Chemin Fieldville

Elevation
— 200

120
Metres

180

Metres

120
Kilometres   2   4   6   8   10

10.2

30. Véloroute des Draveurs

Distance: 20.4 km return
Type: linear
Difficulty: 4 (distance)
Ascent/descent: 133 m
Hiking time: 5+ hrs
Trail conditions: crushed stone
Cellphone coverage: excellent

Uses: walking, biking, snowmobiling
Facilities: benches, garbage cans, interpretive panels, outhouses, picnic tables
Hazards: hunting, poison ivy, road crossings, ticks, wildlife

Finding the trailhead: From the Macdonald-Cartier Bridge, follow Autoroute 5 for 34 km, then turn right onto Route 105/Route 366. In 1 km, turn left at the signalized intersection onto Route 105. Follow it for 21 km; the trail is visible on the left. Turn left opposite Chemin Principal and park.

Trailhead: 45°48'38.9" N, 75°57'09.1" W

Introduction: The Véloroute des Draveurs is a 72 km section of abandoned rail line that has been converted into a recreational corridor. The trail follows the route of an abandoned Canadian Pacific Railway line between Hull and Maniwaki that was completed in 1904. The last regular passenger service was in 1963, and regular freight runs were discontinued in 1968. This section is also the route of The Great Trail (Trans Canada), and its signage may be found along the route.

This is a relatively gentle walk on a wide, crushed-stone pathway, passing through areas of forest, wetlands, and agriculture. There are no grand views, but this trail doesn't have the elevation change usually required to reach a lookout. This Véloroute also features designated rest areas every 5 km. One of these is roughly midway between the communities of Low and Venosta, providing an excellent decision point for those wishing a shorter outing.

Route description: Begin at the Halte (Rest Area) de Low, a covered shelter shading picnic tables and garbage cans with an outhouse nearby. There is also a bilingual information panel. Head north, away from Ottawa/Gatineau, on the wide, crushed-stone track. Passing through the small community of Low, the pathway crosses Chemin Fieldville at 350 m. Gates near the road restrict access to motorized vehicles. There is also the Km 4 marker and a Great Trail sign.

An area of cultivated fields follows, situated in the rolling hills. At 1 km a sign, facing the other direction, indicates the Halte de Low's proximity. About here the trail moves into a forested area, even perceptibly climbing. A wide centre strip of grass grows through the crushed stone.

Passing the Km 5 marker, there is another gate and uncultivated fields border the path. This section rarely remains straight for long, making frequent short turns required to work around the many low hills. At 2 km, a large farmed area is visible to the left, and by the Km 6 marker, the trees have been mostly replaced by cleared land on both sides of the pathway, which passes close to several farm buildings. Respect the many No Trespassing signs. By 2.8 km, the trail begins noticeably to climb, though still gently.

At 3.7 km, the Véloroute reaches Chemin McCrank (dirt), where there are gates across the trail. Shortly after crossing Chemin McCrank, which is bordered by open fields, the trail begins a fairly significant – for an abandoned rail line – descent. And a sign indicates that there is a picnic spot coming up in 1 km.

📍 **4.8 km** The trail reaches very busy Route 105, where the speed limit is 90 kph. Be extremely cautious crossing here. Immediately past the gate on the far side is the Halte de la 105 featuring a picnic table, bench, garbage can, and outhouse shaded by several tall maples. This sits in a pleasant little hollow, and would be an ideal spot for an extended break if not situated so close to the noisy highway.

From here, you may decide whether to end your hike and return to Low, a nearly 10 km total walk, or continue to the next picnic site, which just happens to be in Venosta, 5.2 km further.

Those continuing should enjoy the next section. For perhaps 600 m it parallels Route 105, but then separates, moving into thick forest along a river gorge and descending until it crosses the Rivière à la Truite. The bordering terrain is quite hilly, so sometimes the trail is perched on an embankment and

at other times travels through a cut. This has a quite remote feel, for almost 1.5 km, through mature, brooding spruce, curving and climbing from the river crossing.

Quite suddenly, at about 7.2 km, the path re-enters an area of cultivated fields, bordering both sides of the route, gradually straightening and levelling as it emerges from the ravine. The fields are flat as well, except for one interesting looking hill on your right which, alas, is on private property.

The final kilometre contains numerous landmarks. There is a signpost for the community after Low, Kazabazua, which is 10 km away, and the Km 13 marker. Highway 105 must be crossed again, which involves negotiating the gates and dodging spirited motorists. About 300 m beyond Route 105 is the former train station, now a private residence. Do not confuse it for the picnic grounds, even though there is an interpretive panel there.

10.2 km The pathway reaches the Halte de Low, located just before Chemin Burrough. A bench, table, garbage can, and outhouse, are all to the left of the trail, while the parking area is on the right. Sadly, there is no shade.

The Véloroute des Draveurs continues, but perhaps that is an excursion for another day. For walkers, Venosta will be sufficient. Enjoy a snack, and retrace your path to return to Low.

33. Griffith Uplands Trail

Ontario - North of Highway 7

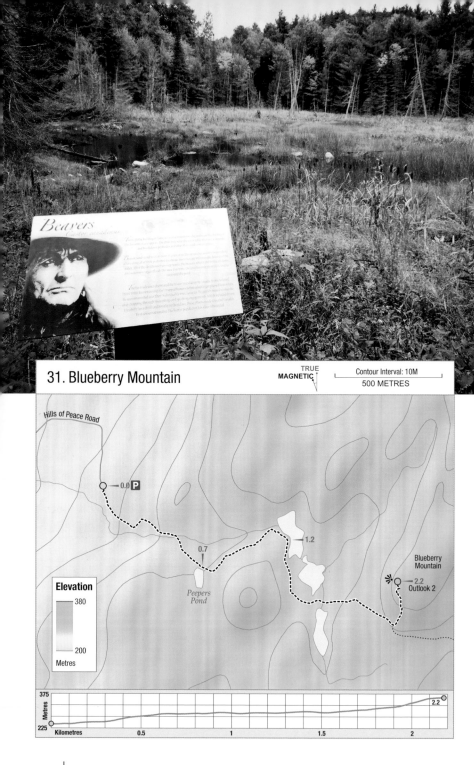

31. Blueberry Mountain

TRUE
MAGNETIC

Contour Interval: 10M

500 METRES

Hills of Peace Road

0.0 P

0.7

1.2

Peepers
Pond

Elevation

380

200

Metres

Blueberry
Mountain

2.2
Outlook 2

375

Metres

225

Kilometres

0.5

1

1.5

2

2.2

31. Blueberry Mountain

Distance: 4.4 km return
Type: linear
Difficulty: 1
Ascent/descent: 126 m
Hiking time: 1+ hrs
Trail conditions: compacted earth, natural surface

Cellphone coverage: poor in first 1.5-2 km; good reception only on top of Blueberry Mountain
Uses: walking, biking, snowshoeing, cross-country skiing
Facilities: benches, interpretive panels
Hazards: ticks, wildlife

Finding the trailhead: From the Highway 416/417 split, follow Highway 417 for 23 km to exit 155. Head left on Highway 49/March Road toward Almonte. In 13 km take the second exit on the roundabout (continue straight), now on Ottawa Street (soon to be Route 16). Keep straight for 28 km, then turn right onto County Road 511. In 6 km, turn left onto French Line — which soon changes to a dirt surface — and after 13 km turn right onto Flower Station Road. In 6.2 km turn right onto Hills of Peace Road. Continue for 1.9 km to the end of the road, beside the house at number 502, and park on the side of the road.

Trailhead: 45°09'53.7" N, 76°40'19.8" W

Introduction: Blueberry Mountain is located on a 500 ha property formerly known as the Alba Wilderness School. In 2009, the owners, the Clifford family, signed an easement with the Mississippi Madawaska Land Trust that specifies that the area "will be permitted to develop naturally into a mature old growth forest." Next to Murphys Point Provincial Park, this is the second largest tract of legally protected land in Lanark County.

A number of routes, usually following old roads, traverse the property. However, only the Blueberry Mountain Trail is well signed. This leads to one of the highest elevations in Lanark County, and a fairly panoramic vista. There is no fee to use this trail, but signing a waiver form, available at the trailhead kiosk, is required.

Although more than 100 m of climb is required, most of it is done gradually, and on a well-defined track. This fairly short hike can probably be enjoyed by most families and novices.

Dogs are permitted off leash but are requested to be on leash near the house because of its free-range chickens.

Route description: There is a trailhead kiosk at the trailhead, with waiver forms and pencils, and a second large blue circular sign advising that Blueberry Mountain is one of "The Seven Wonders of Lanark County." (It is number 4 on the list, apparently.) After signing the waiver, continue along what appears to be a former forest road, now still wide but with bordering vegetation crowding in from the edges. Tall hardwoods entirely shade the path, creating a snug passageway, and it begins to climb almost immediately.

Less than 300 m further is the first of many interpretive panels, this one on bottle gentian. It is found at the start of a small clearing, in which there are a

number of displays honouring funders and sponsors, and another interpretive panel, on staghorn sumac.

Leaving this small clearing, the path makes its steepest climb of the route, which lasts barely 100 m. There are frequent side paths, though most are far less distinct than the main trail.

At 550 m, the trail curves left and crosses a quite elaborate but short bridge over an exceptionally modest creek. At 700 m, a tiny sign identifies the small wet area on the right as Peepers Pond. Curving left around a small knoll, the trail passes several more interpretive panels before it reaches a larger pond/wetland at 1.2 km. Here is another panel, about beavers, including a brief story about Grey Owl and his conservation efforts, and a bench.

The following 400 m are nearly level, and there are additional interpretive panels. My favourite, just beyond 1.6 km, is about a wolf den that was discovered in this area.

9 2 km The route turns left, off the wide track, which continues straight ahead. It is signed, and a bench has been placed across the road on which you have been walking, but it is important not to miss this junction, because otherwise you will just wander off into deeper forest.

Only a short distance remains, but if any section might be challenging to novices, this will be it. The footpath works up a rocky hillside, and one that is steeper than before. Along the way, an interpretive panel about white oak, which surround you, might be of interest.

At 2.2 km, the path emerges from the trees onto a large section of mostly bare rock and wide vistas. Another interpretive panel states that this is Outlook 1. A worn track continues less than 100 m further, to another plaque which states that this is Outlook 2. A footpath appears to continue, but Outlook 2 is the official end of this route.

Enjoy the view and spend a moment contemplating the silence, then retrace the route back to the trailhead.

Great Lakes–St. Lawrence Forest

Canada's second-largest forest region, the Great Lakes–St. Lawrence Forest stretches from southeastern Manitoba to the Gaspé Peninsula, and is a transitional forest between the southern broad-leafed species and the northern conifers. As a result, many boreal species may be found — especially at higher elevations — but the distinguishing conifers are white and red pine and eastern hemlock. Deciduous species such as sugar maple, red maple, red oak, and white elm are common, but the most characteristic hardwood is yellow birch.

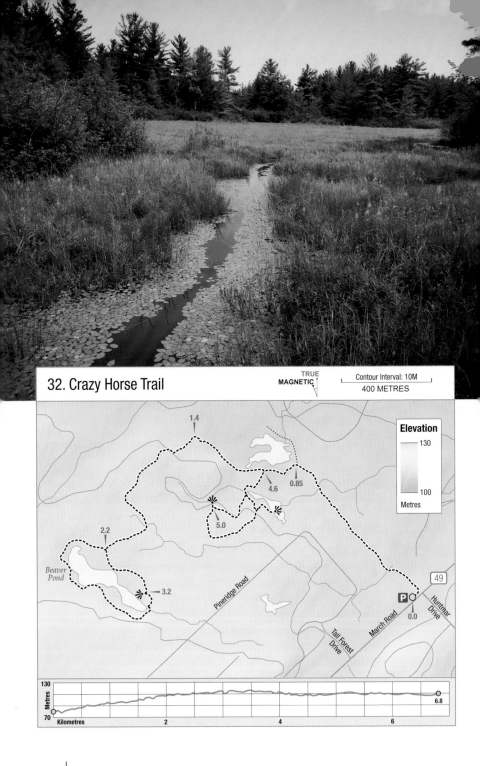

32. Crazy Horse Trail

TRUE
MAGNETIC

Contour Interval: 10M
400 METRES

Elevation

130

100

Metres

1.4

4.6

0.85

5.0

2.2

Beaver Pond

3.2

Pineridge Road

Tall Forest Drive

March Road

Huntmar Drive

49

P

0.0

130

Metres

70

Kilometres

2

4

6

6.8

32. Crazy Horse Trail

Distance: 6.8 km return
Type: linear with loops
Difficulty: 2
Ascent/descent: 35 m
Hiking time: 2+ hrs
Trail conditions: natural surface

Cellphone coverage: excellent
Uses: walking, snowshoeing, cross-country skiing
Facilities: benches, interpretive panels
Hazards: ticks, wildlife

Finding the trailhead: From the Highway 416/417 split, follow Highway 417 for 5.7 km to exit 138. Keep right on March Road North. Follow it for 12 km to the intersection with Huntmar Drive. The trailhead — it is not well signed — is on the right. There is no official parking area, but there is room to park on the right on March Road just beyond Huntmar.

Trailhead: 45°21'02.3" N, 75°59'54.1" W

Introduction: Most trails are named for a geographic feature, or after a neighbouring community, so when you see one named "Crazy Horse" you know there must be a story. To the best of my knowledge, the Lakota war leader who died in Nebraska in 1877 never visited Ottawa. Sure enough, this trail, which was built by the volunteer group Friends of the Carp Hills, was named in honour of an old bar that used to exist on this site. (This might tell us more about these volunteers than we need to know.) In fact, where you park is the bar's former parking lot.

This is a walking-only footpath (with the exception of cross-country skiing in winter) that circles a lovely little pond bordered by small rocky hills quite uncharacteristic of most of the terrain near Ottawa. However, it is also very wet, especially in its first 900 m. What this means for the mosquito population is best left to your imagination. The volunteers intend to improve the boardwalks and other structures, but have dry socks and shoes in your car just in case. Signage is generally good, although I did find it a little confusing on the smaller loop.

I quite enjoyed this little trail, and perhaps more so because it is so close to urban areas, yet feels so remote. The first 900 m, in particular, is bordered on both sides by private property; keep close to the designated path at all times.

Route description: There is an excellent city of Ottawa trailhead sign, including a map, but it is set back a little from March Road, and when I hiked this in July, it was nearly hidden by thick vegetation. A very slender footpath works through the thick brush, signed by orange plastic markers affixed to trees. Almost immediately, houses are visible to the right, and quite close.

At 200 m a long puncheon – a two-plank-wide boardwalk – crosses a small creek and continues through some very soggy ground. At 450 m, the path emerges from the woods into a rocky clearing near a power line. As the path meanders on, houses are no longer visible, but unmarked side trails hint at their proximity.

The worst wet area is encountered at 700 m. The trail is shared with an old vehicle track, which was substantially flooded. There are puncheons here, but they sagged beneath the water's surface when I trod upon them. (Perhaps I should lose weight?) In any case, it was a lively and entertaining couple of hundred metres as I tried to find a dry – okay, less wet – route through this area.

850 m A sign in a pine tree directs trail users left, toward the signed Beaver Pond, and off the vehicle track. The treadway improves immediately, even though a large wetland can be seen to the right. The footpath is slightly elevated on ground that is actually quite rocky, though often with a thin soil cover, and shaded by pine.

Barely 100 m further is the first junction to the side trails, which are signed with yellow markers. Continue straight/right. The main trail threads its way between a small wet area on the left and a larger one on the right. The second junction to the side trails is reached about 100 m later.

Continue on the main trail as it works around the large wet area for another 300 m (or so, depending upon how much rain there has been). But at 1.4 km, the footpath turns left and climbs. Over the next 600 m it crosses several open areas, rocky and sometimes grass covered. Where the grass is high the track is sometimes difficult to see, so watch for the trail markers. About 2.1 km, after a sharp right turn, the route enters another soggy area, passing between two wetlands.

9 2.2 km The path arrives at the Beaver Pond Loop. Heading in either direction returns the hiker to this spot; I chose to head right. This large pond is on the left, and the trail attempts to keep close to it, probably to better observe the amphibian life. However, this means that whenever the water level is high, there are going to be several short sections that are wet, or even underwater.

At about 2.6 km there is a lovely spot with an unobstructed view of the pond, and there is a fair amount of rock covered in pine needles bordering the pond. The surrounding trees contain a significant percentage of softwood, giving this area more of a Canadian Shield appearance. About 300 m later, when crossing the modest outflow of the pond, look left; the old beaver dam that created the pond is quite close.

The best view of the pond is on a very short side trail at 3.2 km, on a small rocky outcrop where much of it is visible. Just 200 m further, the path crosses a channel between the signed Beaver Pond and a smaller pond to the right, after which it returns to the junction at 3.5 km. Retrace the main trail the 1.2 km back to the junction with the side trail, and turn right.

Yellow markers sign this path. Turn right at the junction barely 100 m later, after which the trail — utilizing an old beaver dam as a treadway — curves left around a tiny pond to a second junction. Turn right here as well. From here the path meanders between pine and rocky outcrops. At 5 km, a short side path — these use blue markers — leads to a viewpoint on a rocky hillock.

The next section I found somewhat challenging. The trail is often on moss-covered rock, with the treadway not always clear and markers not visible. The route is a long curve left, reaching another junction about 450 m from the viewpoint. Turn right to another viewpoint, a rock overlooking another pond, about 100 m away.

Return to the junction, and turn right. This completes the loop 100 m later. Recross the beaver dam, keep left at the next yellow trail junction, and reconnect with the main trail at 5.8 km. From here turn right, and retrace the 1 km route back to March Road.

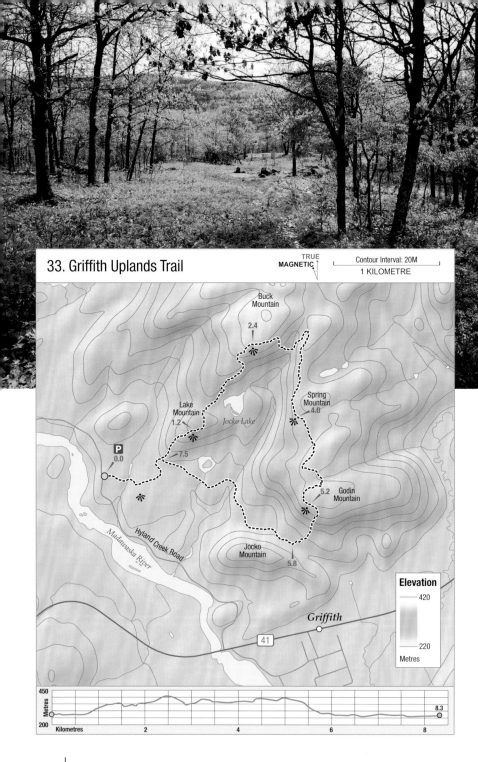

33. Griffith Uplands Trail

TRUE
MAGNETIC

Contour Interval: 20M
1 KILOMETRE

Buck
Mountain
2.4

Spring
Mountain
4.0

Lake
Mountain
1.2

Jocko Lake

7.5

P
0.0

Godin
Mountain
5.2

Jocko
Mountain
5.8

Madawaska River

Hyland Creek Road

Griffith

41

Elevation
420

220
Metres

450
Metres
200

Kilometres   2   4   6   8

8.3

33. Griffith Uplands Trail

Distance: 8.3 km
Type: loop
Difficulty: 3
Ascent/descent: 269 m
Hiking time: 2.5+ hrs
Trail conditions: natural surface, compacted earth

Cellphone coverage: good at trailhead and on hilltops, poor in low areas
Uses: walking, ATVs*, snowshoeing, snowmobiling*
Facilities: none
Hazards: hunting, motorized uses, ticks, wildlife

Finding the trailhead: From the Highway 416/417 split, follow Highway 417 for 74 km, then turn left onto County Road 6 toward Renfrew. In 3.7 km, turn left onto Highway 60/O'Brien Road. Follow it for 1.7 km, then turn left onto Opeongo Road. In 4 km, turn left onto Highway 132. Continue straight/left in 27 km when it merges with Highway 41. In 22 km, turn right onto Hyland Creek Road. The trailhead is on the right in 2.3 km.

Trailhead: 45°15'22.1" N, 77°15'29.2" W

Introduction: Opened in 2010, the Griffith Uplands Trail passes through an area of marble bedrock and uplands forest, something sufficiently uncommon in Ontario that it earned the 5.6 km² area around these four summits the designation of being a provincially significant Area of Natural and Scientific Interest (ANSI).

As a relatively new and not heavily used trail, the treadway is occasionally indistinct. This is especially true on bare rock. Particular care must be taken to watch for trail markers, or rock cairns, and having a trail map is quite important for this route, as is informing someone of where you are and when you expect to return. This is not a route recommended for novices without the company of experienced hikers.

Although this trail is currently maintained by the Township of Greater Madawaska, they are unsure of who originally built it. The trailhead map states that the entire route is 10 km. I measured a considerably shorter distance.

Route description: The parking area, 488 Highland Creek Road, is quite modest, a small space fitting only a few cars. But there is a trailhead sign that features a large map, with the trail beginning from there. The single-track footpath enters the forest immediately, signed by blue paint marks on trees. At 100 m there is a donation box to aid wood ducks.

Although uneven, the route is generally level for its first 700 m, skirting the wet spots of a cedar bog. Then it turns right and climbs up to a forestry road used by ATVs 100 m later. Continue straight; from here a steep climb begins

up Lake Mountain. The next 400 m is straight up, the thick vegetation giving way to scattered trees, rocky outcrops covered in lichen, and an increasingly impressive view behind you.

The route is sometimes difficult to discern through the rocky barrens. Small cairns of rock sometimes mark the track where there are no trees. At 1.2 km it more or less levels for about 100 m, and excellent views are available back toward the Madawaska River.

The path curves left, climbing slightly higher before dropping quite precipitously down through a rock face and into a narrow saddle between two mountains. To the right, small Jocko Lake, snared between the surrounding peaks, beckons appealingly.

However, the path doesn't descend to it. Instead, it climbs again, in a short but challenging ascent through the rocks. By 1.9 km, the worst is finished, and the trail works along a spur, even descending a little before turning left 150 m later and resuming a steep ascent: Buck Mountain.

At 2.2 km, there is a good viewing spot, at an open area. Shortly afterwards, the trail appears to connect with an ATV track, and together they continue to the viewpoint.

2.4 km In a clearing on the slope of Buck Mountain there are good views to the south, toward the Madawaska River. This is almost the highest point on this route—but there is still plenty of climbing remaining.

The ATV track and the footpath soon diverge, and the trail descends Buck Mountain, crossing a tiny creek nearly 500 m later. After that the climb resumes, the trail working past an imposing rock face from about 250 m before turning back 180° and ascending it. On the rock outcroppings shortly after there are good views of both Buck and Lake Mountains.

The path soon appears to share an indistinct vehicle track, at least for a short time, as the route descends again into thicker forest, reaching the next low, wet spot at 3.6 km. There is no view here, behind the crest, but over the next 300 m the path climbs the flank of Spring Mountain. At 4 km, it passes the largest glacial erratic boulder along this route, and just after that there is another good viewpoint on bare rock.

The trail turns left just at the viewpoint, so watch carefully for the markers. About 200 m further there is a short climb, perhaps the steepest on this route, but after 100 m the footpath is running along another ridgeline. At 4.6 km there are two clearings, either one of which could be the viewpoint shown on the trail map.

From the second of these, the path once again turns sharply left – at the clearing – and moves away from the crest. Perhaps 150 m later, the trail rejoins an ATV track, but separates from it, to the right, only 100 m further. Another short, steep climb delivers hikers to the top of Godin Mountain, where the path curves right and enters several open areas before reaching the final viewpoint.

9 5.2 km Arrive at the viewpoint on Godin Mountain, which has the most expansive vista on this route, both south and west. Next to this massive bare rock, a pine is decorated with several First Nations crafted objects, familiarly known as dreamcatchers, hanging from its branches.

Over the next 500 m the trail descends Godin Mountain, often quite steeply. Care must be taken on the slippery rocks and moss. After crossing a boggy area at the bottom, it climbs a few metres to connect with the forestry road, used as both an ATV and snowmobile trail, at 5.8 km; the steep-sided and tree-lined bulk of Jocko Mountain rises directly ahead.

Turn right, and follow this track – through occasional muddy spots – as it winds its uneven way back to the base of Lake Mountain at 7.5 km. At this junction turn left, and retrace the initial 800 m back to the trailhead.

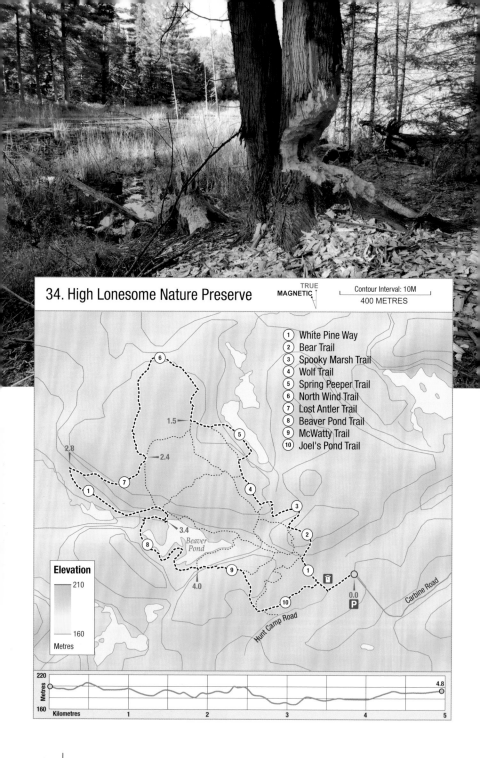

34. High Lonesome Nature Preserve

TRUE
MAGNETIC

Contour Interval: 10M

400 METRES

1. White Pine Way
2. Bear Trail
3. Spooky Marsh Trail
4. Wolf Trail
5. Spring Peeper Trail
6. North Wind Trail
7. Lost Antler Trail
8. Beaver Pond Trail
9. McWatty Trail
10. Joel's Pond Trail

Beaver Pond

Carbine Road

Hunt Camp Road

Elevation

210

160

Metres

34. High Lonesome Nature Preserve

Distance: 4.8 km
Type: loop
Difficulty: 1
Ascent/descent: 73 m
Hiking time: 1.5+ hrs
Trail conditions: compacted earth, natural surface

Cellphone coverage: excellent
Uses: walking, snowshoeing, cross-country skiing
Facilities: benches, garbage cans, interpretive panels, outhouses, picnic tables
Hazards: poison ivy, ticks, wildlife

Finding the trailhead: From the Highway 416/417 split, follow Highway 417 for 38 km to exit 169. Turn left onto County Road 20 toward Pakenham. In 5.8 km, turn left onto County Road 29, then turn right in 350 m onto Waba Road/County Road 20. In 2.9 km, turn left onto Barr Side Road. After 1.6 km, turn left onto Carbine Road (dirt). Continue to the end of the road, in 3.2 km.

Trailhead: 45°19'58.4" N, 76°22'12.8" W

Introduction: From 1884, when it was originally settled, until 1997 this property was farmed and logged. But in 2012, it was donated by the Spicer family to the Mississippi Madawaska Land Trust with the stipulation that it would be preserved in perpetuity. Furthermore, in order to restore it more quickly to its natural state, several of the fields used for agriculture have been replanted with oak, tamarack, maple, and several other original species. The trail system was developed for "public education, health, and enjoyment."

The High Lonesome Trail network is a maze design, which means multiple sections of path connecting at different points to create a wide variety of possible routes. (Having a map can be extremely useful in a maze!) What I have done is generally select the outer perimeter as the profiled route, which means turning right at almost every junction, providing one of the longest walks possible.

This is a lovely property, with beautiful forest, charming beaver ponds, and a well-signed and maintained trail system. High Lonesome is ideal for families and novices as a place to experience the outdoors without a too physically demanding challenge.

Route description: From the parking area, pass the gate and continue along what was the driveway, heading toward the buildings visible ahead. A field, now uncultivated, is on the right. At 150 m, a large sign indicates that the Welcome Centre, with trail maps and washrooms, is to the right. Leave the road, and follow a mown path past an old barn, and a picnic table, to the new Welcome Centre, which has a large number of chairs located around it, a firepit, more tables, and an interpretive panel that outlines the story of this property.

From the Welcome Centre, continue straight on a narrow track through the tall grass along the White Pine Way. About 100 m from the centre, at 300 m, turn right onto the Bear Trail. This quickly climbs onto a wooded knoll and connects to an old forestry road, curving left as it passes through the hardwoods, and dropping back down to a junction with the Spooky Marsh Trail at 550 m.

Once again, turn right. This delightful, narrow footpath, signed with yellow plastic markers, weaves through the trees as it continues down the slope, passing jumbles of rocks, to come close to a marsh. (It doesn't actually look that spooky.) Some of the trees are labelled, according to species, and there are several interpretive panels, making this section both enjoyable and educational.

At 900 m, Spooky Marsh connects to the Wolf Trail, which is one of the principal corridors of this system. Turn right onto this wide forestry road and follow it about 200 m to the Spring Peeper Trail — right again!

Spring Peeper is another slender footpath with red markers, and it drops downhill to another marsh, the edge of which it follows for 200 m before reclimbing the ridge to reconnect with the Wolf Trail. Turn right.

1.5 km Arrive at a junction, where a map is posted. Turn right onto the yellow-marked North Wind Trail crossing a small meadow and reaching the Old Oak Tree, a massive oak dwarfing everything nearby, less than 100 m later. This is another area of mostly hardwoods, with lovely shade.

At just over 1.6 km, the footpath turns sharply left and gently descends for about 200 m before curving left and climbing back up. At 2 km, there is an old rock cairn, possibly once marking a property line. The slender, meandering footpath can sometimes be difficult to follow, and in amongst the thick vegetation, even a little cloud cover can make the trail quite shadowy.

2.4 km The North Wind Trail reaches open Bear Rump Glade, and another junction. On the far side of the clearing it connects with the Wolf Trail, but a few steps before the Lost Antler Trail, with orange markers, branches right. (If you reach the small Inukshuk, you have missed it.) Keep right to follow the Lost Antler Trail, which initially parallels the Wolf Trail but gradually curves right and once again descends a gentle slope.

At 2.8 km, Lost Antler reaches a junction with the White Pine Way – High Lonesome's other major corridor – in a stand of white pine. For the first time, turn left; the signpost there points toward the exit. This section resembles an old road, a marsh on the right, higher ground to the left. After about 350 m, the route curves left and ascends more steeply. Near the top of this climb the trail narrows and curves right, connecting to the end of the Wolf Trail at 3.3 km. Turn right once again and continue to follow the White Pine Way a further 50 m, before turning right onto the orange-marked Beaver Pond Trail, next to a nice interpretive plaque about eastern white cedar.

3.4 km Arrive at a lovely little rest area, at a tranquil spot beside the pond, with several chairs available. For the next 600 m this slender footpath works around the edge of the pond, a truly lovely section. There are additional interpretive panels and even some rocky areas, with great views of the pond and its fauna. This is my favourite section of the system.

At 4 km, turn right at the junction with the blue-marked McWatty Trail. The trail leaves the pond and follows the overgrown remnants of a forestry road. It crosses a low ridge, returning to pleasant, open hardwoods. Continue straight at the junction with the Sleeping Doe Trail, cross an old field, and pass the first junction with the Joel's Pond Trail.

Turn left at this trail's second junction, just a few steps beyond the first and after an interpretive panel for wild sarsaparilla, at about 4.4 km. If you are on the correct route, there will soon be another interpretive panel, on black ash. This red-marked path traces the edge of another small pond, passing a stone viewing bench on an attractive tiny rise labelled Peaceful Point.

At 4.8 km, Joel's Pond Trail ends at the Welcome Centre. To complete this walk, turn right and retrace the 200 m back to the road.

35. K&P Trail – Sharbot Lake

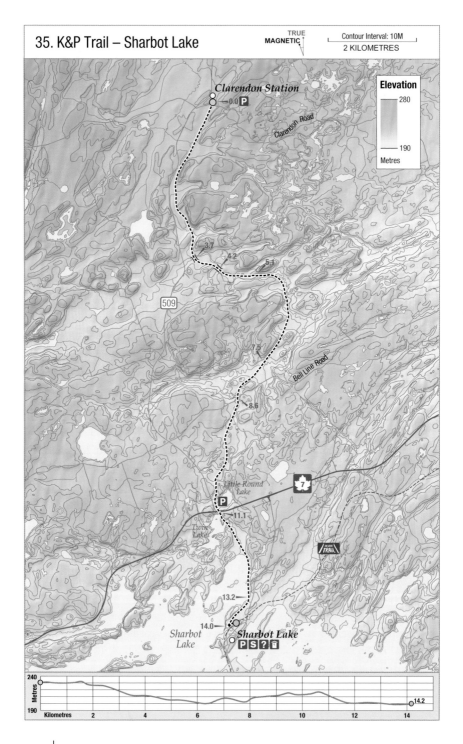

35. K&P Trail – Sharbot Lake

Distance: 28.4 km
Type: linear
Difficulty: 5 (distance)
Ascent/descent: 235 m
Hiking time: 8+ hrs
Trail conditions: compacted earth
Cellphone coverage: no reception
between Clarendon Station and the
Bell Line Road

Uses: walking, biking, horseback
riding, ATVs, snowshoeing, cross-
country skiing, snowmobiling
Facilities: benches, garbage cans,
interpretive panels, picnic tables
Hazards: hunting, motorized use,
poison ivy, road crossings, ticks,
wildlife

Finding the trailhead: From the Highway 416/417 split, follow Highway 417 for
14 km to exit 145, then turn onto Highway 7. Follow it for 93 km, then turn right
on County Road 509. In 9.5 km, turn right onto Clarendon Road (dirt). Park on
the road at a rail trail 400 m further.

Trailhead: 44°52'23.0" N, 76°41'49.3" W (Clarendon Station);
44°46'26.6" N, 76°41'17.2" W (Sharbot Lake)

Introduction: The former Kingston and Pembroke Railway (K&P), also "affec-
tionately" known as the Kick & Push, was abandoned, piece by piece, between
the 1950s and 1980s. Fortunately, the 180+ km corridor was acquired by the
various municipal units along its path and has been preserved as a recreational
pathway.

However, the experience varies on different sections of the K&P. For
example, the 60+ km length from Sharbot Lake to Kingston is surfaced with
either crushed stone or asphalt. So too is the 21 km section from Renfrew to
Calabogie. And between these is a considerable stretch where little work has
been done. There are even a few breaks where bridges and causeways have
been removed.

I find these unimproved sections to be much more natural and interesting,
even though somewhat rougher, and selected this particular stretch because
it ends in the pleasant community of Sharbot Lake. It passes through isolated
areas, with no services anywhere along the route. Those less comfortable with
remote areas might prefer to begin in Sharbot Lake and turn back no later than
the Bell Line Road.

This trail is recommended for experienced outdoors enthusiasts only.

Route description: The former railway station, now a residence, is to the left
of Clarendon Road. Follow the former rail line to the right, heading south. A

commemorative sign honours former reeve of Oso Township Harold Clark, who championed preserving the K&P as a trail.

The track begins wide and solid, with a strip of grass in its middle. It is also quite straight and bordered by thick vegetation. At 600 m, the compacted earth is replaced by loose stones, and 200 m further the forest is replaced by marshy ground and low shrubs. But by 1.2 km, the rough stretch ends as the pathway moves onto drier terrain. Within 200 m, the trail reaches a cluster of houses, each connected by its own path, and County Road 509 is also close on the right.

By 1.8 km, the K&P passes the last house and moves further from the road. The landscape of this highlands area is rocky and studded with small knolls, usually with small marshes and swamps in between. So the K&P describes a curving route between hill and wetland, often with views of each. Connecting paths or roads are frequent, but there is never any doubt about the correct route.

At 3.7 km, the trail reaches a large wet area and crosses its first bridge. Country Road 509 is visible off to the right, as well as a few houses. The first of these is reached about 100 m later. But as the road turns right, the K&P curves left and heads into its most isolated section. The next bridge, somewhat rickety, is at 4.2 km, after which the pathway follows this little stream for a considerable distance, with the ground on both sides usually higher, unless there is wetland.

There are no formal campsites on this route, but at 5.1 km, there is such a nice spot on the right, close to the stream and almost as if it had been cleared deliberately for a tent, that I waypointed it on my GPS in case I can return.

About 350 m further, the trail curves right 90°, still gently descending. It remains fairly close to the stream until about 6.5 km, when it curves slightly right again and begins to climb. However, it soon drops down to the largest wetland thus far, at 7.5 km. In this large wetland is one spot, about 200 m along, where the trail in 2019 was submerged for about 20 m – wet feet are unavoidable. Once past this large marsh the K&P makes its steepest climb, passing through some deeper rock cuts through the hills.

📍**8.6 km** The K&P emerges onto and crosses the Bell Line Road (dirt), where cell reception should be regained. A few houses are nearby, and there are indications that trucks as well as ATVs drive on the K&P. In fact, at 9.4 km there is a house on the left that clearly uses the K&P as their driveway. There are quite a few signs on the trail to warn users of its proximity.

The alternating hills and wetlands resume – including some spots where the trail is almost flooded – punctuated by the tallest vertical rock faces, at about 10.6 km. After this, the pathway distinctly descends, and soon the vehicle noises of Highway 7 begin to intrude.

Little Round Lake becomes visible about 400 m further, and the trail and Highway 509 edge closer together, with a possible parking area to the right just before reaching Highway 7.

📍**11.1 km** The K&P squeezes through a circular metal culvert underneath Highway 7. Once though, Twin Lake is to the right, though quite a bit below the rail trail, and the surrounding hills sport some magnificent white pine trees. Very quickly it becomes clear that this section of trail is also the access road

for cottage owners on this side of the lake. However, the treadway is in excellent condition, and this is actually an attractive section.

By 11.6 km, the path moves away from Twin Lake and into a low, marshy area before reaching the shoreline of Sharbot Lake at 12.3 km. For the next kilometre the K&P follows the water's edge, passing houses, cottages, and docks. At 13.2 km, it passes behind – or through, really – the marina, and crosses Cannon Road immediately after. It then leaves both lake and buildings for 700 m, heading into another area of low, thick vegetated cover.

📍**14 km** The K&P arrives at a junction with the The Great Trail (Trans Canada) in a large open area. There are numerous interpretive panels and houses all around. Turn left, and head onto the trail heading toward Perth, the Central Frontenac Trailway. This is surfaced by crushed stone, and in just 200 m it leads to a charming restored caboose, painted bright red, where there are more benches, interpretive panels, and picnic tables. Sharbot Lake with its amenities is nearby to the right; end your trip here.

Retrace your route to return to Clarendon Station.

Beaver

The many small lakes and wetlands of the Canadian Shield are ideal habitat for beaver, and their dams, lodges, and trail of felled trees may be found throughout the Ottawa region. This largest rodent in North America creates dams as protection against predators and to provide easy access to food during winter. Beavers generally work at night and are prolific builders, each gnawing through an average of 216 trees per year.

During the peak of the fur trade era some two hundred thousand pelts a year were sold to the European market, with the beaver hunted almost to extinction. Because of recent conservation measures, beaver numbers have increased tremendously, and they have returned to many sites where they had disappeared.

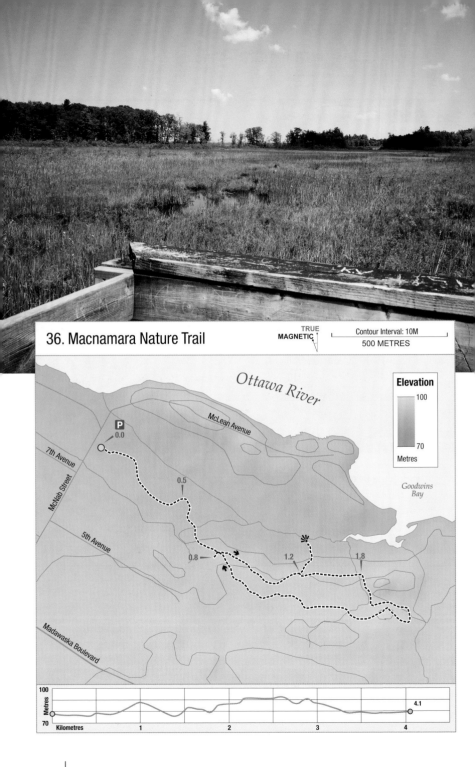

36. Macnamara Nature Trail

TRUE
MAGNETIC

Contour Interval: 10M
500 METRES

Ottawa River

McLean Avenue

Elevation
100

70

Metres

Goodwins
Bay

P
0.0

7th Avenue

McNab Street

5th Avenue

0.5

0.8

1.2

1.8

Madawaska Boulevard

100
Metres
70
Kilometres

4.1

1   2   3   4

36. Macnamara Nature Trail

Distance: 4.1 km
Type: loop
Difficulty: 1
Ascent/descent: 40 m
Hiking time: 1+ hrs
Trail conditions: natural surface

Cellphone coverage: excellent
Uses: walking, snowshoeing
Facilities: benches, garbage cans, interpretive panels
Hazards: ticks, wildlife

Finding the trailhead: From the Highway 416/417 split, follow Highway 417 for 48 km to exit 29. Turn right onto Ottawa Road 29, then left 700 m later on Regional Road 117/Madawaska Boulevard. In 1.9 km, turn right onto McNab Street. The trailhead parking area is on the right in 800 m.

Trailhead: 45°26'18.0" N, 76°20'10.9" W

Introduction: Few trails are located on corporate property, but the Macnamara Nature Trail, created and maintained entirely by volunteers of the Macnamara Field Naturalists' Club, wends through land owned by Nylene Canada Incorporated, whose plant is nearby. This is also part of the Nopiming Crown Game Preserve, one of the few in Ontario on private land. The trail is named for Charles Macnamara, an ardent field naturalist who, in the early twentieth century, documented wild orchids, birds, beavers, and the natural history of the Arnprior area.

His trail passes through some of the lands he lovingly explored, including nineteen numbered interpretive stops of features explained in a trail guide that is available at the trail kiosk. Boardwalks, benches, and viewing platforms make this short route accessible to almost anyone, and it is a wonderful location for an exploration of the natural world of the lower Ottawa Valley.

Remember to bring along some sunflower seeds for the many bird feeders along the trail, and mosquito repellent for yourself.

Dogs are not permitted on this trail.

Route description: At the parking lot, a small kiosk contains trail guides and features a map of the route. A footpath beyond it heads into the forest, a well-defined natural treadway. This quickly narrows, meandering over the low terrain, which gently slopes downwards in the direction of the Ottawa River.

Several side trails connect in, but the correct route is marked with orange signs attached to trees. About 200 m along you reach interpretive stop 2, on your left, and through the mixed hardwoods and softwoods you will probably see a factory on your right. By 400 m the ground becomes so wet that a boardwalk is required, but the path attempts to stay on slightly elevated, and

dry, ground whenever possible. This requires no great climb but does offer a pleasant up-and-down section of hiking.

📍 **500 m** There is a major boardwalk, extending nearly 200 m over a boggy area. Look for showy lady's slipper here in late June and early July. One more short section of boardwalk is crossed before the path finally reaches dry, slightly higher ground.

📍 **800 m** The trail reaches the ruins of a lime kiln, which is interpretive stop 5. This is to the right, and a short side trail leads to its stone foundation. A wooden deck is provided for observation into the former structure. White cedars shelter the area, and fences frame it. The marble outcropping they quarried is off to the side.

Just past the kiln, at about 900 m, the trail splits. Continue straight/left; directly ahead is a bench surrounded by a number of bird feeders – a good place to relax. But the path crosses a tiny stream and meanders uphill through mostly birch and maple. Stop 6, a side trip to the left, takes you to an exposed outcropping of marble. The main trail climbs to the top of an oak-covered ridge, where it continues until about 1.2 km, where the side trail to the wetlands observation tower separates. Turn left and in 150 m the path emerges from the trees to an elevated deck overlooking a marsh.

After you return to the main trail, continue to follow the ridge, making for dry and comfortable walking. At stop 8 there is another bench, where in the fall you can listen to the patter of falling acorns. Just after reaching stop 9, the path works gradually down the hillside, passing beneath some quite tall birch to cross a small boardwalk at 1.8 km.

Across the boardwalk is what the trail guide refers to as an "optional trail," and is not recommended for everyone. This is a much more primitive route with rickety, rotting bridges, signed only with flagging tape and fading splashes of paint, which leads to the banks of the Ottawa River at Goodwins Bay in 750 m. If you make this sometimes wet walk, your reward will be a small bit of sand and some rocks by the water's edge where you can sit and relax.

From here, the main route turns right and climbs back uphill alongside a deeply eroded gorge. It turns left when confronted by a small limestone ridge, about 150 m later, following that past stops 11 and 12. Immediately past 12, at a stand of sumac, the trail turns right and climbs the escarpment, turning right again 50 m later on the crest.

After 200 m the footpath connects to an old woods road and becomes wide enough for two under a canopy of maple. You soon cross a small, unrailed bridge, and 200 m past that, you turn off the wide road to your right onto a footpath that heads down the slope. There is quite a bit of signage, so you

Lady's slipper

should have no problems with navigation. About 200 m down the path there is another bench next to stop 17, which is next to another gorge. A boardwalk conducts you across a small stream, which the path follows past 18 and 19 for the remaining few hundred metres until you complete the loop near the lime kiln.

To return to the trailhead, turn left and retrace the 900 m back to the parking area.

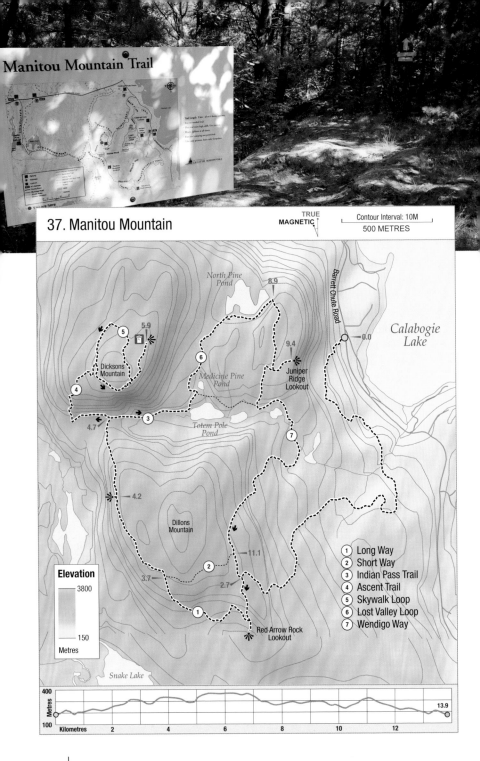

Manitou Mountain Trail

37. Manitou Mountain

TRUE
MAGNETIC

Contour Interval: 10M
500 METRES

North Pine Pond

8.9

Barrett Chute Road

Calabogie Lake

0.0

5.9

5

6

9.4

Juniper Ridge Lookout

Dicksons Mountain

Medicine Pine Pond

4

3

4.7

Totem Pole Pond

7

4.2

Dillons Mountain

11.1

Elevation

3800

2

3.7

2.7

1. Long Way
2. Short Way
3. Indian Pass Trail
4. Ascent Trail
5. Skywalk Loop
6. Lost Valley Loop
7. Wendigo Way

150

Metres

1

Red Arrow Rock Lookout

Snake Lake

400

Metres

13.9

100

Kilometres   2   4   6   8   10   12

37. Manitou Mountain

Distance: 13.9 km
Type: loop
Difficulty: 4
Ascent/descent: 585 m
Hiking time: 4+ hrs
Trail conditions: natural surface

Cellphone coverage: good on hilltops and facing Calabogie Lake; no reception in low areas
Uses: walking, snowshoeing
Facilities: benches, interpretive panels, picnic tables
Hazards: cliffs, ticks, wildlife

Finding the trailhead: From the Highway 416/417 split, follow Highway 417 for 63 km, then turn left onto County Road 508/Calabogie Road. Follow it for 30 km, then turn left onto Barrett Chute Road. The trailhead is on the left, in 1.7 km, at 342 Barrett Chute Road. Park beside the road.

Trailhead: 45°15'51.1" N, 76°46'18.0" W

Introduction: Since shortly after this trail opened in June 2009, it has quickly become known as one of the most admired local options for hiking enthusiasts. Climbing to the top of Dickson Mountain, the summit of the Calabogie Peaks Resort's downhill ski trails, this challenging trek features steep climbs, several expansive vistas, and a first-rate workout for anyone who undertakes it.

This is most definitely not a hike for beginners. However, the signage is quite good, so attempting the section from the trailhead to Red Arrow Rock Lookout, while still challenging novices, might still be enjoyable.

The Manitou Mountain Trail is only one of a maze of pathways visiting several hilltops in a fairly small area. There are a few posts with maps on the route, but carrying a trail map will definitely improve the experience.

Route description: From the start, where there is a kiosk with a map and (possibly) paper copies available, the path heads into the forest and ascends briskly for the first 400 m. The slender footpath is well defined, and the route is marked with paint dabs on trees and signs with directional arrows.

After descending to cross a wet area on a puncheon, at about 700 m, the climb resumes, reaching an old road 200 m further. To the left a dwelling is visible as well as a power line corridor. At about 950 m, a bridge crosses a deeply etched creek bed. As the climb resumes, more of the bordering trees – they provide complete overhead shade – are softwoods.

At 1.2 km, the path makes a 90° turn right, then another 100 m further. Shortly after, it turns left 180°, passing through the first small area of bare rock. By the time of the next creek crossing (this time without a bridge), at 1.7 km, most of the nearby trees are hardwoods again.

Once across, the trail gradually ascends along a former woods road, beautiful hardwood-covered ridges on either side. After 450 m, the path narrows and steepens, squeezing between rocky knolls. Sometimes gentle, sometimes steep, the ascent continues.

2.7 km The trail reaches a junction, where there is a map posted. Turn left, toward the Red Arrow Lookout, along the trail section labelled as the Long Way, and marked by red flashes. Within 250 m it reaches Red Arrow Rock Lookout, an exposed rocky spur that descends thereafter, with an impressive view of virtually undisturbed forest.

Continuing along the Long Way, the path works lower down the ridge on much more difficult, rocky terrain, curving left after 200 m and descending a lovely hardwood-covered slope. After another 100 m, it curves right and reclimbs the mountain, rising more than 50 m over the next 400 m, paralleling a large rock face for much of it.

At 3.7 km, the Long Way connects to the Short Way; turn left and work along the slope of the mountain, with increasingly better views available to your left. After 500 m the trail reaches Manitou Mountain Lookout, perched high above Manitou Lake, overlooking the lower ridgeline opposite. This is a wonderful view, with almost no signs of human habitation. You might notice a painted zigzag pattern on a rock at ground level or several small First Nations totems hanging on a branch; these are the only markers for the lookout.

A rapid descent through a pine slope to Wolf Howl Pond follows to the well-signed junction, where there is a map, with the Indian Pass Trail, at 4.7 km. Turn left, and scramble carefully along the steep slope path for about 200 m to the ominously named Ascent Trail.

Turn right; here you work, struggling up 70 m of elevation over the next 300 m, to its junction with the Skywalk Loop, where there is another map. Turn right, and follow the distinct path, marked by plastic blue diamonds and yellow arrows (it is a cross-country ski trail in the winter). The path immediately moves onto bare rock, and as it curves left, provides views back over Manitou Mountain and Manitou Lake. After 300 m, the Skywalk Loop branches: turn left, away from the ridge, but follow the Skywalk Trail for another 250 m.

5.9 km The footpath emerges onto a panoramic view at the Top of Calabogie ski hill with views of Calabogie Lake and far to the north and east. To the left is a shelter, with picnic tables and outhouse nearby. Enjoy the view and definitely have a snack, then retrace the 250 m to the junction and resume following the Skywalk Loop, which is a meandering path round the top of Dickson Mountain that remains among the trees.

Once at the junction with the Ascent Trail, at about 6.8 km, descend the steep slope and return to the Indian Pass junction, at 7.4 km. Turn left, onto the orange-flashed Indian Pass Trail, which descends gently for 500 m to small Totem Pole Pond, the imposing cliff of Dickson Mountain visible through the trees on your left. At the pond, Indian Pass turns left and makes a short, ugly 100 m climb to reach the junction with the Lost Valley Loop, beside tiny Medicine Pine Pond.

Turn left and follow this lovely path – marked with red – as it winds through attractive mixed forest and low rock ridges, and along North Pine Pond. At the end of the pond, at 8.9 km, there is an indistinct junction, with the Lost Valley Loop turning right more than 90°. After a pleasant meander over the undulating terrain, it reaches the side trail to the Juniper Ridge Lookout, 600 m further. Turn left, and climb the low ridge; there is a rope to assist.

9.4 km The Juniper Ridge Lookout has a marvellous view of Calabogie Lake – it is actually directly above, and barely 500 m from where you started. However, plenty of hiking remains. Return to the Lost Valley Loop, and turn left to follow it as it descends to connect with the Wendigo Way, near another small pond, at 9.8 km. There is a map at this junction.

Turn left onto Wendigo Way, which mostly descends for the next 400 m, crossing a small brook and skirting a large pond. Watch carefully for the path's orange markers, particularly as it passes through an area of tall softwoods and very indistinct treadway. Once the climb resumes, it continues all the way to its junction with the Short Way at 11.1 km. Keep straight/left; barely 150 m further it reaches the junction with the Long Way, where there is a map.

Turn left, and retrace the 2.7 km – mostly downhill! – back to the trailhead.

38. Ottawa Valley Recreational Trail

TRUE
MAGNETIC

Contour Interval: 10M
2 KILOMETRES

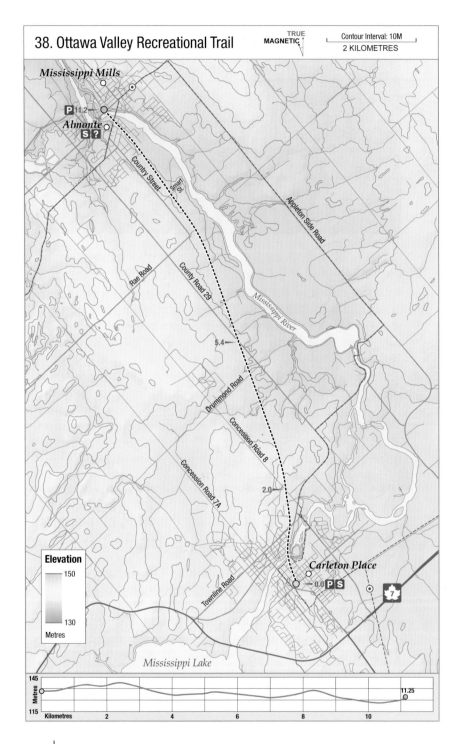

Mississippi Mills

P 11.2

Almonte
S ?

Country Street

Smart St.

Appleton Side Road

Rae Road

County Road 29

Mississippi River

5.4

Drummond Road

Concession Road 8

Concession Road 7A

2.0

Carleton Place

0.0 P S

7

Elevation
150
130
Metres

Townline Road

Mississippi Lake

145
Metres
115
Kilometres   2   4   6   8   10

11.25

38. Ottawa Valley Recreational Trail

Distance: 22.5 km return
Type: linear
Difficulty: 5 (distance)
Ascent/descent: 59 m
Hiking time: 6+ hrs
Trail conditions: asphalt, crushed stone

Cellphone coverage: excellent
Uses: walking, biking, horseback riding, ATVs, snowshoeing, cross-country skiing, snowmobiling
Facilities: garbage cans, picnic tables
Hazards: motorized uses, poison ivy, road crossings, ticks, wildlife

Finding the trailhead: From the Highway 416/417 split, follow Highway 417 for 14 km to exit 145, then turn onto Highway 7 towards Carleton Place/Toronto. Continue for 22 km, then turn right onto Franktown Road. Follow it for 1.7 km, angling left as it becomes Moore Street. Turn sharply right onto Lake Avenue East, then left in 50 m onto Beckwith Street. Carleton Place Farmers' Market is on the right; park there. The trail is on the far side.

Trailhead: 45°08'15.6" N, 76°08'29.0" W

Introduction: Eastern Ontario was once criss-crossed by competing railways, but as the automobile reduced first passenger and then local freight traffic, most of these became uneconomical and were abandoned. One of these, a 296 km long corridor from Smiths Falls to Mattawa, is being developed into a recreational trail. In October 2018, Lanark County officially opened its 61 km section from near Smiths Falls to near Arnprior. As of 2020, only a few portions in Renfrew County and the Township of Papineau-Cameron have been completed, but there are plans to complete the entire link over the coming decade.

This is an exceptionally easy pathway for walking: a wide, crushed-stone surface and very little elevation change. However, it is quite long, so walkers who don't want to spend their entire day can choose to do only a section. For that, I recommend starting either around Almonte, which has a number of connected shorter walking routes, or near Carleton Place, where the OVRT passes within 150 m of the start of the Rotary Centennial Trail, which follows the Mississippi River.

I found this route excellent for birding, observing both eastern bluebirds and scarlet tanagers in the trees alongside this pathway. There is little in the way of dramatic scenery, but the countryside is quite lovely, and both communities have restaurants and other amenities quite close to the trail.

seabamirum, CC BY 2.0

Scarlet tanager

Route description: From the parking area, in the middle of downtown Carleton Place and close to all manner of amenities, walk up to the pathway. It features a parallel asphalt strip and a crushed-stone track. An information sign directs walkers and cyclists onto the asphalt and ATVs, horseback riders, and snowmobiles onto the crushed stone.

Turn left and follow this wide, bi-surfaced pathway through the community. By the time it reaches the impressive bridge crossing the Mississippi River, 600 m from the start, the trail has already crossed three streets. At each of these are gates, restricting the pathway to one lane, and a stop sign facing trail traffic.

The bridge, asphalt surfaced, with steel fencing and two viewing platforms, is one of this trail's highlights, and it provides scenic views in both directions along the river.

From the bridge, the wide track continues past homes, crossing several more quiet streets, and parallels Mullett Street for some distance before reaching busy, four-lane Townline Road East at 1.2 km. There is no crosswalk here, so exercise particular caution when crossing. On the opposite side, the asphalt strip disappears, and the entire pathway is surfaced with crushed stone. The neighbouring buildings change as well, becoming almost entirely commercial and industrial.

2 km Upon reaching, and crossing, Concession Road 8, the OVRT leaves the community of Carleton Place and moves into a long stretch of rural terrain. Young trees border the pathway; they're not very tall so there is no shade at all. The land appears quite flat, with very little evidence of changing elevation.

After crossing Concession Road 8, the pathway makes a gradual and almost imperceptible curve left before settling into a long straight section. Farms become visible, particularly as the trail approaches unpaved Drummond Road, at 4.6 km.

5.4 km The trail reaches County Road 29, crossing in an 80 kph speed zone. Traffic whizzes by pretty fast, so crossing may take some time. The former railway crossed at a diagonal, but the route has been rebuilt so that trail users have a perpendicular spot to scamper across.

Another long straightaway follows, with cultivated fields alternating with small patches of forest. Old cedar rail fences border much of it, and there are some lovely apple trees along this stretch, which are extremely attractive when blossoming.

At about 7.3 km, another gradual left turn begins, as well as an equally barely noticeable climb. Both end by the time the trail crosses beneath a power line and passes the electrical substation, at 8.2 km. About 700 m further, Smart

Street must be crossed, after which there is increasing evidence that the pathway is approaching Almonte.

By 9.5 km, new housing developments can be seen on the left. The trail is separated somewhat from the buildings, but as connecting paths have been built, expect more dog walkers and families. A bit of a boggy area on the left provides a buffer, but just before the trail reaches John Street, at 10.6 km, the path abruptly emerges into the middle of the community.

Almonte's library and farmers market are on the left, but a fence separates them from the trail. About 300 m further, and the OVRT reaches Bridge Street, the centre of Almonte, with the Old Town Hall off to the right, and businesses all around.

Cautiously cross the street, and continue a little further. Within a few metres you are on a bridge crossing the Mississippi River, and the view here may be even better than from the bridge in Carleton Place – debate among yourselves – particularly with all the restored older buildings nearby.

Eastern bluebirds

📍**11.2 km** At the far end of the bridge, the trail reaches Main Street East, next to the Old Flour Mill building. This is a good place to turn back, although the OVRT continues at least another 26 km to Arnprior. After a visit in Almonte, retrace the route to return to Carleton Place.

39. Shaw Woods

TRUE
MAGNETIC

Contour Interval: 20M
500 METRES

Elevation
200

120
Metres

Shaws Pond

4.6

Bulger Road

P 0.0

4.4

5.2

3.3

3

2.4

2

Pine Pavilion

1.2

Snake River

9

Basswood Road

① Snake River Trail
② Connaught Trail
③ Northern Trail
④ Johnny's Lookout Trail

⑤ Old Growth Trail
⑥ Great Gully Lake Trail
⑦ Pinery Trail
⑧ Trillium Loop Trail

220

Metres

120

Kilometres

1   2   3   4   5   6   7

7.1

39. Shaw Woods

Distance: 7.1 km
Type: loop
Difficulty: 2
Ascent/descent: 87 m
Hiking time: 2+ hrs
Trail conditions: compacted earth, natural surface
Cellphone coverage: limited reception

on Connaught and Northern Trails
Uses: walking, snowshoeing
Facilities: benches, garbage cans, interpretive panels, outhouses, picnic tables
Hazards: poison ivy, road crossings, ticks, wildlife

Finding the trailhead: From the Highway 416/417 split, follow Highway 417 for 79 km, then turn left onto County Road 20/Bruce Street. In 3.1 km, turn right onto Highway 60/Stewart Street. Follow it for 21 km, then turn right at the junction with County Road 5. In 7.5 km, continue straight onto County Road 9/Bulger Road. The Shaw Woods parking area is on the left in 11 km at 2065 Bulger Road.

Trailhead: 45°37'59.9" N, 77°04'01.6" W

Introduction: The Shaw Woods Outdoor Education Centre is a registered charitable not-for-profit society created in 2010 and managed by volunteers. It began to develop education and recreation facilities on the 200 ha Shaw Woods Nature Preserve. Including 50 ha of old-growth forest, this property, which had been owned by successive generations of the Shaw family since its original settlement in 1847, was protected by them in cooperation with the Nature Conservancy of Canada.

In recent years, an extensive trail network of at least 14 km and a wide variety of school education programs have been offered. Institutions of higher learning, such as Algonquin College and the University of Guelph, conduct field research projects on this rare fragment of preserved original growth forest.

The property is bisected by Bulger Road, with a portion of the trail network on each side. The route I have selected includes some on each side, so those wishing a shorter walk can choose which loop they prefer. This is an excellent place for children and novices, although they might begin with the west side route through the old-growth forest first.

Route description: At the parking area is a sturdy trailhead kiosk with a map of the West Side trails, brochures, and sundry general information. To reach the East Side trails, continue along the dirt road — it is identified as being for bus parking — toward a building complex, where there are outhouses, the Pine

Pavilion (a large open-sided shelter with picnic tables), and a wide variety of structures used for the school education programs.

A footpath parallels Bulger Road for about 100 m, before it turns left and crosses at an excellent signalized pedestrian crossing. Once across, the route passes a metal gate, then a kiosk with a map of the East Side trails, and reaches Shaws Pond and the Snake River at 200 m.

Interpretive panels and displays, such as the two large grinding stones used in the former Shaw gristmill, are everywhere, and a considerable amount of time can be spent reading them. A log bench faces the pond just before the dam, a 1962 replacement for the original impoundment.

At the far end of this small dam, the trail splits; turn right, toward the Snake River Portage. There is an excellent signpost here, as at all junctions. For the next 500 m the path works alongside the Snake River, a rocky ridge hugging the left. The treadway is dry and covered in pine needles. Keep straight at the next junction, 200 m later and just after interpretive post 35, which is almost where the portage ends.

Beyond this the track gets a bit rougher, including one spot where a board-walk is required. By post 38, where the river opens up into broad wetlands, the trail makes a sharp turn left and climbs up the rocky ridge to post 39, steeply enough that a rope is provided for assistance. (The pine-needle-covered rocks can be slippery.)

The path reaches the junction with the Snake River and Connaught Trail at 1.2 km; turn right onto the latter. (Those wishing a shorter, easier hike should turn left here.) There is no map, nor does the Outdoor Centre provide one for the Connaught Trail. However, this is reasonably well signed, with additional interpretive posts, and the treadway is usually easy to follow. This slender foot-path wanders over the gentle landscape, skirting small wetlands and passing through dense forest – a pleasant walk but with few views.

2.4 km Arrive at the junction with the Northern Trail, which states that it is 1.8 km long. The Connaught Trail continues, but I found this to be challenging to follow, and it ends without notice on a remote dirt road far from houses and with no cell reception.

So turn left onto the Northern Trail, which continues to wander through the mixed forest. Snowshoe markers are the most frequent signs, and the occasional interpretive posts, but mostly there are no markers. Fortunately, much of the route follows an old woods road and is quite easy to follow. (Watch for a more than 90° turn left at 3.3 km.) This section is also slightly hillier than the Connaught Trail. Hardwoods soon come to dominate, making this a wonderful route in the fall.

At about 3.8 km, a trail sign indicates the boundary of the Shaw Woods property, and about 200 m further the Northern Trail connects to the Snake

River Trail. Keep straight/right, on a much more well-defined footpath, which immediately climbs a short hill, then connects to the Johnny's Lookout Trail at 4.4 km. Turn right, toward the lookout, continuing straight at the next junction.

4.6 km Johnny's Lookout is a large, railed wooden platform, with a bench and interpretive information, situated on a ridge above Shaws Pond. The view is excellent and, although unshaded, is a pleasant spot to spend some time observing.

From the lookout, return the 75 m to the last junction and turn right. The trail descends the short, steep hill to Shaws Pond, which it continues alongside to complete the loop at the end of the dam at 5.2 km. Turn right, and retrace the 300 m back to the parking area.

From the western trail kiosk, turn right onto the Old Growth Trail. This 1.6 km loop is amazing, traversing an ancient forest, one of the few places that perhaps closely resembles how the woodlands appeared to the first Europeans, before logging and farming so radically altered the landscape.

I found this section quite affecting, and hope that you will as well. Far better than I could, the Visitor's Guide, which might be available at the kiosk or can be downloaded from the outdoor centre's website, describes what you are viewing. Remember to turn left at the junction with the Great Gully Trail, about 1 km from the kiosk, and keep straight when it reaches the Pinery Trail. Complete the final 600 m to return to the parking area.

40. Wilno – Barry's Bay

TRUE
MAGNETIC

Contour Interval: 20M
2 KILOMETRES

40. Wilno – Barry's Bay

Distance: 19.4 km return
Type: linear
Difficulty: 4 (distance)
Ascent/descent: 124 m
Hiking time: 5+ hrs
Trail conditions: compacted earth, natural surface
Cellphone coverage: good throughout

Uses: walking, biking, horseback riding, ATVs, snowshoeing, cross-country skiing, snowmobiling
Facilities: benches, garbage cans, interpretive panels
Hazards: hunting, motorized vehicles, poison ivy, road crossings, ticks, wildlife

Finding the trailhead: From the Highway 416/417 split, follow Highway 417 for 79 km, then turn left onto County Road 20/Bruce Street. In 3.1 km, turn right onto Highway 60/Stewart Street. Follow it for 21 km, then turn right at the junction with County Road 5. Continue on Highway 60 for 62 km, then turn right onto Wilno Road North. Turn left onto Smaglinski Stoppa Parkway and park alongside the road on the right.

Trailhead: 45°30'39.8" N, 77°33'40.8" W

Introduction: This trail follows the former route of the Ottawa, Arnprior, and Parry Sound Railway, which operated from 1897 to 1959, carrying lumber from what is now Algonquin Park and grain from Lake Huron to the St. Lawrence. This was once a very busy railway, with a train passing every twenty minutes.

Although this former rail line is used by ATVs and is an official snowmobile trail, the treadway is very rough, and there are several washouts where the pathway is submerged for short distances. This is not a suitable route for new hikers, and only mountain bikers will find this comfortable. Then again, its very roughness was a quality that appealed to me.

Route description: Begin at the Polish-Kashub Heritage Museum, where the former rail line runs alongside the display buildings and is surfaced with crushed stone. Turn right, crossing the Smaglinski Stoppa Parkway and immediately moving onto a much rougher surface. As this is primarily a snowmobile route, little maintenance is performed on anything usually covered in snow – such as the treadway.

On the right is a large open area, which was mostly filled with logs when I was there. The path parallels Highway 60, out in the open and quite close to it. In fact, the museum remains in sight for well over 500 m. About 700 m from the start, the hillside on the right is being excavated. The trail is actually on an

embankment here, and higher than Highway 60, although it dips about 400 m later when it crosses a driveway.

Shortly after this, the rail-trail curves right, behind a small hill and diverging from the road, reaching a lovely small pond at 1.6 km, which is also lower than the trail. From here the treadway improves somewhat, although there are still occasional dodgy patches.

By the time it reaches a larger pond, 400 m further, the treadway is excellent, and tall pines shade it. Watch for turtles both in the pond, and in the creek that parallels the pathway. About 2.7 km, an informal track branches right to connect to a nearby road – which happens to be the Smaglinski Stoppa Parkway.

Soon the trail is passing close to, and slightly above, this road. To the right is large Albert Lake, and houses are soon visible. By 3.4 km, Highway 60 is close again on the left, and when the trail crosses the Smaglinski Stoppa Parkway, at 3.6 km, they are only a few metres apart. Kretzel Lake is visible on the left.

4 km Only a thin buffer of trees separates trail from highway, as they run parallel to reach the Pecarski Road, where there is a sign stating that the trail is maintained by the Opeongo Snowbirds Snowmobile Club. The pathway continues, a long straight route, and about 200 m further Highway 60 curves away to the left, though houses are still visible almost up to a well-signed turnoff to the Mountain View Motel.

The treadway often alternates between a sandy surface, when dry, and a rocky one, where wet. At this intersection, it is quite sandy. From here, the route enters true Canadian Shield terrain, with small, softwood-covered hills flanking the pathway, and frequent ponds, marshes, creeks, and other wetlands inhabiting the low ground.

The trail essentially follows the narrow Sherwood River for the next several kilometres and passes a number of wetlands and ponds. A small bridge crosses the stream at 5.7 km. Just after one particularly messy area, where there is a large gravel pit to the right, it crosses Airport Road, at 6.3 km.

After the next small bridge, at 7.3 km, the largest open water pond fills the low ground to the right. The trail curves left around it. This is quite a lovely section, with beaver, waterfowl, and muskrats seemingly unconcerned by my passage. At 8.3 km, the trail leaves the river, although there is a short section that is washed out just where the ponds ahead drain into it.

Some 200 m further, and the pathway becomes a slender causeway, barely higher than the waters bordering it. At another, larger washout, at about 8.6 km, wading the shallow submerged track is the only option.

From here, the path begins to climb, where it passes between two knolls. There are at least two deep erosion runnels where bicyclists will probably need to carry their bikes across. The path curves gradually right and levels out, and houses come into sight at 9.5 km.

9.7 km After a short section shared with cars, the trail reaches Highway 60 in Barry's Bay, with a restaurant just across the road. Stop here for a snack, or turn around and retrace the route back to Wilno.

50. Tip to Tip Trail

41. Charleston Lake Provincial Park

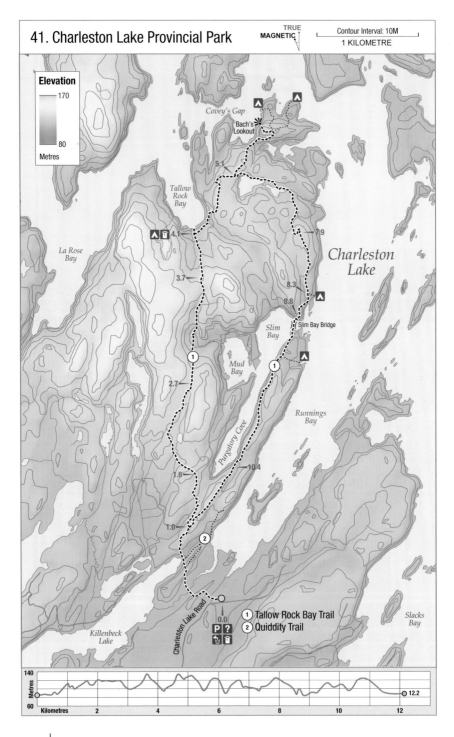

TRUE
MAGNETIC

Contour Interval: 10M
1 KILOMETRE

Elevation

170

80

Metres

Covey's Gap

Bach's
Lookout

5.1

*Tallow
Rock
Bay*

4.1

*La Rose
Bay*

3.7

7.9

*Charleston
Lake*

8.3

8.8

Slim Bay Bridge

*Slim
Bay*

2.7

1

*Mud
Bay*

1

*Runnings
Bay*

Purgatory Cove

10.4

1.6

1.0

2

Charleston Lake Road

0.0

P ?

① Tallow Rock Bay Trail
② Quiddity Trail

*Killenbeck
Lake*

*Slacks
Bay*

140

Metres

60

Kilometres

2   4   6   8   10   12

12.2

41. Charleston Lake Provincial Park

Distance: 12.2 km
Type: loop
Difficulty: 4 (rugged terrain)
Ascent/descent: 318 m
Hiking time: 3+ hrs
Trail conditions: natural surface
Cellphone coverage: weak in the first few kilometres, but excellent in the remainder

Uses: walking, snowshoeing
Facilities: benches, campsites, garbage cans, outhouses, picnic tables
Hazards: cliffs, poison ivy, ticks, wildlife

Finding the trailhead: From the Highway 416/417 split, follow Highway 416 for 76 km, then turn onto Highway 401 West. In 43 km, take exit 675, then turn right onto Mallorytown Road/County Road 5. In 550 m, turn left onto County Road 2, then right onto County Road 4 in 500 m. Continue for 16.6 km, turn right onto County Road 3. In 4.1 km, turn right onto Woodvale Road. Turn left onto Charleston Lake Road in 1.2 km. Follow the paved surface for 1 km to a parking area, on the left past the park gatehouse. There is a fee to enter the park.

Trailhead: 44°30'13.9" N, 76°02'18.8" W

Introduction: Charleston Lake Provincial Park comprises almost 2,400 ha of crown land scattered on the shores and islands of large Charleston Lake. The park is a popular summer destination, and its 200+ campsites are filled almost every weekend. A wide variety of hiking options are available within its boundaries, including the Blue Mountain Trail, which requires canoe travel to access the trailhead.

The Tallow Rock Bay Trail, however, is my recommendation. It is the longest trek available in the park, taking one into its most remote corners. A variety of backcountry campsites are found along its route, accessible only by foot or water, and there are several lookouts, side trails, and a floating bridge. There is some relatively challenging terrain in places and a considerable amount of climbing required. Accordingly, it rates a higher difficulty level than is usual for this distance.

Route description: There is a large map posted at the trailhead, which the Tallow Rock Bay Trail shares with the Quiddity Trail. From the parking area, the first 500 m is quite easy, a wide, crushed-stone track that passes over two marshy areas on long boardwalks. There is a bench after the first boardwalk and another on a platform in the second, longer boardwalk.

Once the boardwalk ends, so does the crushed stone, and there is a sign stating that wheelchair travel is not recommended. At 600 m, the Quiddity Trail splits to the right; keep left, and at the canoe portage 85 m further, continue straight.

Crossing a small stream, the trail climbs and becomes more rugged. Pine and cedar dominate the forest here, instead of the hardwoods at the trailhead. If you notice fences to the left, this is the extreme eastern edge of the park, and these mark its boundary. The trail is usually quite distinct, but watch for signage marking the route: a light-blue diamond with a white hiker symbol inside.

At the next junction, at about 1 km, Tallow Rock Bay loop splits west and east. Turn left onto the west loop, where within 10 m there is a Km 1 marker. The trail meanders nicely, dodging both frequent rocky outcroppings and wet areas. It often parallels these rocky ridges and is frequently covered in pine needles.

By 1.6 km, hardwoods once again are in the majority, and the terrain becomes easier. Watch for a massive oak with branches like tines on a fork (difficult to miss, actually), almost the only old tree in the area. About 300 m further, a puncheon (narrow boardwalk without railings) crosses an open wet area. For the next several hundred metres, the path alternates between moving through small stands of trees and fairly open ground – probably farmland reforesting. The trail narrows often to little more than a slender track through the high grass. Expect ticks!

The open ground mostly ends once the trail begins a noticeable descent, at about 2.7 km. Look on the right about 150-200 m later, and you should see an abandoned cabin just off the trail. The 3 km marker is found just after the path skirts around a small wet area – it is usually dry in summer.

For the next several hundred metres the trail runs up between two ridges, steadily climbing. About 400 m in, some vertical rock faces to the left rise more than 20 m high. Cresting on a pine-covered ridge at about 3.7 km, the trail reaches its highest point along this route. From here, the next 600 m is a pleasant descent through lovely hardwood-covered slopes.

4.1 km Just above Tallow Rock Bay, the trail splits. A short path leads down to the water's edge, where there is a picnic table nestled between two stony ridges and a small beach. This is also a camping area, so an outhouse is also available.

From here the main route becomes more challenging, initially following the edge of the lake over quite rocky ground. About 200 m from the junction

is a signpost naming the camping areas ahead, and immediately afterwards begins this hike's toughest climb, a steep trudge up a rocky hillside. At 4.7 km, it reaches a high point, where there are areas of open rock, with pine and cedar predominating. For the next 400 m the path works through this somewhat exposed terrain. On the longer stretches of moss-covered rock, trail markers are frequently mounted on posts.

5.1 km The side trail to the Covey's Gap and Captain's Gap campsites – and to Bach's Lookout – splits left, and the junction is well signed. Entry to these campsites is restricted to registered campers, but the lookout has one of the best vistas on this hike and is open to all. Turn left to reach it.

Initially, more bare rock is traversed, but the path soon descends – first gently, then more steeply. Then, almost immediately, all that elevation is regained, reaching the junction for the routes to each campsite at 5.8 km. Turn left, Bach's Lookout is on the sign. Barely 30 m further, this path splits again, with Bach's Lookout to the left.

Only 100 m remains, until the path ends on open rock – and a cliff – over-looking Covey's Gap, a narrow channel connecting Charleston Lake with Tallow Rock Bay. Enjoy the view, then retrace the route back to the main trail, turning left onto it at 6.7 km.

The path immediately descends sharply to edge around the signed Beaver Pond, at the outflow of which you will get an excellent view of the dam and its elaborate construction. After this, you will need to cross several ridges, which involves constant climbing and descending through narrow gaps in the rocky terrain. Few views are available, even though several times large areas of bare rock are crossed.

By 7.9 km, after the trail crosses a tiny brook and makes two 180° turns in quick succession, the trail heads resolutely south. It continues to work its way through quite challenging rocky terrain, and then it begins a long, gradual descent – but with frequent short climbs. At 8.3 km, the path to the Hidden Bay campsite branches left; continue straight.

Perhaps the greatest surprise of the trail occurs 300 m later, when the trail, essentially at lake level, suddenly climbs about 20 m through a narrow fissure in a rock face.

8.8 km Once through, the path descends to reach the floating Slim Bay Bridge, less than 100 m past the Km 7 marker. This is a fascinating structure, quite long and bobbing slightly as you cross the mouth of Slim Bay. On the far side,

the trail is much gentler, wider, and almost rock free. Bob's Cove campsite is to the left, 300 m further. The path climbs again and crests above Slim Bay at about 9.6 m, with some of the best views of this walk.

From here, the path descends again, moving away from the water's edge although still providing the occasional glimpse. At 10.4 km, it is actually quite close to the end of Slim Bay at Purgatory Cove. One remaining significant climb remains before reaching the junction that marks the completion of the loop. From here, retrace the 1 km back to the trailhead.

Frontenac Arch

The Frontenac Arch is a broad and ancient granite ridge, situated between Ottawa and Kingston, which joins the Canadian Shield to the Adirondack Mountains. The topography of the region is rugged: steep, rocky slopes and ridges, typical of the Precambrian Shield and vastly different from the lowlands south of the Ottawa River near the city. Charleston Lake and Frontenac Provincial Parks are both found within the Arch's boundaries.

In 2002, UNESCO designated this region as the Frontenac Arch Biosphere Reserve, one of only thirteen in Canada. A biosphere reserve is defined as an area with important natural and ecological value where people live, work, and enjoy a variety of economic and recreational activities based on respect for the environment.

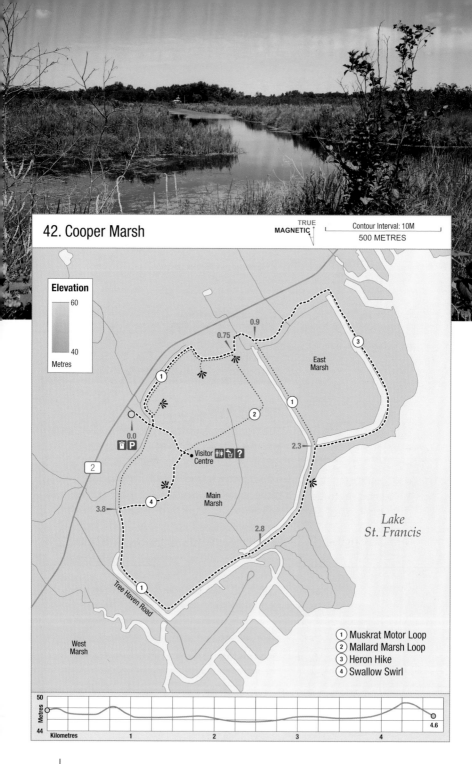

42. Cooper Marsh

TRUE
MAGNETIC

Contour Interval: 10M
500 METRES

Elevation

60

40

Metres

0.9

0.75

East
Marsh

1

0.0

2

2

1

2.3

Visitor
Centre

3.8

4

Main
Marsh

*Lake
St. Francis*

2.8

1

Tree Haven Road

West
Marsh

1 Muskrat Motor Loop
2 Mallard Marsh Loop
3 Heron Hike
4 Swallow Swirl

3

50

Metres

44

Kilometres

1

2

3

4

4.6

42. Cooper Marsh

Distance: 4.6 km
Type: loop
Difficulty: 1
Ascent/descent: 3 m
Hiking time: 1+ hrs
Trail conditions: compacted earth, crushed stone, natural surface

Cellphone coverage: excellent
Uses: walking, snowshoeing
Facilities: benches, garbage cans, interpretive panels, outhouses, picnic tables
Hazards: poison ivy, ticks

Finding the trailhead: From the Highway 417/174 split, follow Highway 417 about 55 km to exit 58. Turn right onto Highway 138 for 32 km, then turn left onto County Road 44. In 1.6 km, turn right onto County Road 42. Follow it for 4.2 km, turning onto Highway 401 toward Montréal. After 21 km, take exit 814, then turn right onto County Road 2. Cooper Marsh is on the left in 3.2 km.

Trailhead: 45°06'58.8" N, 74°31'04.0" W

Introduction: This pleasant little trail system built around a wetland, teeming with more than 130 species of birds and a similarly wide variety of plant life, is excellent for a family walk. Novice hikers, too, might enjoy this as an easy introduction to the activity.

Managed by the Raisin River Conservation Authority, Cooper Marsh sits on the north shore of Lake St. Francis, a wide stretch of the St. Lawrence River. It is an important part of the habitat restoration projects being undertaken to repair damage to wildlife habitat caused by the flooding that accompanied the opening of the St. Lawrence Seaway. Work on Cooper Marsh began in the 1980s and continues to the present as a partnership between conservation authorities, naturalists, and groups such as Ducks Unlimited.

Route description: From the parking area, where there is a lovely picnic spot including outhouses and a billboard-sized map display, head along the gravel access road toward the Visitor Centre. Immediately after crossing one of the small water drainage channels, at about 100 m, you reach the junction with Muskrat Motor Loop, which is marked with a yellow sign, and the Mallard Marsh Loop, signed in red.

Turn left, onto a slender crushed-stone and grass-covered track. In a few steps the Mallard Marsh Loop branches off to the right. Keep straight/left: you are Muskrat Motoring!

This trail follows one of the impoundment embankments: wide, flat, and dry, and initially paralleling Highway 2, which, though hidden by the 2+ m high vegetation, is quite audible.

In summer, which is when I hiked Cooper Marsh, the grasses are lush, thick, and tall. So when the trail passes through the marsh, expect limited viewing possibilities. These grasses create a living wall that parts only occasionally, perhaps if there is a breeze, to permit glimpses of what is beyond. On the other hand, the birdlife is quite animated, particularly with raucous red-winged blackbirds constantly announcing their presence.

At 500 m there is another junction with the Mallard Marsh, and a bench. These junctions are signed with symbols, not names – so that's a muskrat, not a rat or a beaver. Keep left to remain on Muskrat, the trail now grass surfaced.

Curiously, Muskrat and Mallard parallel each other only a few metres apart for the next 200 m. They reconnect several times, finally at a viewing platform. If you are comfortable, use the Mallard Marsh Loop until the platform; it is more scenic.

But if you remain on Muskrat, it immediately reaches a connector to the highway; keep right on the broad grass pathway, which runs alongside the trees until it reaches the viewing platform and picnic table, at 750 m.

Muskrat curves left again, away from the marsh, and within 100 m it reaches another open area where there is another connection to Highway 2. The trail curves right, past some beehives and a small garden. There is an unsigned three-way junction; keep straight as the others are informal tracks.

900 m Arrive at the junction with the Heron Hike, and then turn left onto Heron. This becomes a narrower track and even occasionally features some overhead shade. Much of this route follows a track – or sometimes more than one – mown through the tall grass. Whichever one you follow doesn't matter; they all arrive at the same place.

On the right is the East Marsh, which in summer shows very little open water. To the left, Highway 2 and some houses are often visible across the fields. After 400 m, when it almost appears as if the trail will emerge onto the road or a small marina, Heron Hike makes a sharp 90° right turn.

The path is now wider and arrow-straight for nearly 500 m, and the bordering vegetation, though thick, is not high enough for much shade. Much of it is sumac, and catbirds appear to enjoy using its cover to emit their taunting mewls. Some benches are located where there are gaps in the brush. At about 1.8 km, the trail begins a long, gradual curve right, connecting back to Muskrat Motor Loop at 2.3 km.

Turn left onto Muskrat. About 100 m further there is a very large raised platform, on the left, which provides views of shallow Meadow Bay and the broad St. Lawrence River beyond it. Some benches are built into the platform. The Muskrat Motor Loop here is grass surfaced and very wide; four could comfortably walk side by side. Once you are off the platform, thick alders block sight of the river, but occasional views of the Main Marsh, to the right, are possible.

By 2.8 km, private properties located just outside Cooper Marsh can be seen to the left. This is also a spot where several of the drainage channels converge, and it probably offers the best view of the Main Marsh available on Muskrat. The Visitor Centre can be seen quite well from here.

For the next 500 m private houses are visible, and I found the views of their boats and docks rather appealing. The trail narrows, and at 3.3 km it turns sharply right. For the next 250 m, Tree Haven Road, the access to the private houses, is just on the opposite side of a drainage channel. Then the path curves right, and vegetation once again encloses it.

3.8 km The junction with the Swallow Swirl is reached. Turn right, leaving Muskrat once again, and follow a boardwalk as it wends through the main marsh. Several interpretive panels, usually at special viewing platforms, help identify the many distinguishing plants that grow in this wetland.

For 350 m the boardwalk curves through the marsh, including an excellent view of an occupied osprey nest. At about 4.2 km, the boardwalk connects to the mainland again and ends. To the left are a picnic table and another viewing platform. The path continues directly ahead, and in 100 m it reaches the Visitor Centre.

This is a delightful and interesting structure and an excellent place to enjoy a snack, as there are picnic tables on the marsh-facing side. Inside, in addition to the interpretive material, are washrooms and drinking water. Another viewing platform, also a good viewpoint for an osprey nest, is in the back.

Once you are finished at the Visitor Centre, follow the gravel entrance road the 300 m back to the Highway 2 trailhead and the end of this walk.

43. Forêt Larose

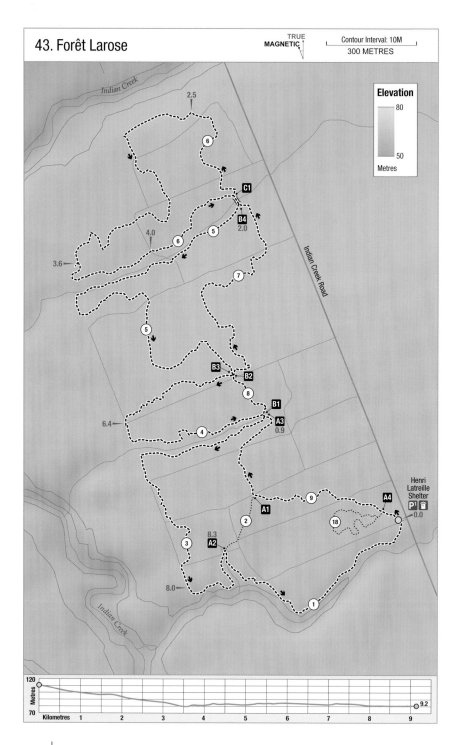

TRUE
MAGNETIC

Contour Interval: 10M
300 METRES

Elevation

— 80

— 50

Metres

Indian Creek

2.5

6

C1

B4
2.0

4.0

6

5

3.6

7

5

Indian Creek Road

B3

B2

8

B1

6.4

A3
0.9

4

Henri
Latreille
Shelter

9

A4

A1

2

18

8.3
A2

3

P1

0.0

8.0

1

Indian Creek

120

Metres

70

Kilometres 1   2   3   4   5   6   7   8   9

9.2

43. Forêt Larose

Distance: 9.2 km
Type: loop
Difficulty: 2
Ascent/descent: 20 m
Hiking time: 2+ hrs
Trail conditions: natural surface
Cellphone coverage: excellent

Uses: walking, biking, snowshoeing, cross-country skiing
Facilities: benches, garbage cans, outhouses, picnic tables
Hazards: high usage, poison ivy, ticks, wildlife

Finding the trailhead: From the Highway 417/174 split, follow Highway 417 about 25 km to exit 88. Turn left onto Regional Road 33, then turn right in 750 m onto Russland Road. In 6.7 km, turn left onto Saumure Road (Ottawa County Road 8). Continue straight on Indian Creek Road, which in 750 m will change to a dirt road. Turn left 2.1 km later at a junction to stay on Indian Creek Road. Continue 1.1 km further to arrive at the P1 Forêt Larose parking area and the trailhead.

Trailhead: 45°22'32.8" N, 75°14'33.0" W

Introduction: Attempting to accurately describe this route is a challenge, because it contains so many twists and turns that the adjective "sinuous" is somehow both inadequate and likely to be overused. This path system was primarily designed for mountain bikers, although walkers are permitted to use it. As a result, the trail rarely remains in a straight line, and it delights in weaving among the trees in sharp, tight corners, one after another, after yet another – until it becomes difficult to recall in which direction it is actually heading.

This is one of three – at time of writing – loops of similar trails available in the Forêt Larose. I walked all of them, but I selected this one because its design of stacked loops permits choosing a shorter route if desired.

Careful attention must be paid at all times for cyclists. I encountered quite a few when I hiked this, and listening for their approach was as helpful as watching for them.

Route description: Start at P1, where an outhouse, garbage cans, excellent map, and the large Henri Latreille Shelter with its picnic tables, are all sheltered beneath a stand of tall, stately red pine. Begin on Trail 9, its signpost hosting a blue mountain bike symbol immediately below the number. Hikers are permitted on the trail, but the primary use is by cyclists.

The trail is a slender dirt track seemingly swept through the pine-needle-covered forest floor, clearly visible in the sparse second layer of hardwoods scattered beneath the towering pines. Almost immediately the first junction,

A4, is reached, where there is a map, with Trail 18 branching left. Continue on the meandering Trail 9. Its design as a mountain bike path becomes most evident in the corners, which are banked to permit bicycles to whip around them easily. These give walkers a sense of being on a rollercoaster route.

At 250 m, the path crosses the first of many dirt or grass-surfaced forest access roads. These roads are themselves recreational pathways for walkers, cyclists, and other uses not permitted on the mountain bike route, such as horses and dog sleds. There is a sign on the opposite side where Trail 9 continues.

Shortly afterwards there are two unsigned connections with small loops intended for more adventurous cyclists; keep right at both. At 600 m, at the next forest access road, is junction A1. Trail 2 turns left while Trail 9 crosses the road; continue on Trail 9.

900 m Junction A3 sits on the edge of a low gully and is the decision point for the first loop. Trail 3, to the left, circles back 2.1 km to the P1 Trailhead. For a longer hike, turn right and cross the ravine over an unrailed bridge, reaching junction B1 on its far side.

There is a map here, and this is the start of a second, quite small – 1.2 km total – loop. Again, keep right, now on Trail 8.

Junction B2 is only 200 m further, reached just after crossing another forest access road. Keep right there, and again at B3 just a few steps later. Your route now follows Trail 7, where the forest beneath the pines is a bit thicker, limiting visibility somewhat, and the ground is a little more uneven than previously. It is still very easy walking, with no rocks, few tree roots, and virtually no perceptible elevation change, except in the gullies.

Trail 7 continues the weaving pattern of previous trails, crossing forest access roads, and includes another small advanced cyclists' loop. At times, to the right, Indian Creek Road can be seen as well.

2 km Junction B4 is located alongside another ravine, and it is the decision point for whether to include the fourth and final loop or select a shorter walk by turning left. Another narrow, unrailed bridge traverses the low, wet ground, and on the opposite ridge is junction C1. The path is Trail 6 in both directions; keep right.

Once again this is a winding, sinuous track. About 200 m later are some of the most open and attractive stands of pine on the entire route, where the trail is a distinct track cleared through their needles and the trees stand like pillars in a cathedral. This is followed by an area of thick vegetation where nothing but the immediate trail is visible.

At 2.5 km, just after crossing another forest access road, a sign indicates "Jump" (for mountain bikers) to the right. This time keep left, because the jump is just that, an area for cyclists to play. Trail 6 skirts a small gully, which deepens as you proceed. About 100 m further, the path straightens, a deep gully on the right, and incorporates numerous small artificial bumps to enliven the cyclist's ride. This area is named Rollers/Tabletop.

Less than 200 m later, the route makes a surprisingly sharp 90° left turn, away from the gulch and Rollers/Tabletop. This is actually the most distant point from P1, although most of the walking still remains. For a considerable distance, the path works its distinctively torturous route through the forest, with only occasional forest access road crossings and small side loops worth remark.

3.6 km Trail 6 arrives at the Mini Side Winder, another advanced diversion option into a gully. At the top sits a picnic table, and this is actually a rather nice spot to sit and have a snack. There is even entertainment in watching cyclists dashing into and through the uneven ground to the right.

From here, the trail turns left again, keeping the lower ground to the right. On one of its straightest sections thus far, Trail 6 traces the crest of the ravine. At 4 km, a forest access road crosses the ravine. Continue straight, past Le Bol à Frank, another advanced cyclists' play area. Your route continues alongside this gully, as it shallows, until it returns to junction C1 about 350 m later.

Recross the bridge, and at B4, where there is a map, turn right and follow Trail 5 alongside the opposite edge of the same gorge until it turns left, and away, at 5 km. I quite enjoyed this section, and now that you know Trail 6 is just opposite, you might notice some other trail users on it. Once it leaves the ravine, Trail 5 appears to follow a former forest track for nearly 100 m, before curving left and resuming its snaking route through the essentially level ground. However, this is also another area of tall pine stands, which I find rather appealing.

At about 5.6 km, the path moves into some thicker vegetation, and there is no visibility along the winding route. After about 300 m, it reaches junction B3. Keep right, and right again at B2 a few steps away onto Trail 4.

What follows is the most wiggling section of a trail system distinguished by its winding design. It's almost comical how often and how quickly it curves. But after crossing another forest access road, at 6.4 km, the path soon reaches another ravine, where it turns left and follows back to junction B1, at 7 km.

Turn right, crossing the now shallow gully to A3, and right again onto Trail 3. This follows the ravine for nearly 500 m before turning left, and away from it. This section is one of the most well defined, suggesting that it might also be the most often used.

8 km After more of its typical meandering, the trail reaches another fairly deep ravine, where it turns left again. These slopes are more deeply eroded, so the path sometimes must curve around small side gullies. In the deepest of these, at 8.3 km, junction A2 connects with Trail 2 at a forest access road. Keep right, and continue alongside this attractive ravine, where some cedars shade the slope.

This is now Trail 1, which follows the shallowing ravine until just before reaching Indian Creek Road, when it curves left and returns to P1, completing the loop.

Bourget Desert

By the mid-1800s, forestry and burning to clear for agriculture had wiped out the original forest covering Eastern Ontario. That proved disastrous for the sandy soils in what is now known as Forêt Larose. Erosion, silted and choked rivers, and out-of-control wildfires resulted in it being known as the Bourget Desert.

In 1928, Russell County purchased 490 ha from private landowners and, directed by Ferdinand Larose, began an aggressive reforestation program. Additional land was purchased as the program expanded, and in the 1940s and 1950s up to one million trees were being planted annually, mostly red pine, white pine, and white spruce.

By 2016, more than 18,000,000 trees had been planted, with the first seedlings planted in 1928 being more than 28 m tall. Forêt Larose now covers 10,944.7 ha, and is the second largest man-made forest in Ontario.

(Photo courtesy of United Counties of Prescott and Russell)

43. Forêt Larose

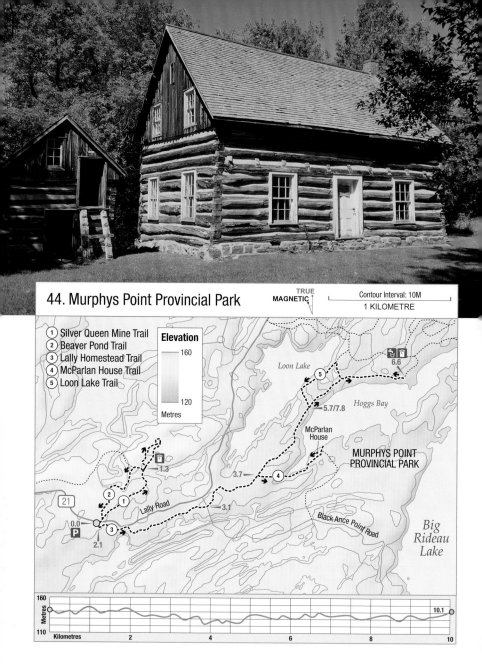

44. Murphys Point Provincial Park

TRUE
MAGNETIC

Contour Interval: 10M

1 KILOMETRE

1 Silver Queen Mine Trail
2 Beaver Pond Trail
3 Lally Homestead Trail
4 McParlan House Trail
5 Loon Lake Trail

Elevation

160

120

Metres

Loon Lake

6.6

5.7/7.8

Hoggs Bay

McParlan
House

3.7

4

MURPHYS POINT
PROVINCIAL PARK

1.3

2

1

Lally Road

3.1

21

0.0

P

3

2.1

Black Ance Point Road

Big
Rideau
Lake

160

Metres

110

Kilometres

2

4

6

8

10

10.1

44. Murphys Point Provincial Park

Distance: 10.1 km
Type: loop
Difficulty: 2
Ascent/descent: 88 m
Hiking time: 2+ hrs
Trail conditions: compacted earth, natural surface
Cellphone coverage: excellent

Uses: walking, biking*, snowshoeing, cross-country skiing
Facilities: benches, campsites, drinking water, garbage cans, interpretive panels, outhouses, picnic tables
Hazards: poison ivy, road crossing, ticks, wildlife

Finding the trailhead: From the Highway 417/416 split, follow Highway 417 West 14 km to exit 145. Turn onto Highway 7, and continue 56 km to Perth, then turn left onto Drummond Street West. At 2.7 km, turn right onto South Street, then left onto County Road 1/Rideau Ferry Road just 150 m later. Follow County Road 1 for 5.9 km, then turn right onto County Road 21/Elm Grove Road. Drive for 11 km to the main park entrance.

There is a fee to use the trails, and this can only be purchased in the main park area. Once you have your pay-and-display permit, return to County Road 21 — now named the Lally Road — and turn left. After 2.5 km, the well-signed parking area is on left; the trail starts across the road.

Trailhead: 44°46'03.1" N, 76°15'17.8" W

Introduction: Murphys Point Provincial Park is a compact, but diverse, natural preserve bordering the Rideau Waterway near the community of Perth. It boasts considerable attractive hardwood forest cover, camping, numerous short walking paths, canoe access, swimming, archaeological sites, and former mines, and is bisected by the wandering Rideau Trail — all situated on the rolling, interesting topography of the Frontenac Arch.

This route is made up of two distinct sections, each of which can be walked separately. The shorter, at 2.1 km, takes you to the site of the former Silver Queen Mine. The other, at 8 km, heads to McParlan House, a former farm and an archaeological site, and into the camping area. Both are suitable walks for families, although the latter is considerably longer. Neither features particularly difficult terrain.

Route description: From the parking area, cross Lally Road and enter the Silver Queen Mine Trail, where an interpretive panel describes the mine that once worked this area. The path follows an old road, on which cyclists are permitted, though immediately there is a junction with the Rideau Trail/Beaver Pond Trail, which is for walking only. Continue straight, along the road. The numbered posts you sight work with the Silver Queen Mine Trail interpretive booklet, available at the park office, which is a superb companion to this walk and will greatly add to the experience of this trail.

After working over the rolling terrain, at 600 m the path reaches a junction; continue straight/right. On the right is a picnic table, an interpretive panel, and an impressive full-size display of a mine's wagon – including replica horses – protected by an overhead shelter. Less than 50 m beyond that is another junction; turn left.

The next several hundred metres are fascinating, as the trail works along the base of a hillside and visits the remains of a site where mica, feldspar, and apatite were mined. In this 700 m loop, you will find numerous pits where the minerals were extracted, some open and fenced, some gated and shut, with old equipment and samples of the minerals. There is also a restored bunkhouse, and in the adjacent field there are numerous picnic tables, making it a pleasant location to sit and relax. There is also an outhouse nearby.

Return to the wagon display and the junction there, at 1.3 km. Turn right onto the Beaver Pond Trail and into thick forest cover. Less than 100 m further is another junction; turn left. The winding path works alongside a large wetland – the eponymous beaver pond – until it turns away and reconnects to the old road. Turn right, and in 50 m you return to Lally Road.

2.1 km Return to the parking area and walk to its far end, where there is a large trailhead kiosk, which includes a map. Turn left onto the Lally Homestead Trail, but follow the orange triangles that mark the Rideau Trail down the

small hill, past an old foundation, and across the grassy field toward the old farm buildings: the Lally Homestead. A grass-covered pathway passes left of the two standing buildings and briefly connects with Lally Road before veering right and into the forest. (There is a sign indicating that the campground is 3.1 km distant.)

The path becomes pleasantly uneven, an unimproved track traversing numerous low rocky ridges

—mostly grass covered, but occasionally bare rock. Leaving this rocky ground, the forest opens up into attractive hardwoods, providing wonderful views of the contoured ground around you. At 3.1 km, the trail crosses Black Ance Point Road.

The path widens now, resembling a former settlement road, though it continues shaded beneath a magnificent hardwood canopy. About 200 m later it seems to reach a junction; turn right, following the broad path and the orange Rideau Trail markers.

3.7 km The path reaches the junction with the McParlan House Trail. Turn right, and descend the old road down to lake level, 200 m later, bordered by wonderful hardwood-covered ridges. At Black Creek, 200 m beyond that, a sturdy bridge, constructed by Rideau Trail Association volunteers, crosses the rocky ravine.

McParlan House, an archaeological site and the reconstruction of a former homestead, sits in a small field about 300 m further. There is a picnic table there, and just beyond the house a side path reaches a pleasant spot beside Hoggs Bay. A sign indicates that the park's trail ends here, but that the Rideau Trail continues 3 km to the park boundary — it keeps going all the way to Kingston, actually.

Retrace the 650 m back to the main trail junction, and turn right toward the campground. The broad track is easy walking, through lovely hardwood-topped slopes, and there isn't much climbing required. About 400 m from the junction, Hoggs Bay — part of Big Rideau Lake — can be glimpsed to the right, and at 5.7 km there is a four-way junction, with a canoe portage crossing your route. Continue straight, now on the Loon Lake Trail.

Cedar rail fences soon line the path, and 300 m further it reaches the park campground at a campsite access road. Turn right, and follow this road through the camping area, always keeping on the track closest to the water.

6.6 km You reach the sandy beach, where there are picnic tables, garbage cans, canoe rental, a water tap — even a playground — and an interpretive panel: a good place for a break. From here, retrace the 550 m on park road back to the trail. However, turn right, and continue along the road for an additional 150 m. There, the Loon Lake Trail turns left and traces the lake's shoreline for nearly 400 m, until it reaches the canoe portage.

Turn left, away from the water, and follow the portage track less than 200 m to the junction with the path from the Lally Homestead Trail. Once there, turn right, and retrace the 2.2 km back to the trailhead.

45. New York Central Fitness Trail

TRUE
MAGNETIC

Contour Interval: 10M

2 KILOMETRES

Eadie Road

St. Guillaume Road

St. Pierre Road

P ℹ
6.0

5.5

S
Embrun

2.5

Notre Dame Street

Bay St

St-Onge

1.3

Castor Street

3

4.0

Castor River

P
0.0

St. Andre Road

S
Russell

Elevation

80

60

Metres

6

74

Metres

Kilometres   1   2   3   4   5   6

64

45. New York Central Fitness Trail

Distance: 12 km return
Type: linear
Difficulty: 2
Ascent/descent: 22 m
Hiking time: 3+ hrs
Trail conditions: asphalt
Cellphone coverage: good throughout

Uses: walking, biking, inline skating, snowshoeing, cross-country skiing
Facilities: benches, garbage cans, outhouses, picnic tables
Hazards: high usage, poison ivy, road crossings, ticks, wildlife

Finding the trailhead: From the Highway 174/417 split, follow Highway 417 for 17 km to exit 96. Turn right onto Highway 41 and follow it for 2.3 km, then turn left onto Regional Road 8. In 1.4 km, turn right onto Frontier Road, which curves left in 1.6 km, becoming Burton Road. This curves right in 950 m to become North Russell Road. Follow it for 6.8 km, then turn left into the parking area just after crossing the trail. Or park on the right, in the Russell Fairgrounds lot.

Trailhead: 45°15'46.4" N, 75°21'41.0" W

Introduction: Eastern Ontario might seem like an unlikely place to find a trail named the New York Central, but between 1898 and 1957, this route was part of a railroad system connecting Ottawa with New York City. As air travel siphoned off passenger traffic, and Northern Ontario lumber found other markets, the railway was abandoned. In 1979, the township of Russell purchased some of this property and converted it for recreational purposes.

If you want to see an example of how a properly managed trail can become a treasured community resource over time, you must visit the New York Central. Almost every house along the route has its own link connecting to the pathway, and residents use it constantly. Every time I have visited, it has been active with multi-generational family groups and young children. This is a great community trail.

Currently, the developed section extends from Route 200, just west of Russell, to Notre Dame Street in Embrun. Many residents hope that someday it might be possible to extend the trail into the city of Ottawa. I have chosen to profile only the section beginning at Concession Street in Russell because there is good parking available to start the walk. The trail actually continues west another 2.3 km, and itself is a very pleasant stroll.

Route description: From the parking area, head right (east) in the direction opposite to Concession Street. The pathway is paved with a yellow centre line, making it easy to follow. In 2010 the area to the left was field, but now it's new housing. Instead of being at the edge of Russell, as it once was, the trail currently separates the older part of the community from the newer.

Several connecting side paths have been developed to the newer neighbourhood on the left, and a power line now parallels the pathway. In 2019, the new construction ended at Eadie Road, about 1.3 km from the start. For the next kilometre your route, almost as straight as an arrow, continues through a luxuriant hardwood forest, interrupted only by a power line corridor 300 m from Eadie Street. Two benches with a garbage can have been placed between road and power line.

Another two bench/garbage can combinations are located at about 2.2 km, and by then you will have probably noticed that the trail appears to be approaching a busy road. There are also more houses here, some having built quite elaborate connections to the trail.

♀2.5 km The trail reaches busy County Road 3; on the Russell side it is Castor Street, and on the Embrun side it is Notre Dame Street. Although well signed on the highway and the trail and marked by a crosswalk, this is an extremely dangerous intersection, and there have been accidents. Cross carefully.

Once across, the trail parallels the road but is insulated somewhat inside a buffer of pleasant hardwoods, interrupted only by one farmer's road. There are even a few additional benches. However, just 300 m from County Road 3 the trail crosses the entrance to the busy local dog park. But for nearly 1.2 km it is an uninterrupted straight section, and quite pleasant.

At 3.7 km there is another potentially challenging road crossing, this time at the entrance of the Russell Sports Dome. Immediately after this, the pathway moves into an area of considerable commercial activity, where street and driveway crossings are frequent.

♀4 km The trail reaches the intersection of Notre Dame Street and Saint-Guilliaume Road, which since 2010 has been redeveloped into a roundabout. To traverse this, the pathway curves right around it, passing several business entrances, before crossing Notre Dame on a marked crosswalk, and continuing left up Saint-Guilliaume until it has crossed several more business entrances and Bay Street. Got that? It's easy to see when you are there. However, this is a busy and intricate roadway system that is also challenging for motorists. Take your time navigating it.

At 4.1 km, just the other side of Bay Street, is a bench and rest area. (Not surprising, really.) You can stop here and check to see if you still have all your limbs or, if heading in the return direction, steady your nerves before venturing into the roundabout.

The remainder of the trek lacks any additional drama. Until the next road crossing, St. Pierre Road, at 5.5 km, the trail proceeds into Embrun. As in Russell, newer housing is gradually taking over the cultivated fields on the left, while the older businesses and homes on the right are shaded by mature trees and almost all have their own private trail entrance. Expect lots of young children wobbling around on the path; proceed slowly.

After crossing St. Pierre Road, the pathway gently curves right, and deep, lush forest once again shrouds the route, and it seems as if the community has been left behind.

6 km The trail emerges from its sylvan cocoon to end at a parking area on Notre Dame Street in Embrun's downtown. Benches, a garbage can, a covered picnic table, and an outhouse are nearby, as is the old train station building. This is a great opportunity to wander into the nearby restaurants and other businesses of Embrun. When you are ready, retrace your route to Russell.

46. Prescott-Russell Recreational Trail

TRUE
MAGNETIC

Contour Interval: 10M
4 KILOMETRES

Elevation
90
40
Metres

46. Prescott-Russell Recreational Trail: Vankleek Hill

Distance: 30.4 km return
Type: linear
Difficulty: 5 (distance)
Ascent/descent: 74 m
Hiking time: 8+ hrs
Trail conditions: asphalt, crushed stone
Cellphone coverage: excellent

Uses: walking, biking, snowshoeing, snowmobiling
Facilities: benches, garbage cans, interpretive panels, outhouses, picnic tables
Hazards: poison ivy, road crossings, ticks, wildlife

Finding the trailhead: From the Highway 417/174 split, follow Highway 417 for 86 km, then turn at the exit onto Highway 34/County Road 34. Turn left towards Vankleek Hill. Continue for 8.4 km, then turn left into the trailhead parking area.

Trailhead: 45°32'04.7" N, 74°38'43.0" W

Introduction: The Prescott-Russell Recreational Trail, which traverses the rural farmlands east of Ottawa, opened in June 2004. Officially it extends 72 km, from the Quebec provincial border to the city limits of Ottawa, but the first 3 km from the Quebec border hasn't been restored and is only used by snowmobiles and ATVs, so it's really only 69 km. It was constructed on the abandoned rail bed of the former Montreal-Ottawa line – yet another recreational repurposing of abandoned industrial infrastructure.

The section between the communities of Vankleek Hill and St-Eugène connects two of the five Trailhead Pavilions constructed on this pathway, all of which feature maps, picnic tables, garbage cans, and outhouses. This section passes through some of the least populated areas along the Prescott-Russell Trail. And although this isn't a comfortable distance for a day hike, the generally flat terrain makes it easy walking. This should be a restful, pastoral experience, regardless of the distance one actually travels.

Route description: From the pavilion, which is marked Km 19, follow the trail to the right/east. The treadway is asphalt here, and heading in the direction of Ottawa, but it is crushed stone toward Quebec. You must immediately cross busy Highway 34. Exercise extreme caution, as it is an 80 kph zone.

Once you are safely across and through the narrow gap in the gate across the pathway – having read all the regulatory signage, naturally – the wide crushed-stone pathway extends off toward the horizon.

Cultivated fields flank the pathway on both sides, though there is often a border of trees close to the rail trail. At 1 km you will encounter something rare: the pathway crosses an operating rail line. About 800 m further, after the trail passes beneath a power line, it moves into a thickly forested area where there are fewer houses and no fields.

At 3.2 km, a bridge crosses the ravine cut by tiny Little Rideau Creek, and once across, cropland again becomes visible. The first bench is located at the Km 15 marker, though apparently for no other reason: there is no special view. Around the Km 14 marker are a number of interpretive panels about agriculture in Prescott-Russell. By this point the pathway is straight, no trees border it, and some of the corn has been planted so close to the edge of the trail that it becomes a hedge when full grown.

Farm equipment both crosses and uses the trail, sometimes roughing the treadway, but any farmers I met were always cautious and courteous around trail users.

6.7 km The trail crosses County Road 12, the first road since Highway 34. Signs on the trail label it and every road crossing. Directly ahead, in sight and distinctly audible, is Highway 417. The trail crosses beneath it 300 m from County Road 12, under two massive bridges that were built when the pathway was still an operating railroad.

Beyond this the trail appears less heavily used. Grass has grown up through much of the crushed stone, and the bordering trees and scrub appear to crowd toward the centre. It is also quite apparent that the route is distinctly, though modestly, descending, which it will do all the way to St-Eugène. There are more interpretive panels along this section as well, though some are repeats of panels seen earlier on the route.

The next road crossing, at Cunning Road, is at 9.2 km, and the next bridge, crossing Cat Creek, is 2 km beyond that, at 11.2 km. The surrounding lands are entirely given over to agriculture and are quite open. Directly ahead, the hills you see in the distance are those of Rigaud, Quebec.

At 12.6 km, there is a stop sign on the trail. A large farm straddles both sides of the trail, and the ruts provide well-defined evidence that its equipment frequently crosses. Be careful here, especially because the farmers may not be expecting many trail users.

Perhaps 500 m further, there is a sign that states that the pavilion is 2 km distant. At 14.1 km, the trail reaches Regional Road 14, and St-Eugène. Once across the road, the treadway is surfaced in asphalt.

Interestingly, despite being in a community, at first only a few houses are visible, and those are all to the right. Only 500 m further, after crossing another bridge (also over Cat Creek), it seems as though we are in a village, although the trail appears to be at its northern edge. At 14.9 km, Mill Street crosses the trail to create a parking area for the pathway.

15.2 km The path arrives at the St-Eugène Pavilion, with its outhouse, picnic tables, garbage cans, map, and information panels. It is situated in a large, grass-covered, and well-mown field. Access to the community's businesses can be through Mill Street or Regional Road 14.

Less than 1 km of maintained trail remains until it ends at Moore Road, should your curiosity require some extra distance to satisfy. Beyond that the unmaintained abandoned rail line exists and can be followed into the nearby community of Rigaud, Quebec, although it is quite rough at many spots.

Retrace your route back to Vankleek Hill.

Abandoned Railroads

Railroads were the superhighways of the late nineteenth and early twentieth centuries, the only practical method to move goods and people over land before the invention of the automobile. Every community vied for a railway connection: having a rail station meant prosperity and growth; being passed by meant decline and economic stagnation.

By the end of World War II, however, railroads were unmistakably in decline, and all but the most profitable routes were abandoned. Yet their role in transportation is not over, for in the past two decades thousands of kilometres of rail lines have been converted to recreational trails for walking, cycling, and cross-country skiing.

47. Rideau Trail – Westport

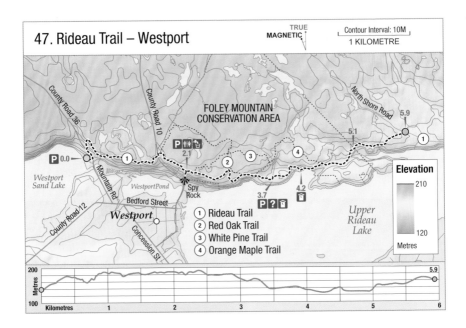

FOLEY MOUNTAIN
CONSERVATION AREA

TRUE
MAGNETIC

Contour Interval: 10M
1 KILOMETRE

① Rideau Trail
② Red Oak Trail
③ White Pine Trail
④ Orange Maple Trail

County Road 36
County Road 10
North Shore Road
Mountain Rd
County Road 12
Concession St.

Westport
Sand Lake

WestportPond

Bedford Street

Westport

Spy
Rock

Upper
Rideau
Lake

Elevation
210
120
Metres

5.9
5.1

0.0
2.1
3.7
4.2

Metres
200
100
Kilometres   1   2   3   4   5   6
5.9

Rideau Trail

Stretching 387 km between Ottawa
and Kingston, the Rideau Trail is one
of the longest signed and maintained
hiking trails in Canada. Beginning
within sight of the Parliament
Buildings in downtown Ottawa,
the Rideau Trail meanders through
urban areas, farmlands, suburban
forests, and wilderness areas as it
wends its way along National Capital
Commission paths, country roads,
provincial parks, and private lands.

The trail is maintained by
volunteers, and its three clubs — Ottawa, Perth, and Kingston —
regularly organize group hikes, snowshoeing, or cross-country
skiing throughout the year. For more information, see www.
rideautrail.org.

47. Rideau Trail – Westport

Distance: 11.8 km return
Type: linear
Difficulty: 3
Ascent/descent: 392 m
Hiking time: 3+ hrs
Trail conditions: compacted earth, crushed stone, natural surface

Uses: walking, snowshoeing, cross-country skiing*
Facilities: benches, garbage cans, interpretive panels, outhouses, picnic tables
Hazards: cliffs, hunting, poison ivy, road crossings, ticks, wildlife

Finding the trailhead: From the Highway 416/417 split, follow Highway 417 for 14 km to exit 145, then turn onto Highway 7. Continue for 23 km, then turn left onto Highway 15. In 12 km, turn right onto County Road 10/Perth Road. At Drummond Street in Perth, in 22 km, turn left; after 1.4 km, turn right onto South Street. Continue straight, on County Road 10, for 29 km to Westport, then turn right onto Bedford Street. In 850 m, turn right onto Mountain Road/ Regional Road 36. In 650 m, turn left into the Lion's Hall parking area.

Trailhead: 44°41'07.2" N, 76°24'36.1" W

Introduction: The centre section of this route lies within the Foley Mountain Conservation Area, part of the Rideau Valley Conservation Authority. Although "mountain" might seem an ambitious name for a granite knob barely 80 m high, the view from the Spy Rock observation platform is panoramic. Foley Mountain sits on the edge of the Frontenac Arch, an extension of the Canadian Shield, so the sedimentary soils and lush farmland spreading away to the south look to be part of another world – which, geographically speaking, it almost is.

Foley Mountain holds an important place in the history of the more than 300 km long Rideau Trail connecting Kingston with Ottawa. It was here, on November 7, 1971, that the footpath was officially opened. One of the highlights of this walk is the bronze plaque, affixed to a massive boulder, commemorating that event.

This is a challenging walk with considerable elevation change and occasionally rocky terrain, but it is eminently worthwhile. Once in the Conservation Area, other footpaths are available, and well signed, should a shorter or less hilly walk be desired.

Route description: From the parking area next to Westport Sand Lake, return to the highway and turn left, walking on the shoulder. Watch for the Rideau Trail's distinctive orange triangle markers on power poles and trees. After about 200 m uphill, cross the road and enter the forest.

The route immediately becomes a slender, none-too-distinct footpath weaving its way up the hillside between trees and rocky outcroppings. Fortunately, there are frequent Rideau Trail markers, and it isn't possible to travel far without seeing the next one.

At 400 m, near the crest, the path turns right nearly 180°, then actually descends a little as it works its way back across the rocky slope. At 700 m, a tiny plank bridge crosses a narrow, rock-littered ravine, after which it climbs to an area of bare rock and scattered cedar, about 150 m further.

The route levels somewhat and becomes more open, providing better views. Jack pine and cedar predominate. There is one shallow gully, crossing a larger brook on a modest bridge, before returning to bare rock and continuing to reach Perth Road/County Road 10 at 1.6 km.

Head left, alongside the road, toward the entrance to the Foley Mountain Conservation Area. After only about 50 m, you should be able to spot a Rideau Trail sign across the road: cross; follow that footpath. This is a very wide track, and it generally parallels both the hillcrest and the entrance road, though buffered from both by forest.

Within 200 m, picnic tables appear in small clearings, and there are many informal trails. Watch the signage to keep on the correct path.

2.1 km The path intersects a boardwalk and crushed-stone trail. Turn right and walk down to Spy Rock, with its scenic overlook of the community of Westport and Upper Rideau Lake.

Return to the junction and continue a short distance along the crushed stone, toward the parking area. Just before reaching it, the Rideau Trail branches right onto a natural-surface footpath. To the left, you might notice some of the park buildings, where there are washrooms and drinking water is available. The next section might get confusing at times. Much of the distance crosses bare rock, with cedar scattered thinly, so there is often some distance between markers. In addition, there are many informal side trails. However, your route is marked by both the Rideau Trail orange triangles and plastic markers for the Conservation Area's Red Oak Trail.

At 2.9 km, the trail turns sharply right, begins to descend distinctly, and moves out of the cedar and into an area of hardwoods. It continues to wind down the hillside, with one little climb until it reaches a junction, where there is a trail map, at 3.2 km. The Red Oak Trail turns left; continue straight/left on the Rideau Trail, which now shares the path with the White Pine Trail.

The steepest descent follows, along a gorgeous hardwood ridge. About 250 m further, at the next junction, the White Pine Trail splits left; continue along the Rideau Trail, which it now shares with the Orange Maple Trail. This is a beautiful forest, all maple of varying ages. A roped-off pathway is to the right, heading toward the lake at Meditation Point.

3.7 km The trail reaches the park's Interpretive Centre, and as the path emerges from the trees, on the right is the bronze plaque commemorating the opening of the Rideau Trail. There is a picnic area to the right, with benches and garbage cans, and there are outhouses nearby. On the opposite side of the building is a trailhead kiosk, with a posted map and paper copies available.

On the lake side is a broad crushed-stone path, the Jack Hebert Mobility Trail. Your route continues straight, on what appears to be a parking area, barricaded at its far end. Signage is poor in this area, but you continue beyond the parking area and along a former road, keeping the lake to the right.

At 4.2 km, the road ends at what is called a "natural swim area" — a beach — where no dogs are permitted. There are picnic tables, barbeque pits, an interpretive panel, and an outhouse. The Rideau Trail (with the Orange Maple Trail) continues on a footpath quite close to the shore of Little Bay.

After only 150 m, the trail turns away from the water and heads uphill, and at 4.5 km it reaches another junction where there is another map. The Orange Maple Trail heads left; the Rideau Trail branches right, dropping back down the hillside then working between two ridges alongside a small brook, which it crosses 200 m from the junction, and again 200 m beyond that.

5.1 km A sign announces that you are leaving the Foley Mountain Conservation Area and entering private property. Use of the trail is permitted, but you must remain on the path. Hunting can occur on these lands during the appropriate season.

The much narrower footpath meanders over the forested hillside, crossing a private road, just above Big Bay, 500 m later. It continues uphill, the forest changing back to cedar as it moves into some open areas and bare rock.

At 5.8 km, the route begins to descend, and a quiet paved road can soon be seen to the left. The trail reaches the North Shore Road, close to some houses, nearly 100 m later. The Rideau Trail continues right, following the road. You should turn back here, and retrace your route to the start.

Red-winged Blackbird

As you hike past a wetland or farming area, expect to hear the distinctive "oak-a-lee" song or "chek" call of the red-winged blackbird. One of the most numerous birds in North America, the all-black male often displays its bright red shoulder patches as it flits between cattails chasing insects. The striped brown female, in contrast, looks almost like a large sparrow. Migration begins in September or October, and they are one of the first birds to return in April.

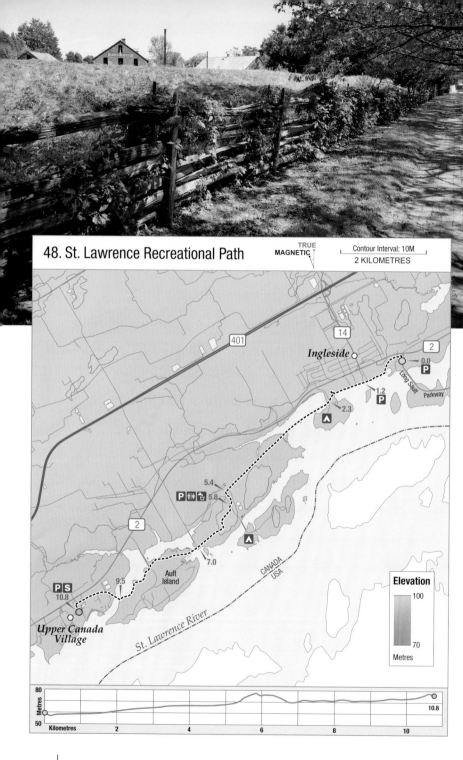

48. St. Lawrence Recreational Path

TRUE
MAGNETIC

Contour Interval: 10M
2 KILOMETRES

401

14

2

Ingleside

0.0 P

1.2 P

2.3

5.4

P 5.8

7.0

CANADA
USA

9.5

Ault
Island

10.8
P S

*Upper Canada
Village*

St. Lawrence River

Elevation
100

70
Metres

80

Metres

50

Kilometres   2   4   6   8   10

10.8

48. St. Lawrence Recreational Path

Distance: 21.6 km return
Type: linear
Difficulty: 4 (distance)
Ascent/descent: 57 m
Hiking time: 6+ hrs
Trail conditions: asphalt, crushed stone
Cellphone coverage: excellent

Uses: walking, biking, snowshoeing, cross-country skiing
Facilities: benches, garbage cans, interpretive panels, outhouses, picnic tables
Hazards: poison ivy, road crossings, ticks, wildlife

Finding the trailhead: From the Highway 417/174 split, follow Highway 417 for 33 km to exit 79. Turn south onto County Road 5, which will become County Road 12 in 8 km. Continue an additional 30 km, then turn right at the junction with County Road 14. Follow County Road 14 for 14 km to the junction with Highway 2. Turn left, and 700 m later turn right onto Long Sault Parkway. Turn into the parking area immediately on the right. The trail begins in the northeast corner of the parking area.

Trailhead: 44°59'52.1" N, 74°58'27.4" W

Introduction: The 200 km between Kingston and the Quebec border is known as the St. Lawrence Heritage Corner, and it is home to a variety of parks and recreational areas. Within 100 km by air of Ottawa, that includes Upper Canada Village, the Upper Canada Migratory Bird Sanctuary, the Long Sault Parkway, and a large number of day-use area parks, campgrounds, and recreational trails.

The St. Lawrence Recreational Trail extends for nearly 75 km between the communities of Lancaster and Morrisburg, although it follows roads in some sections. However, between the west end of the Long Sault Parkway and Upper Canada Village, it is a well-maintained path with abundant facilities, including camping – excellent for families and groups. It also passes through the Upper Canada Migratory Bird Sanctuary, which has its own extensive network of footpaths. The 22 km profiled might be too far for some, but there are many spots along the way that are themselves worthwhile destinations, so there are opportunities aplenty to turn this into a shorter, but no less enjoyable, trek.

Route description: From the parking area, the asphalt-surfaced pathway makes its meandering way, by 600 m, to the edge of the St. Lawrence River. Most of this area is grass covered, though many large hardwood trees dot the area. Busy Highway 2 is often visible, to the right, though not too noisy. At 1.2 km, there is a parking area, with a bench, used often by recreational paddlers; watch for them crossing the trail.

For another 600 m, the pathway crosses this open terrain, with extensive views out onto the river and over the wildflower-speckled fields, keeping quite close to the river. Then it turns sharply to curve around a narrow inlet before moving briefly away from the water.

2.3 km The trail crosses Killamey Road, which is the entrance to the Farran Park Campground. There is a Waterfront Trail map here, which states that this section is part of the Lower Seaway Valley Trail. As you will notice on the map, this is almost the only section of the Seaway route that is not mostly on road. There are also picnic tables, benches, and garbage cans nearby, and the campground store is less than 20 m to the left. For casual walkers, this could be a turning point.

Pass through a narrow gate; there is soon open water on both sides of the trail. This next 1 km is quite lovely as the trail crosses a narrow causeway. At its far end, the trail moves into the thickly wooded grounds of the Upper Canada Migratory Bird Sanctuary, leaving open water behind. It is still very wet through here, however, with ditches on both sides of the trail filled with still water. Expect hordes of hungry mosquitoes!

For the following 1 km, which is quite straight, thick forest and wet ditches line the path. However, shortly after a footpath joins in from the left, the woods open up somewhat on the right, providing better views of a marshy area popular with waterfowl and amphibians. Several of the Sanctuary's walking paths connect to and use the asphalt pathway.

At 5.4 km, the trail makes a tight turn left and soon passes through another gate. Less than 100 m further, the pathway leaves the asphalted surface to continue on a crushed-stone treadway. And just beyond that on the left is the Stephanie Grady Educational Pavilion, which shelters several picnic tables and features several interpretive panels.

5.8 km The trail reaches the Upper Canada Migratory Bird Sanctuary Interpretive Centre. Besides featuring information about the sanctuary, it acts as a general store for nearby campers, so drinking water is available. On the grounds nearby are benches, garbage cans, and picnic tables. Maps of the trail are posted just outside the centre, and not only is there parking for cyclists, but there is also a repair station. The Interpretive Centre is another excellent turnaround spot for those desiring a shorter hike (after a snack and cool drink, of course!).

The pathway continues, crossing Morrison Road – incidentally, it returns to an asphalt surface – and passing through large, untended fields dotted with

bluebird nesting boxes. This section features the most noticeable hills on this route, though it is still quite gentle.

The trail continues out of sight of the river until about 7 km, when the path emerges from thick forest. About 100 m further, Aullsville Road (gravel) connects on the right. The trail crosses another short causeway/dike, then pops back into dense forest. We are now on Ault Island.

The trees restrict views of the water until about 8 km, when it might be visible on the right. Most of the vegetation is hardwoods, so in summer the canopy is lush. However, about 400 m later, when the path crosses Ault Island Road (paved), more tall pine borders it, and the water to the right is quite visible.

The trail meanders along the island's shoreline until 9.5 km, when it turns sharply right and crosses a very sturdy, but short, bridge to reconnect with the mainland. Stop a moment on the bridge to enjoy the view.

Barely 200 m further, the dedicated pathway abruptly ends at a dirt road; you are actually now in Upper Canada Village. Turn left and almost immediately turn right again onto a paved road. This is a park road, so traffic is light. Follow this through the park maintenance and administration area until, at 10.6 km, you reach the main parking area. Turn left onto a brick-lined walkway bordered by a handsome cedar-rail fence.

10.8 km Arrive at the entrance to Upper Canada Village. Canteens and other services are to the left, and in the summer this is an extremely busy spot! When you are finished your visit, retrace your route back to Long Sault Parkway.

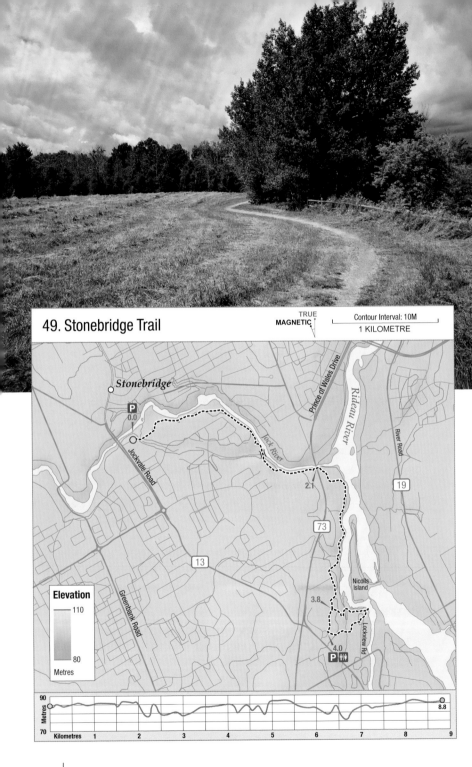

49. Stonebridge Trail

TRUE
MAGNETIC

Contour Interval: 10M

1 KILOMETRE

Stonebridge

P
0.0

Jockvale Road

Prince of Wales Drive

Rideau River

Jock River

2.1

River Road

19

73

13

Greenbank Road

Nicolls
Island

3.8

4.0

P

Lockview Rd

Elevation

110

80

Metres

Metres
90
70
Kilometres   1   2   3   4   5   6   7   8   9

8.8

49. Stonebridge Trail

Distance: 8.8 km return
Type: linear
Difficulty: 2
Ascent/descent: 54 m
Hiking time: 2+ hrs
Trail conditions: asphalt, compacted earth, crushed stone

Cellphone coverage: excellent
Uses: walking, biking, snowshoeing, cross-country skiing
Facilities: benches, garbage cans, picnic tables
Hazards: poison ivy, ticks

Finding the trailhead: Take exit 129 on Highway 417, turning south onto Greenbank Road. Follow it for 10 km to Jockvale Road. Turn left, and follow it for 800 m, turning right onto Longfields Drive. The parking area is on the left, marked by a large Stonebridge Trail sign, in 300 m. The path begins at its far end.

Trailhead: 45°15'43.3" N, 75°43'54.1" W

Introduction: This is a pleasant walk in an area that has rapidly developed into suburbia. Its two halves are quite different, with the first 2 km almost always being within sight of houses, and the final 2 km at times feeling more remote than they actually are because of the dense tree cover. Being so close to both the Jock and the Rideau Rivers makes this a worthwhile hike for novices and families.

Route description: From the parking area, the trail is a wide crushed-stone pathway, with wide mowed strips on each side. (This is to reduce the growth of poison ivy and lessen the chance of brushing up against a tick.) After 225 m, it reaches a large area of playgrounds, houses, and softball and soccer areas: W.C. Levesque Fields. The trail circles these; keep left, close to the treeline, where the trail works its way closer to the Jock River. At least one side path leads down to the water's edge. After nearly 600 m paralleling the field, you reach another junction. Again, keep left where the paths heads into an area of larger, older trees.

There are many side trails, mostly leading toward the river, through this too brief, 200 m forested stretch. Then the taller trees disappear, leaving no shade, and for 300 m it is semi-open. Fortunately, you next enter an area of high cedar, which provides your best view so far of the Jock River, on your left. The trail meanders around a gully and passes under a couple of towering maples. At 1.5 km you emerge from the forest again; on your right is a water control structure, gated, with houses behind it. The trail bends left, descends a set of stairs, then crosses a bridge level with the Jock River.

On the far side of the bridge there is a little lookout to the left. Then the trail climbs the embankment, passes through another stand of trees, and emerges almost into the backyards of a neighbourhood. One of the properties contains its own observatory – not something you see in most backyards. A side trail connects to the street, Marwood Court.

The trail finally moves away from houses for a time, heading back into forest. This is perhaps the most attractive section thus far, situated on the bank above the river, wide and surfaced with crushed stone. Sadly, after only a few hundred metres you hear the sounds of heavy traffic, and on your right the grounds of Capital Memorial Gardens crowd the path.

2.1 km The trail drops, curving, and at 2.1 km it passes underneath the massive steel-and-concrete Prince of Wales Drive road bridge. Directly ahead, you can see the Jock feed into the Rideau River. From the bridge, the path climbs, curving right, and moves into an area of spruce – and incidentally into Beryl Gaffney Park. About 220 m later, gates narrow the trail where it crosses a private drive. After a further 90° right turn it should be possible to view the Rideau, on the left, through thickening vegetation. Short side paths lead to the waterline.

For the first time the area feels somewhat remote, traffic noises muted and the trees tall and sheltering. About 300 m later, a metal bridge crosses a narrow – but deep – gully, then 300 m further a much larger bridge traverses a considerably deeper ravine. After the second bridge, the trail splits; to the left there is a bench overlooking the water, while the main trail – stay on it – turns right and parallels the ravine until it reaches a gate at the end of Hazelwood Way. The left route reconnects just before the gate, at 3.4 km.

The path resumes 100 m later, at the far end of this short cul-de-sac. Less than 100 m later, there are a couple of benches on the left, where maybe there was once a lookout. But the trail has moved away from the water, the sight of which is now blocked by trees. About 300 m from Hazelwood Way there is a path junction. Turn left, and immediately cross a short wooden bridge.

3.8 km The trail splits again. Keep straight/right on the broader track. Remain on the broadest crushed-stone path, and barely 200 m further you arrive at a large open area and trailhead parking for Maple Hill Park, where there are garbage cans, washrooms – and oodles of regulatory signage. Turn left onto a slightly separated crushed-stone pathway that crosses a field. (This is now an off-leash dog area.)

The track narrows considerably as it enters the forest, and it then descends a small hillside to cross a wet area 200 m from the parking area. This part was a bit rough when I went through, but the crushed stone resumes on the far side. The path pops out of the trees, then meanders across another field, reaching the end of Lockview Road, where there is a large Beryl Gaffney Park sign, at 4.4 km.

The crushed-stone path, now reduced to a slender thread through the grass, continues through the field for another 100 m, until it reaches the treeline and makes a sharp left turn. To the right is an informal footpath. I recommend it, but be warned that it is slippery and steep. Clambering down the uneven slope will deliver you to the edge of the Rideau River directly below, with excellent views of a dam that builds up the water level for the Rideau Canal locks at Nicolls Island. These are the best water views available on this route.

Back up top, the crushed-stone track turns left and traces the treeline for 200 m before re-entering the forest, descending a staircase, and crossing a little brook on an impressive set of massive flat(ish) boulders. The trail climbs back out of this modest gully, then works its way back to the main trail. Numerous side paths diverge; keep on the crushed stone. It arrives at the junction 200 m before the Maple Hill Park parking area, at 5 km.

Turn right and retrace your route the 3.8 km back to the starting trailhead.

50. Tip to Tip Trail

TRUE
MAGNETIC

Contour Interval: 10M
500 METRES

Dwyer Hill Road

Donnelly Drive

Burritts Rapids

Rideau Canal

River Road

0.0

Rideau River

1.9

2.4

Burritts Rapids Road

County Road 23

Elevation

110

80

Metres

100
Metres
10

Kilometres

1

2

2.4

50. Tip to Tip Trail

Distance: 4.8 km return
Type: linear
Difficulty: 1
Ascent/descent: 62 m
Hiking time: 1+ hrs
Trail conditions: compacted earth, crushed stone, natural surface
Cellphone coverage: excellent

Uses: walking, snowshoeing, cross-country skiing
Facilities: benches, drinking water, garbage cans, interpretive panels, picnic tables, outhouses
Hazards: poison ivy, road crossing, ticks

Finding the trailhead: From the Highway 416/417 split, follow Highway 416 south for 41.7 km to exit 34. Turn right onto County Road 43 and continue for 13.5 km, then turn right onto the Burritts Rapids Road/County Road 23. In 2.8 km, turn right onto River Road. The trailhead is on the left in 350 m at the Rideau Canal-Burritts Rapids Lock parking area.

Trailhead: 44°58'56.5" N, 75°47'09.2" W

Introduction: With the development of the Rideau Canal (1827–1832), a small island was created at Burritts Rapids, where a settlement had already been established by United Empire Loyalists in 1793. The trail, as its name suggests, begins at one end of this island and continues to its opposite tip, a slim sliver of a ridge that provides good views of both the canal's artificial channel and the original course of the river, over which there is a low dam.

This is an exceptionally pleasant location for a family walk, a short distance with minimal elevation gain. I recommend beginning at the Burritts Rapids Lockstation, both because of its amenities and also because it is an attractive, family-friendly spot. There is a restaurant just across River Road, while Merrickville with its many businesses is just 11 km distant.

Route description: From the parking area, follow a narrow crushed-stone pathway down to the Burritts Rapids Lock and its lockstation. The surrounding area is a pleasant picnic ground, with numerous picnic tables, washroom facilities, drinking water, and several interpretive panels.

Cross the canal on the wooden lock doors; on the far bank is a Tip to Tip Trail signpost that includes a map. It states that the total distance is 4 km. (I recorded it as a little bit longer, but I start and finish at the edge of the parking lot.)

The route is obvious and straightforward; turn left and follow a slender footpath that parallels the waterway. It begins as a grass-covered track, rarely more than a metre from the river's edge, with surprisingly thick vegetation bordering it once it leaves the proximity of the lockstation. There are even a few places where there is overhead shade. However, there is always an excellent view of the busy waterway and its frequent passing pleasure craft.

At about 700 m, houses can be seen to the right, though you initially remain in a sheltered forested corridor. But at 850 m, the pathway emerges into the community of Burritts Rapids, connecting to Centre Street, and adjacent to some attractive houses. Additional interpretive panels recount the history of the community.

Signs direct you left, across a mowed lawn and seemingly through people's backyards. You should remain close to the vegetation and the river.

📍**1 km** The path reaches – and crosses – Grenville Street, right beside the Burritts Rapids Swing Bridge. On the far side of the street is another picnic area, with benches, a large interpretive panel, and another map of the trail.

The route continues on the far side of the lawn, now resembling a seldom-used roadway and comfortably wide enough for two to walk side by side. It soon returns to the river's edge and quickly moves away from houses.

By 1.3 km, the river noticeably begins to widen, and there is a horse farm visible on the far bank. Within another 200 m, you should be able to catch glimpses of water to your right as well, through the vegetation. The path distinctly ascends a low ridge, climbing about 5 m above river level. At 1.8 km, there is an observation platform, with a bench, on the left.

📍**1.9 km** The pathway splits; turn right, and descend to a dam. This was constructed across the original route of the Rideau River, and is designed to keep the water level sufficiently high in the canal channel for its uses. I found this had the most expansive views anywhere along this route, and I noticed some interesting waterfowl and raptors while on the dam's small, fenced platform.

Return to the junction and turn right to continue along the trail. The roadway surface ends and now the occasional tree root peaks through the treadway. Vegetation to the sides is thicker and crowds the centre more, and there is a high overhead leafy canopy. The surrounding trees are older, and there is more pine. I found this the most attractive woodland of this hike.

📍**2.4 km** The trail reaches the end of the long, narrow spit of land separating the Rideau River from the canal. There is a small hole in the vegetation that permits a view upstream, where Parks Canada has placed two of its iconic red chairs. An informal track works down the hillside to the water's edge, but no better view can be gained from there.

Enjoy the restful surroundings for a few moments, or enjoy a snack, and when ready retrace your route back to the Burritts Rapids Lockstation.

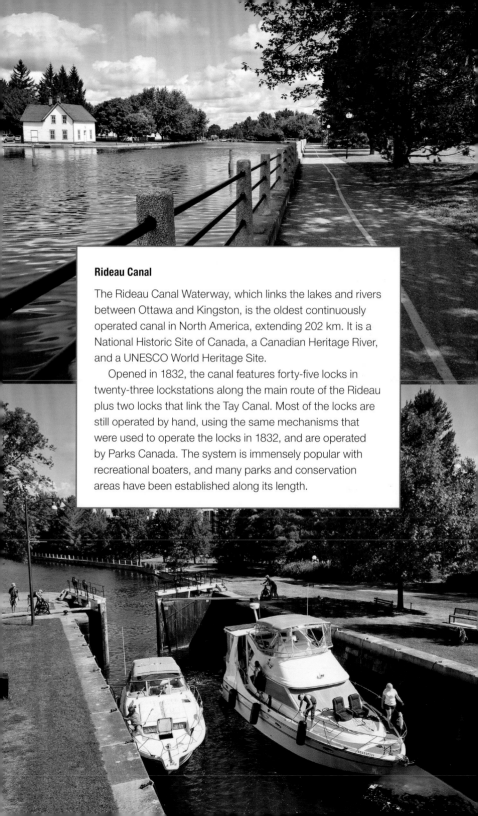

Rideau Canal

The Rideau Canal Waterway, which links the lakes and rivers between Ottawa and Kingston, is the oldest continuously operated canal in North America, extending 202 km. It is a National Historic Site of Canada, a Canadian Heritage River, and a UNESCO World Heritage Site.

Opened in 1832, the canal features forty-five locks in twenty-three lockstations along the main route of the Rideau plus two locks that link the Tay Canal. Most of the locks are still operated by hand, using the same mechanisms that were used to operate the locks in 1832, and are operated by Parks Canada. The system is immensely popular with recreational boaters, and many parks and conservation areas have been established along its length.

Acknowledgements

I consulted a large number of people while researching the routes featured in this edition, and many others for trails that I hiked but ultimately decided not to include. Everyone was cooperative, proud of their particular trail, and eager to make my work easier by providing whatever information that they thought could help. Their enthusiasm and commitment to trail development and usage was infectious; I want to thank them all, and I apologize that there isn't room enough in one volume to showcase every path that I sampled. The region enjoys a rich and exciting variety of trails.

Unlike a normal recreational walk, when I travel on a route that I wish to profile for a book, I am frequently stopping for photographs, recording data for maps, constantly checking cellphone reception, and continuously making notes about the trail and its surroundings. That isn't particularly enjoyable for others, so in all my previous works, I walked almost every route by myself. For this edition of *Hiking Trails of Ottawa*, however, my good friend Ron Hunt accompanied me on many of my hikes. He was patient when I shushed him (often), cheerful when I insisted that we stop so that I could examine whatever suddenly captured my attention, and was never disappointed when my exploration of a possible new route didn't measure up. He supported my efforts wholly and for that has my gratitude.

No book belongs solely to the author. A published work, particularly one as complex as a hiking guide, is a collaborative effort: cartographer, editors, proofreaders, and designer. I have been extremely fortunate that every one of the people involved in this project is excellent in their area of expertise, and their talent has made this work one of the best examples of its genre available in Canada. To them, I acknowledge my debt, and extend my thanks.

Finally, I wish to thank those who use this book. When I created my first guide, in the dimly remembered days before the Internet, finding accurate information on hiking and biking locations was almost impossible. Oddly, despite the many websites now available, reliable sources can still be challenging to find. I have always written my guides with new and casual hikers in mind, creating a book that will tell you of enjoyable routes and enable you to find your way and walk comfortably, knowing that you have a reliable guide in your pack. Thank you for your interest in Canada's outdoors.

Michael Haynes is one of the leading authorities on trail development in Canada. He has been named a trail hero by the Ontario Trails Council and has authored thirteen trail guides, including the first edition of *Hiking Trails of Ottawa, the National Capital Region, and Beyond* and the two-volume *The Best of The Great Trail*. A regular commentator for CBC Radio, Haynes's travel writing has also appeared in *Ottawa Magazine*, *Saltscapes*, and *Explore*.

Over his thirty years of work in trails, Michael Haynes has been Executive Director of the Nova Scotia Trails Federation, a member of the Canada Walks Advisory Committee and a founding Board Member of Canada Bikes. He has served on the Province of Ontario's Trails Coordinating Committee and the Public Health Agency of Canada's Advisory Committee for Active Transportation, the Steering Committee for the Ottawa Pathway Patrol, and Ottawa's Public Advisory Committee on Segregated Bike Lanes. He has also worked as a consultant on several trail development plans, including the Municipality of North Grenville and the Municipality of Chatham-Kent.